Scott Foresman · Addison Wesley

# enVisionMATH® 2.0

## Volume 1 Topics 1-8

## Authors

**Randall I. Charles**
Professor Emeritus
Department of Mathematics
San Jose State University
San Jose, California

**Janet H. Caldwell**
Professor of Mathematics
Rowan University
Glassboro, New Jersey

**Juanita Copley**
Professor Emerita, College of Education
University of Houston
Houston, Texas

**Warren Crown**
Professor Emeritus of Mathematics
Education
Graduate School of Education
Rutgers University
New Brunswick, New Jersey

**Francis (Skip) Fennell**
L. Stanley Bowlsbey Professor
of Education and Graduate and
Professional Studies
McDaniel College
Westminster, Maryland

**Stuart J. Murphy**
Visual Learning Specialist
Boston, Massachusetts

**Kay B. Sammons**
Coordinator of Elementary Mathematics
Howard County Public Schools
Ellicott City, Maryland

**Jane F. Schielack**
Professor of Mathematics
Associate Dean for Assessment and
Pre K-12 Education, College of Science
Texas A&M University
College Station, Texas

## Mathematicians

**Roger Howe**
Professor of Mathematics
Yale University
New Haven, Connecticut

**Gary Lippman**
Professor of Mathematics and Computer
Science
California State University East Bay
Hayward, California

PEARSON

Glenview, Illinois     Boston, Massachusetts     Chandler, Arizona     Upper Saddle River, New Jersey

## Contributing Authors

**Zachary Champagne**
District Facilitator, Duval County Public Schools
Florida Center for Research in Science,
Technology, Engineering, and Mathematics
(FCR-STEM)
Jacksonville, Florida

**Jonathan A. Wray**
Mathematics Instructional Facilitator
Howard County Public Schools
Ellicott City, Maryland

## ELL Consultants

**Janice Corona**
Retired Administrator
Dallas ISD, Multi-Lingual Department
Dallas, Texas

**Jim Cummins**
Professor
The University of Toronto
Toronto, Canada

## Texas Reviewers

**Theresa Bathe**
Teacher
Fort Bend ISD

**Chrissy Beltran**
School Wide Project Coordinator
Ysleta ISD

**Renee Cutright**
Teacher
Amarillo ISD

**Sharon Grimm**
Teacher
Houston ISD

**Esmeralda Herrera**
Teacher
San Antonio ISD

**Sherry Johnson**
Teacher
Round Rock ISD

**Elvia Lopez**
Teacher
Denton ISD

**Antoinese Pride**
Instructional Coach
Dallas ISD

**Joanna Ratliff**
Teacher
Keller ISD

**Courtney Jo Ridehuber**
Teacher
Mansfield ISD

**Nannie D. Scurlock-McKnight**
Mathematics Specialist
A.W. Brown Fellowship-Leadership Academy
Dallas, TX

**Brian Sinclair**
Math Instructional Specialist
Fort Worth ISD

ISBN-13: 978-0-328-76720-5
ISBN-10: 0-328-76720-4

10  V003  17 16

Look for these digital resources in every lesson!

# Digital Resources

 Go to PearsonTexas.com

 **Solve**
**Solve & Share** problems plus math tools

 **Learn**
**Visual Learning Animation Plus** with animation, interaction, and math tools

 **Glossary**
**Animated Glossary** in English and Spanish

 **Tools**
**Math Tools** to help you understand

 **Check**
**Quick Check** for each lesson

 **Games**
**Math Games** to help you learn

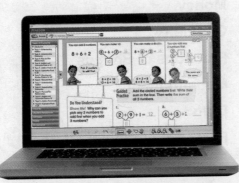

**eText**
The pages in your book online

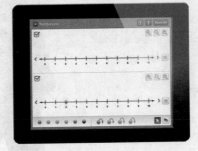

**PearsonTexas.com**
Everything you need for math anytime, anywhere

## Key

Number and Operations

Algebraic Reasoning

Geometry and Measurement

Data Analysis

Personal Financial Literacy

Mathematical Process Standards
are found in all lessons.

**Digital Resources at PearsonTexas.com**

Solve    Learn    Glossary

Check    Tools    Games

And remember the pages in your book are also online!

# Contents

## Topics

## TOPIC 1 — Understanding Addition

4 and 2 is 6.

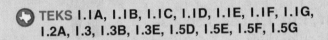

$$4 + 2 = 6$$
$$2 + 4 = 6$$

2 and 4 is 6.

Hi, I'm Jada. This shows you can add in any order.

TEKS 1.1A, 1.1B, 1.1C, 1.1D, 1.1E, 1.1F, 1.1G, 1.2A, 1.3, 1.3B, 1.3E, 1.5D, 1.5E, 1.5F, 1.5G

## TOPIC 2 — Understanding Subtraction

6

$$6 - 4 = 2$$

Hi, I'm Alex. This shows you can subtract to find a missing part.

TEKS 1.1A, 1.1B, 1.1C, 1.1D, 1.1E, 1.1F, 1.1G, 1.3, 1.3B, 1.5D, 1.5E, 1.5F

## TOPIC 3
# Five and Ten Relationships

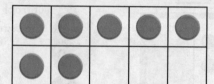

Hi, I'm Marta. This shows that 7 is 2 more than 5.

⭐ TEKS 1.1A, 1.1B, 1.1C, 1.1D, 1.1E, 1.1F, 1.1G, 1.2A, 1.3C

## TOPIC 4
# Addition and Subtraction Facts to 12

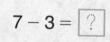

$7 - 3 = \boxed{?}$

$3 + \boxed{?} = 7$

Hi, I'm Jackson. You can think addition to subtract.

⭐ TEKS 1.1A, 1.1B, 1.1C, 1.1D, 1.1E, 1.1F, 1.1G, 1.3, 1.3C, 1.3D, 1.3E, 1.3F, 1.5D, 1.5G

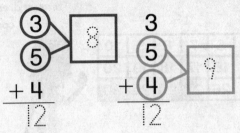

# Volume I

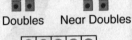

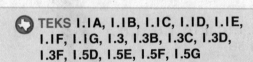

## TOPIC 7 — Counting and Number Patterns to 100

| 1 | 2 | 3 | 4 | 5 | 6 | 7 | 8 | 9 | 10 |
|---|---|---|---|---|---|---|---|---|----|
| 11 | 12 | 13 | 14 | 15 | 16 | 17 | 18 | 19 | 20 |
| 21 | 22 | 23 | 24 | 25 | 26 | 27 | 28 | 29 | 30 |

> Hi, it's Jada again. You have to pay attention to the tens and ones digits when counting!

★ TEKS 1.1A, 1.1B, 1.1C, 1.1D, 1.1E, 1.1F, 1.1G, 1.5, 1.5A, 1.5B

---

## Volume I

## TOPIC 8 — Tens and Ones

| Tens | Ones |
|------|------|
| 1 ten | 27 ones |

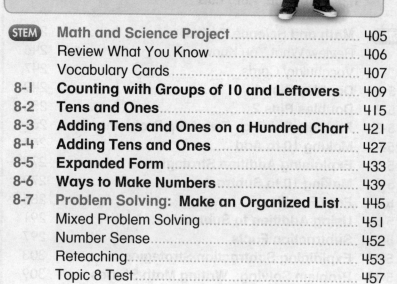

$$37 = 10 + 27$$

> Hi, it's Daniel. You make and break apart numbers in many different ways.

★ TEKS 1.1A, 1.1B, 1.1C, 1.1D, 1.1E, 1.1F, 1.1G, 1.2B, 1.2C, 1.3A

## TOPIC 9
## Numbers to 120

100, 101

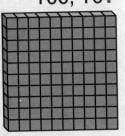

Hi, it's Marta again. Counting above 100 is just like counting below 100.

⭐ TEKS I.IA, I.IB, I.IC, I.ID, I.IE, I.IF, I.IG, I.2B, I.2C, I.5, I.5A, I.5B, I.5C

## TOPIC 10
## Comparing and Ordering Numbers to 120

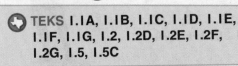

42 is greater than 24.

42 ⊗ 24

Hi, it's Alex again. Compare these numbers by comparing tens first.

⭐ TEKS I.IA, I.IB, I.IC, I.ID, I.IE, I.IF, I.IG, I.2, I.2D, I.2E, I.2F, I.2G, I.5, I.5C

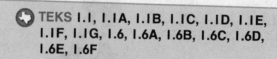

**Volume 2**

## TOPIC 11 — Money

25¢   10¢   5¢   1¢

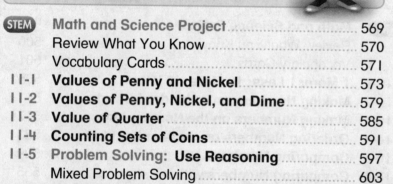

Count quarters, then dimes, then nickels, then pennies.

Hi, it's Jada again. Start with the coin that's worth the most.

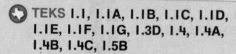

⭐ TEKS 1.1, 1.1A, 1.1B, 1.1C, 1.1D, 1.1E, 1.1F, 1.1G, 1.3D, 1.4, 1.4A, 1.4B, 1.4C, 1.5B

## TOPIC 12 — Geometry

Hi, it's Carlos again. One way to sort shapes is by the number of sides.

⭐ TEKS 1.1, 1.1A, 1.1B, 1.1C, 1.1D, 1.1E, 1.1F, 1.1G, 1.6, 1.6A, 1.6B, 1.6C, 1.6D, 1.6E, 1.6F

## Volume 2

### TOPIC 13 — Fractions of Shapes

*Hi, it's Emily again. Both rectangles are divided into fourths.*

⭐ TEKS 1.1A, 1.1B, 1.1C, 1.1D, 1.1E, 1.1F, 1.1G, 1.6G, 1.6H

### TOPIC 14 — Measurement

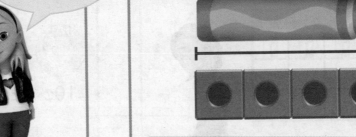

*Hi, it's Jackson again. The crayon is about 4 cubes long.*

⭐ TEKS 1.1, 1.1A, 1.1B, 1.1C, 1.1D, 1.1E, 1.1F, 1.1G, 1.7, 1.7A, 1.7B, 1.7C, 1.7D, 1.7E

## Volume 2

**TOPIC 15 — Data**

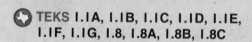

> Hi, it's Marta again. I can use the data to see what drinks students like.

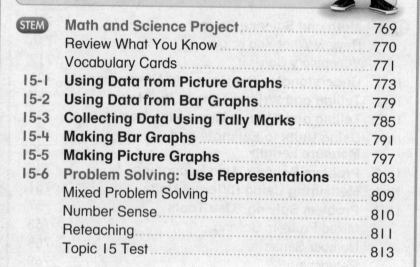

TEKS I.IA, I.IB, I.IC, I.ID, I.IE, I.IF, I.IG, I.8, I.8A, I.8B, I.8C

**TOPIC 16 — Personal Financial Literacy**

> Hi, it's Daniel again. When you save money, you have more money.

10¢   20¢   30¢   40¢   50¢

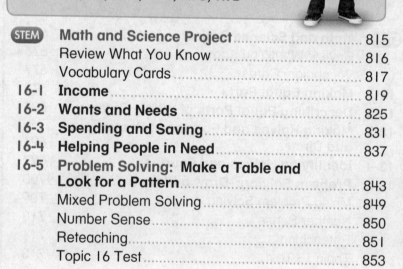

TEKS I.IA, I.IB, I.IC, I.ID, I.IE, I.IF, I.IG, I.9, I.9A, I.9B, I.9C, I.9D

Volume 2

# Step Up to Grade 2

These lessons help prepare you for Grade 2.

 TEKS 2.1A, 2.1B, 2.1C, 2.1D, 2.1E, 2.1F, 2.1G, 2.2, 2.2B, 2.2D, 2.4, 2.4B, 2.6, 2.6A, 2.6B

Name _____

# Writing Numbers 0 to 4

Practice writing the numbers 0–4.

1. 0 0 0 0 0 0 0

2. 1 1 1 1 1 1 1

3. 2 2 2 2 2 2 2

4. 3 3 3 3 3 3 3

5.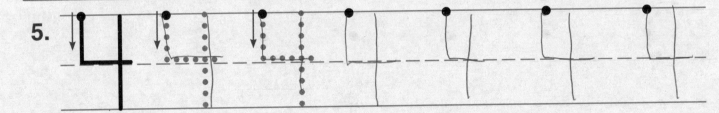

# Writing Numbers 5 to 9

Practice writing the numbers 5–9.

1.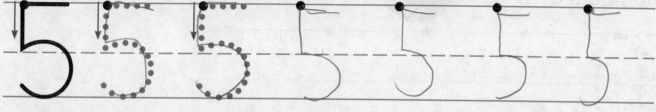

2.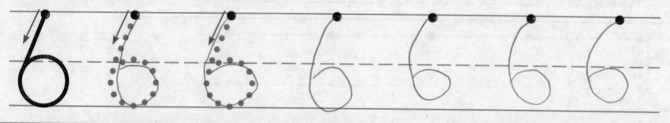

3.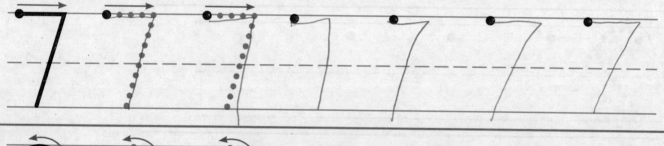

4.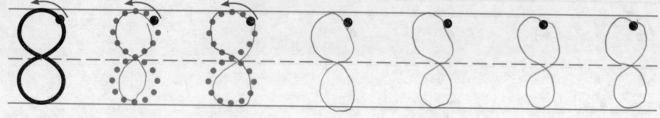

5.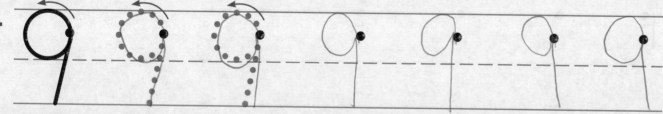

Name _____

# Comparing Numbers Through 5

> Write the number that tells how many.
> Then circle the number that is less.

**1.**

  (2)    3

**2.**

  2    1

**3.**

  3  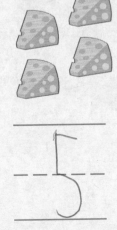  5

**4.**

  ___    4

# Comparing Numbers Through 10

Write the number that tells how many.
Then circle the number that is greater.

1.

7

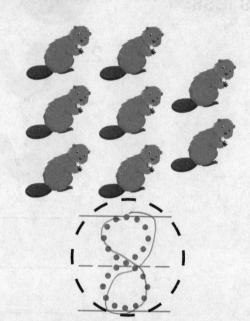

(8)

2.

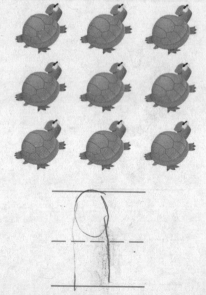

9

6

**Grade 1** | Readiness

Name Amory Cox

# Shapes

Color each shape below.

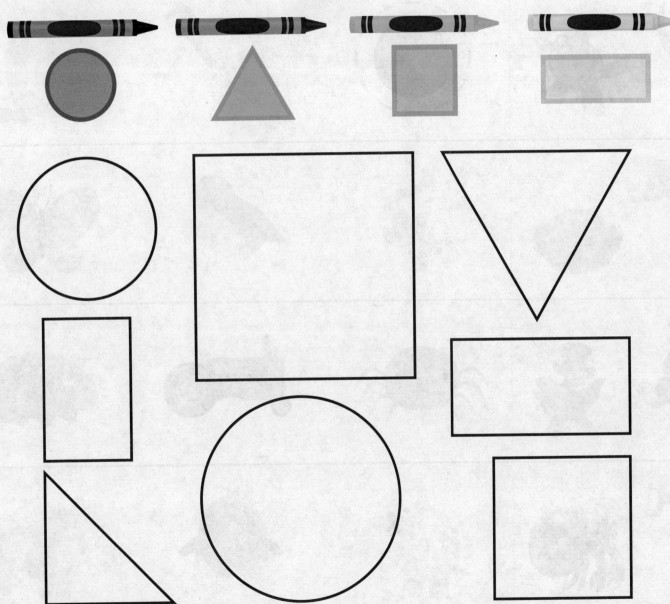

# Sorting by One Attribute

Name the color of the toys in the group.
Then circle the toy that belongs in the group.

1. green

2. gray

3. Brown

4. red

**Grade 1** | Readiness

Name _____

# Picture Graphs

**1.** Color a picture on the graph for each color of apple.

Circle your answer.

**2.** Are there more  or  ?

**3.** How many more?   ( I more )   or   2 more

# Real Graphs

1. Place a red cube on the graph for each red boat.
   Place a blue cube on the graph for each blue boat.

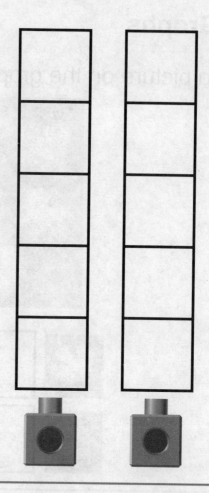

---

Circle your answer.

2. Are there fewer  or  ?

3. How many fewer?   I fewer   or   2 fewer

**Grade 1** | Readiness

# Understanding Addition

**Essential Question:** What are ways to think about addition?

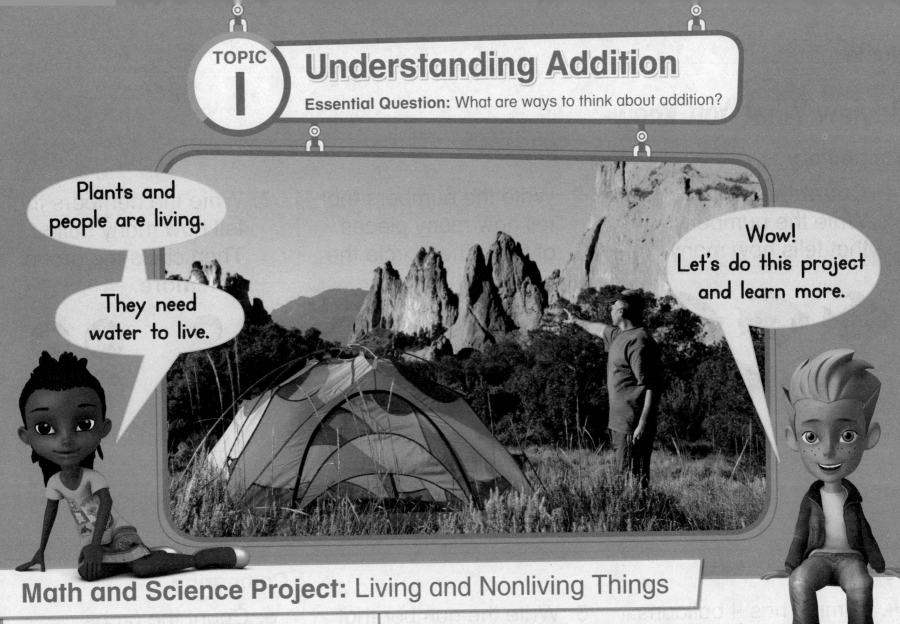

Plants and people are living.

They need water to live.

Wow! Let's do this project and learn more.

## Math and Science Project: Living and Nonliving Things

**Find Out** Talk to friends and relatives about living and nonliving things. Ask them to help you find living and nonliving things around your house.

**Journal: Make a Book** Show what you found out. In your book, also:

• Draw 2 living and 2 nonliving things.

• Make up and solve addition problems about the living and nonliving things in your house.

Name _____

# Review What You Know

## Vocabulary

**1. Count** the fish.
Write the number
that tells how many.

5

2. Write the numbers that
tell how many pieces
of fruit. Then circle the
group with **fewer**.

2    4

3. Write the numbers that
tell how many balls.
Then circle the group
with **more**.

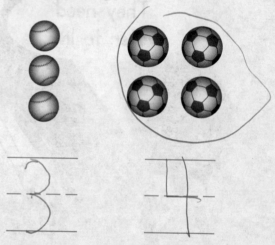

3    4

## Counting

4. Tammy has 4 balloons.
Draw a picture of her
balloons.

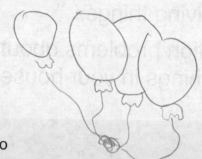

5. Write the number that
tells how many cats.

6

## Comparing

6. Count the crabs.

How many more red
crabs than blue crabs
are there?

1 more        2 more

Topic 1

## My Word Cards

Study the words on the front of the card.
Complete the activity on the back.

### pattern

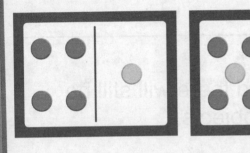

### in all

There are 4 birds **in all**.

### part

2 and 3 are parts of 5.

### whole

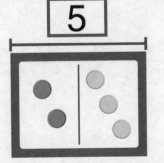

The **whole** is 5.

### plus

5 + 4

5 **plus** 4

This means 4 is added to 5.

### add

5 + 3 = 8

# My Word Cards

A __5,5__

is a piece of a whole.

---

If I add 4 objects to
I object, then I have
5 objects

_____.

If I add I0 object
to 5 objects then
i have I5 objects.

---

I can arrange 5 objects
in any

__Way__

and there will still be
5 objects.

---

I use a plus sign to

__add numbers.__

---

2 __+__

2 equals 4.

---

When I add all of the
parts, I make a

__robot.__

# My Word Cards

Study the words on the front of the card.
Complete the activity on the back.

## sum

$2 + 3 = 5$

↑

**sum**

## equals

$5 \ + \ 2 \ = \ 7$

5 plus 2 **equals** 7.

## addition sentence

$6 + 2 = 8$

This is an **addition sentence.**

## join

**Join** 2 groups to add.

## addend

$6 + 5 = 11$

↑ ↑

**addends**

# My Word Cards

Use what you know to complete the sentences.
Extend learning by writing your own sentence using each word.

I can write an

_thirt_

_____

_____

to add.

4 plus 4 = 8

_____ 8.

The answer to an addition sentence is called the

_____

_____.

In the addition sentence 6 + 4 = 10, the 6 is an

_number_

_____.

I can use addition to

_a se ____ er_

_____

2 groups.

Name _____

**Solve & Share**

Show 5 counters on your mat so they are easy to count. Show 5 counters on your mat so they are harder to count. Draw your counters. Then use digital tools to solve the problem.

⭐ TEKS 1.2A Recognize instantly the quantity of structured arrangements. Mathematical Process Standards 1.1B, 1.1C, 1.1D, 1.1E.

**Digital Resources at PearsonTexas.com**

Solve  Learn  Glossary  Check  Tools  Games

Easy To Count

5

Hard To Count

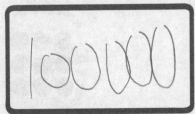

5

You can use patterns to see numbers.

7

What numbers do these patterns show?

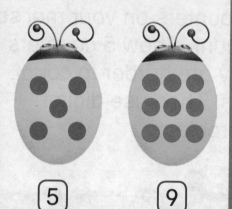

5    9

These patterns each have 2 groups with the same number of dots.

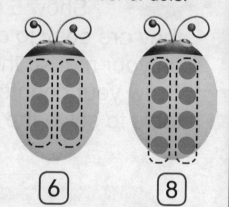

6    8

## Do You Understand?

**Show Me!** How is the 6 pattern like the 8 pattern? How is it different? because those patterns have 2 groups with the same numbers of dots.

## ☆ Guided Practice ☆  Write the number of dots.

1.

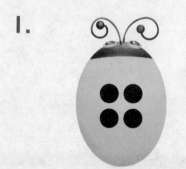

4

2.

6

3.

9

4.

5

© Pearson Education, Inc. 1

Name _____

Write the number of dots.

5.  5

6.  7

7.  3

8.  9

9.  8

10.  4

11.  6

12.  5

13.  8

14. **Extend Your Thinking** Draw the missing dot pattern.

15. Jake uses 5 counters.
He makes a dot pattern.
What pattern can Jake make?
Draw a dot pattern to show your answer.

16. Melina made 4 dot patterns for 6.
She made 1 pattern wrong.
Which pattern did she make wrong?

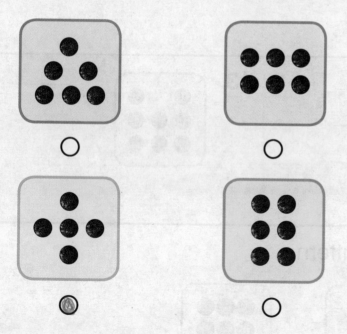

17. **Extend Your Thinking** What is your age? Draw a dot pattern to show the number.

10 ten

Name _____

**Another Look**

You can use patterns to show numbers.

This pattern shows 3.

This pattern shows  6 .

🏠 **HOME CONNECTION**
Your child recognized the number of dots in patterned arrangements without counting.

**HOME ACTIVITY** Play a game using a dot cube or dot tile to help your child recognize number patterns for 3 through 9 without counting.

Write the number each pattern shows.

**1.**

4

**2.** ★★★★
★★★★

8

**3.**

5

**4.**

9

# Write the number of dots.

**5.**  7

**6.**  5

**7.**

**8.**  9

**9.**  6

**10.**  4

---

**11.** Which number does the pattern show?

4     7     10     14

○     ◉     ○     ○

**12. Extend Your Thinking** Sandy drew patterns for numbers in order. Draw the dots for the missing pattern.

Name _____

**Solve & Share**

Make patterns to show 6 with red and yellow counters. Draw 2 of the patterns you make. Tell why they are good patterns for 6.

★ TEKS 1.2A Recognize instantly the quantity of structured arrangements. **Mathematical Process Standards 1.1B, 1.1C, 1.1D, 1.1E, 1.1F.**

Digital Resources at PearsonTexas.com

Solve  Learn  Glossary  Check  Tools  Games

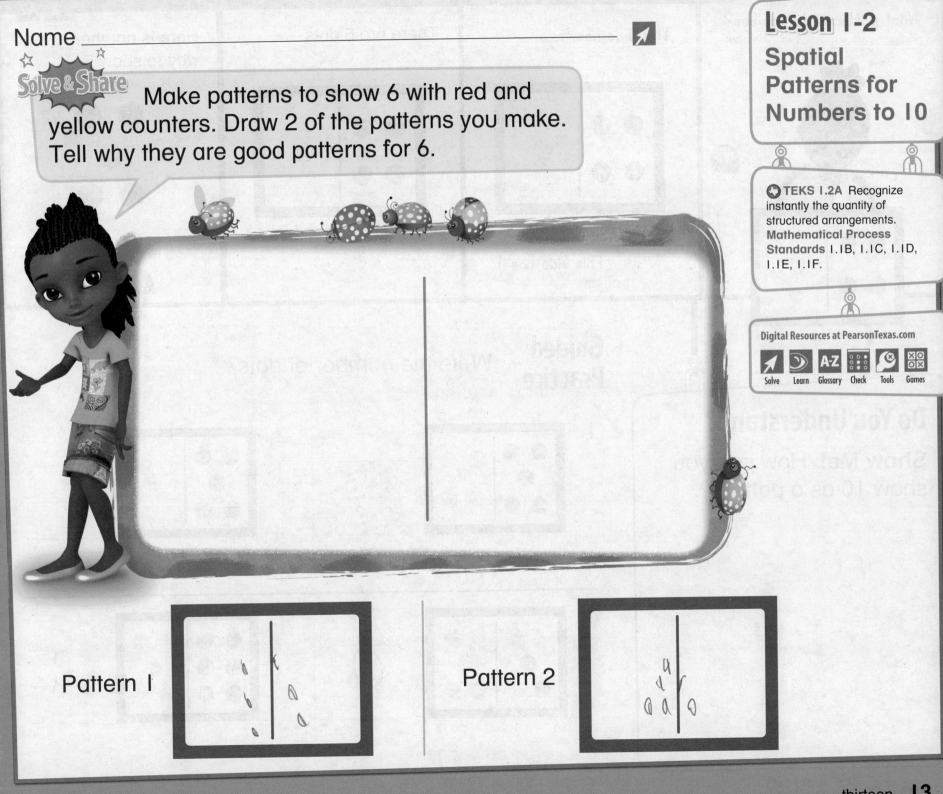

Pattern 1

Pattern 2

 What patterns do you see?

 This side has 4.

This side has 1.

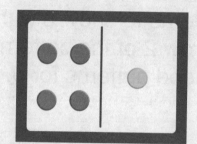 There are 5 dots.

 Here is another way to show 5.

## Do You Understand?

**Show Me!** How can you show 10 as a pattern?

## ☆ Guided Practice ☆  Write the number of dots.

1. 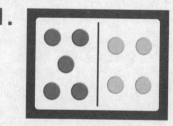  9

2.   6

3.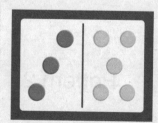

4.

© Pearson Education, Inc. 1

**Topic 1 | Lesson 2**

Name _____

Write the number of dots.

**5.**

\_ \_ \_ \_ \_

**6.**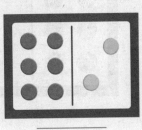

\_ \_ \_ \_ \_

**7.**

**8.**

\_ \_ \_ \_ \_

**9.**

**10.**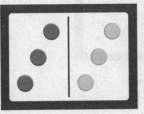

**11. Extend Your Thinking** Kira made a pattern for 9. Draw dots to show 2 different patterns that Kira could have made.

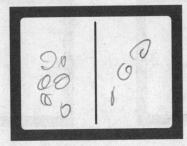 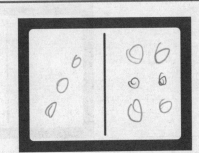

12. Mike had 6 puzzles.
   Now he has 10 puzzles.
   How many new puzzles did Mike get?

   Draw dots to complete the pattern.
   Write the number.

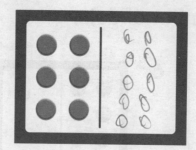 

4 new puzzles

13. Which is **not** a pattern for 7?

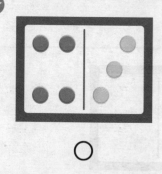 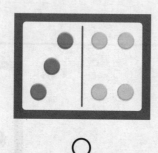 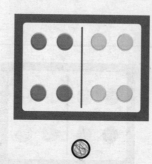 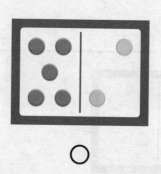

   ○            ○            ◉            ○

14. **Extend Your Thinking** Write a number between 4 and 10.
   Draw 3 different patterns for your number.

7

 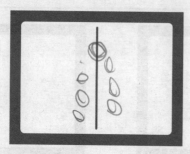 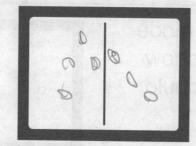 

Name _____

## Another Look  You can use patterns to show numbers.

This side shows 4.

This side shows 2.

5 ⑥ 7

④ 5 6

This is a pattern for 6.

🏠 **HOME CONNECTION**
Your child recognized the number of dots in two-part patterned arrangements without counting. He or she also used two-part patterns to show numbers.

**HOME ACTIVITY** Play a game using pennies to help your child use two-part patterns to show the numbers 3 through 10. Together, say aloud the two parts followed by the total number of dots in the pattern.

Circle the number the pattern shows.

**1.**

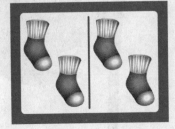

④ 5 6

**2.**

6 ⑦ 8

**3.**

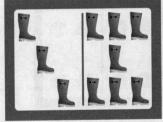

7 9 ⑩

**4.**

8 ⑩ 12

# Write the number of dots.

**5.** 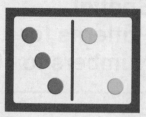 5

**6.** 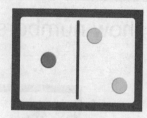 3

**7.**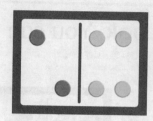

**8.** 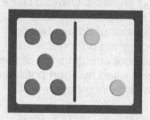 7

**9.** 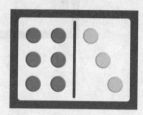 9

**10.**

**11.** Jim drew dots to show a pattern for 10. Which could be his pattern?

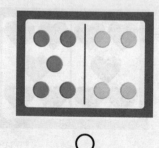
○

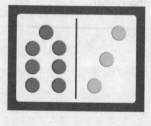
◉

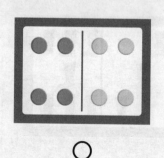
○

○

**12. Extend Your Thinking** Tom has 7 dots. He puts some dots on one flag and the rest of the dots on the other flag. Can he put the same number of dots on each flag?

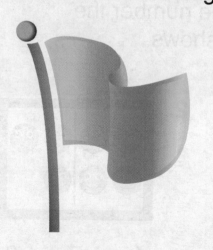
Yes

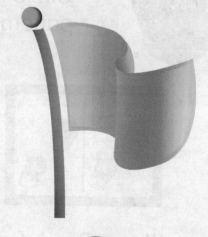
No

Name _____

**Solve & Share**

For each problem, drop 6 counters on the ice cave. Write the number of counters that land inside and outside the ice cave. What is the same about each drop? What is different?

⭐ TEKS 1.3B Use objects and pictorial models to solve word problems involving joining, ... within 20 and unknowns as any one of the terms in the problem ... . Mathematical Process Standards 1.1C, 1.1D, 1.1F.

Digital Resources at PearsonTexas.com

Solve   Learn   Glossary   Check   Tools   Games

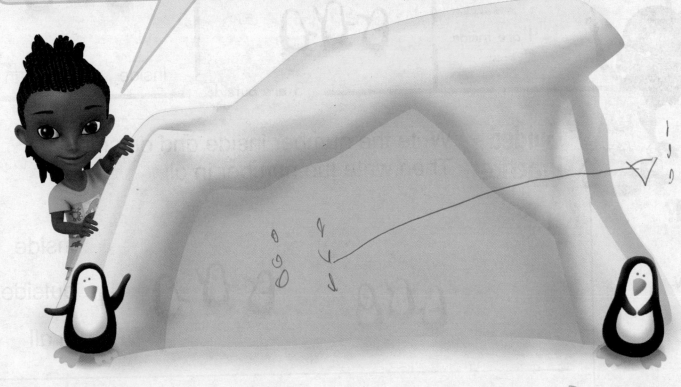

1. 3 inside 3 outside

2. 3 inside 3 outside

3. 3 inside 3 outside

4. 3 inside 3 outside

There are 7 penguins **in all**.

Some of the penguins are inside the ice cave.

4 are inside.

Some of the penguins are outside the ice cave.

3 are outside.

| 4 | 3 | 7 |
|---|---|---|
| inside | outside | in all |

## Do You Understand?

**Show Me!** What is another way to show 7 using counters?

☆ **Guided Practice** ☆  Write the number inside and outside. Then write the number in all.

1.

3  inside
3  outside
6  in all

2.

____ inside
____ outside
____ in all

© Pearson Education, Inc. 1

Name ____________________

## Independent Practice

Write the number inside and outside. Then write the number in all.

**3.**

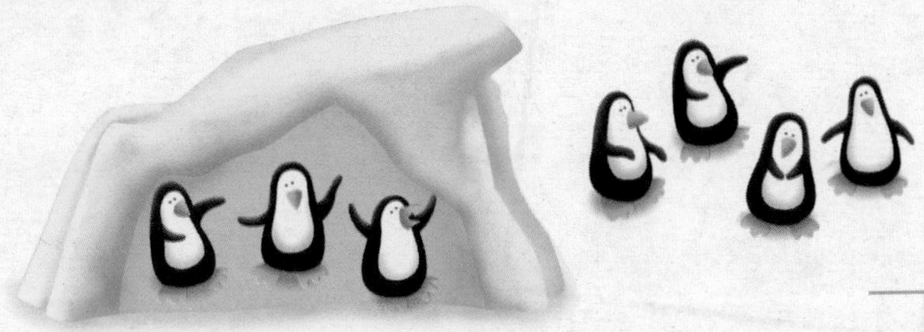

___ inside ___ outside ___ in all

**4.**

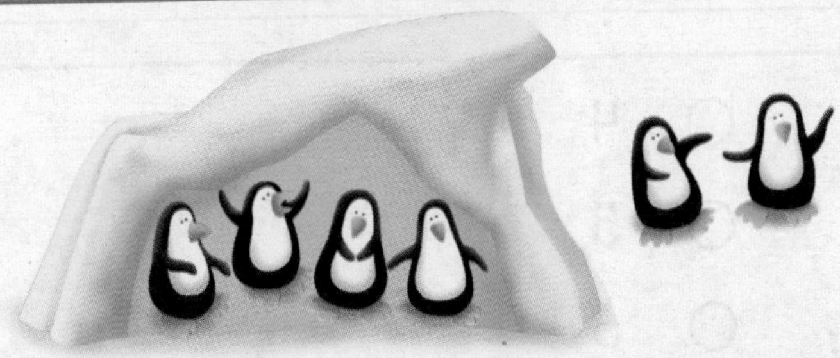

___ inside ___ outside ___ in all

**5.**

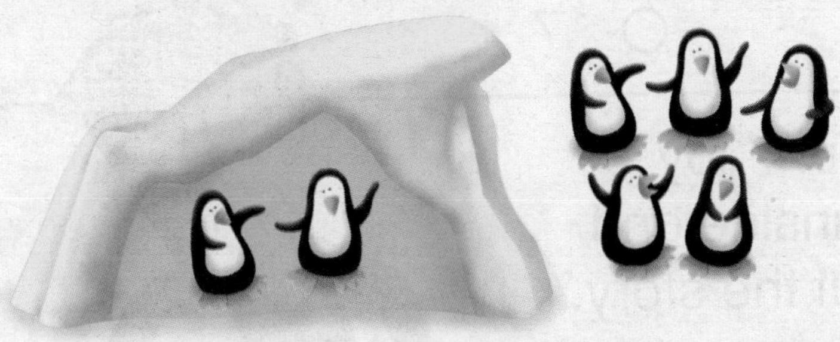

___ inside ___ outside ___ in all

**6. Extend Your Thinking** Dan used dots to show the number 6. He put some dots inside the circle and the rest outside the circle. Show 2 different ways Dan could have used.

**One Way**

**Another Way**

Solve each problem below.

**7.** Ben put 3 toy trucks inside the box.
He put 4 toy trucks outside the box.
How many trucks are there in all?

Draw a picture to solve.

_____ trucks

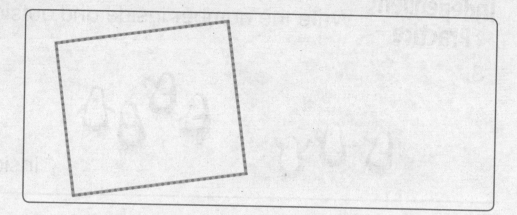

**8.** Ana hides 6 blocks.
She hides 1 block under the chair.
She hides the rest under the table.
How many blocks does Ana hide under the table?

○ 4
○ 5
○ 6
○ 7

**9. Extend Your Thinking** Write a sentence about 7 toy
cars. Draw a picture to match. Put some cars inside and
some outside. Then write numbers to tell about the story.

_____

_____

_____

_____ inside

_____ outside

_____ in all

**Another Look** You can use different ways to make 6.

3 and 3

5 and 1

Write the numbers that show ways to make 6.

1.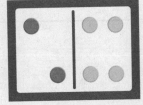

___ and ___

2.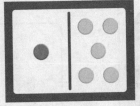

___ and ___

3.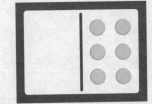

___ and ___

4.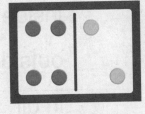

___ and ___

5.

___ and ___

6.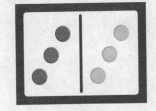

___ and ___

Write the number inside and outside.
Then write the number in all.

**7.**

____  ____  ____
inside  outside  in all

**8.**

____  ____  ____
inside  outside  in all

**9.**

____  ____  ____
inside  outside  in all

**10.**

____  ____  ____
inside  outside  in all

**11.** Marlen drew 7 tiles in all.
☆ She drew 4 tiles inside a circle.
She drew the rest outside.

How many tiles did she draw
outside the circle?

○ 7

○ 5

○ 3

○ 1

You can draw a
picture to help.

**12. Extend Your Thinking**
Tito has 6 white mice.
Some mice are inside the cage.
Some mice are outside the cage.

Draw a picture to solve.
Then write the numbers.

____ inside

____ outside

____ in all

Name _____

For each problem, show a different way to cover each balloon with 1 blue or 1 red tile. Write the number of each tile. Does the number of blue or red tiles change the total number of balloons?

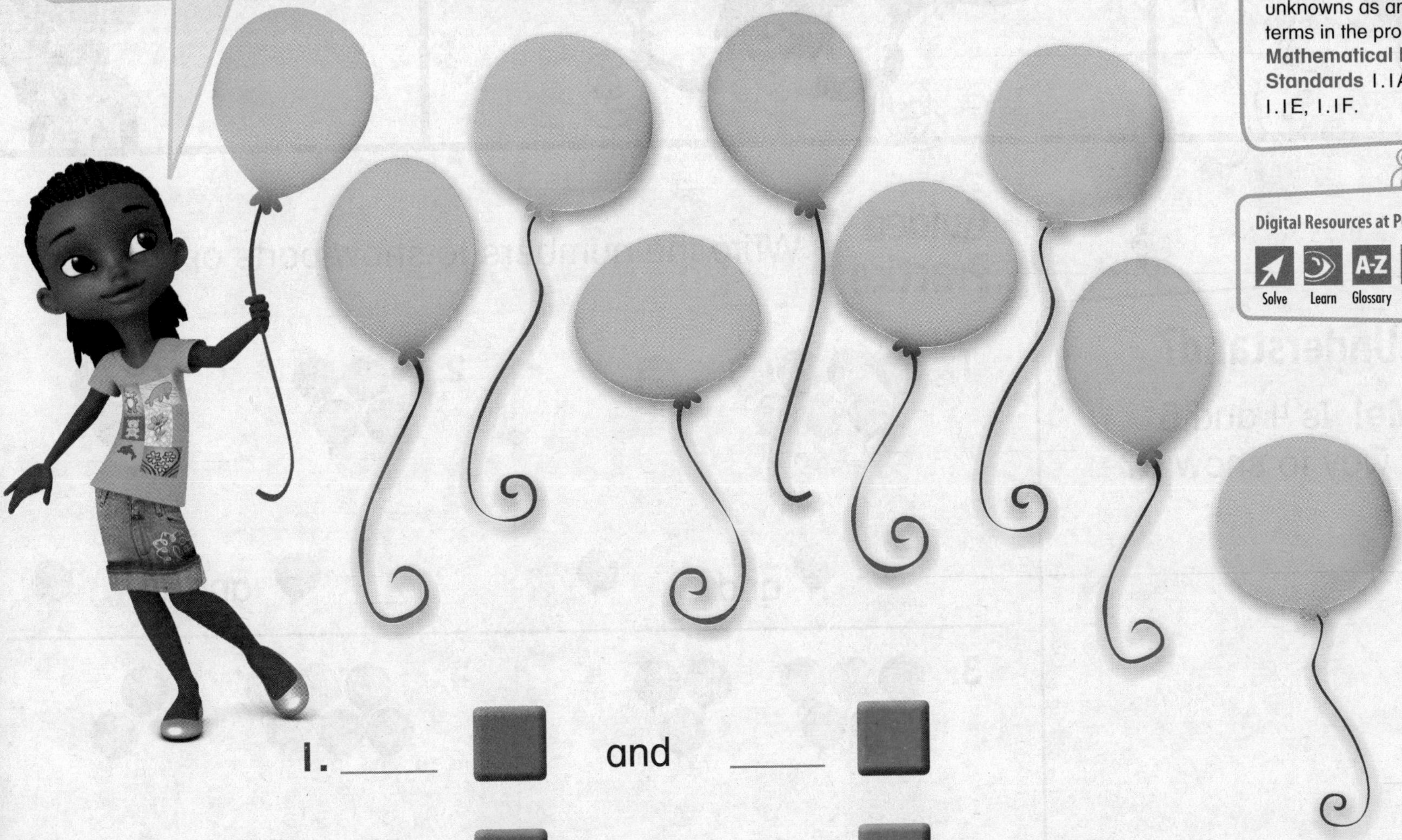

⭐ **TEKS 1.3B** Use objects and pictorial models to solve word problems involving joining, … within 20 and unknowns as any one of the terms in the problem … . **Mathematical Process Standards 1.1A, 1.1C, 1.1D, 1.1E, 1.1F.**

Digital Resources at PearsonTexas.com

| Solve | Learn | Glossary | Check | Tools | Games |

1. _____ ⬛ and _____ ⬛

2. _____ ⬛ and _____ ⬛

Kami has a set of 8 balloons in all.

**Part** of the set is blue.

4 are blue.

Part of the set is green.

4 are green.

The **whole** set is 8 in all.

_4_ blue  _4_ green  _8_ in all

↑ part   ↑ part   ↑ whole

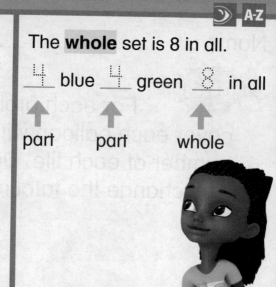

## Do You Understand?

**Show Me!** Is 4 and 5 another way to show 8? Explain.

## ☆ Guided Practice ☆

Write the numbers to show parts of 8.

1.
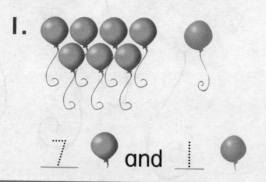

_7_ 🎈 and _1_ 🎈

2.

____ 🎈 and ____ 🎈

3.

____ and ____ 🎈

4.
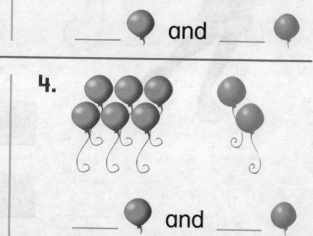

____ 🎈 and ____ 🎈

© Pearson Education, Inc. 1

**Independent Practice**

Write the numbers to show parts of 9.

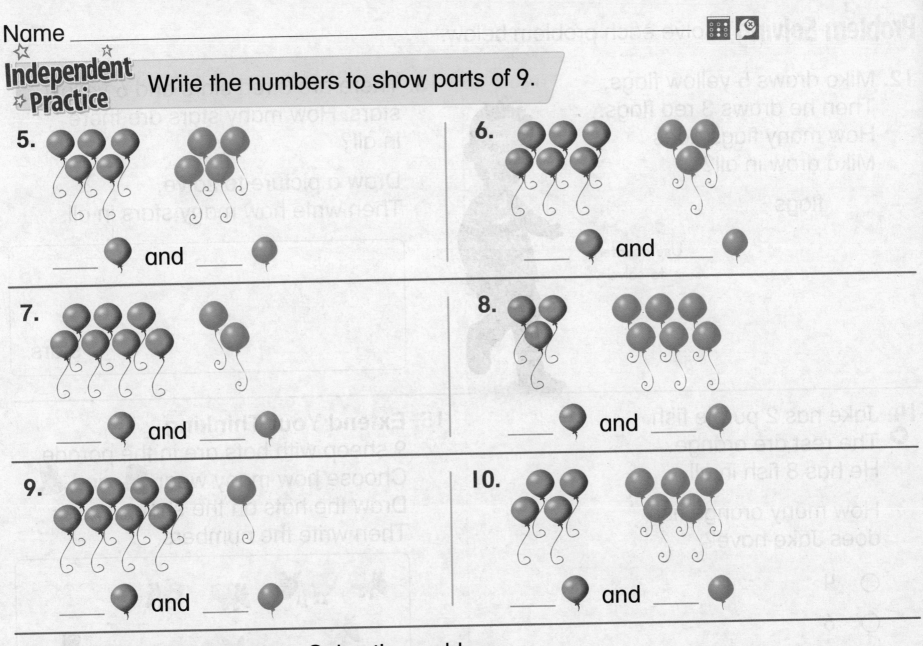

5. ___ 🎈 and ___ 🎈

6. ___ 🎈 and ___ 🎈

7. ___ 🎈 and ___ 🎈

8. ___ 🎈 and ___ 🎈

9. ___ 🎈 and ___ 🎈

10. ___ 🎈 and ___ 🎈

11. **Extend Your Thinking** Solve the problem.

There are 9 hats in all. 3 are red.
The rest are yellow. How many hats are yellow? _____ yellow hats

12. Miko draws 5 yellow flags.
Then he draws 3 red flags.
How many flags does
Miko draw in all?

_____ flags

Use counters to solve.

13. There are 3 red stars and 6 yellow stars. How many stars are there in all?

Draw a picture to solve.
Then write how many stars in all.

_____ stars

14. Jake has 2 purple fish.
⭐ The rest are orange.
He has 8 fish in all.

How many orange fish
does Jake have?

○ 4

○ 6

○ 8

○ 10

15. **Extend Your Thinking**
9 sheep with hats are in the parade.
Choose how many wear 🎩 and 🎩.
Draw the hats on the sheep.
Then write the numbers.

_____

_____

_____ in all

Name _____

**Another Look** You can use different ways to make 8.

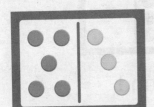

5 and 3

4 and 4

 **HOME CONNECTION**
Your child identified different ways to make 8 and 9.

**HOME ACTIVITY** Give your child 8 pennies and draw a large circle. Have your child place some pennies inside the circle and the rest outside. Then have your child tell how many are inside, how many are outside, and how many there are in all. Give your child 1 more penny and repeat the activity.

Write the numbers that show ways to make 8.

1.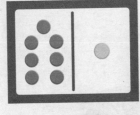

___ and ___

2.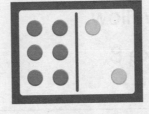

___ and ___

3.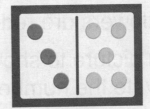

___ and ___

4.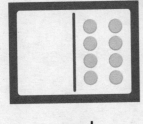

___ and ___

5.

___ and ___

6.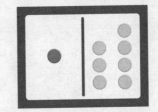

___ and ___

Write the numbers to show parts of 9.

**7.**

_____ ● and _____ ●

**8.**

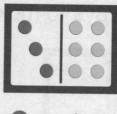

_____ ● and _____ ●

**9.**

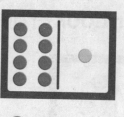

_____ ● and _____ ●

**10. Algebra** The whole is 9.
One part is 3.
The other part is _?_ .

4 ○  5 ○  6 ○  7 ○

**11. Algebra** The whole is 9.
One part is 1.
The other part is _?_ .

9 ○  8 ○  7 ○  6 ○

**12. Algebra** The whole is 9.
One part is 7.
The other part is _?_ .

2 ○  5 ○  7 ○  9 ○

**13. Extend Your Thinking** Max sees 8 flowers.
Some flowers are red. The rest are yellow.

Draw a picture to show a way to make 8.
Then write the numbers.

_____ and _____ is 8.

Name ______________________

Solve & Share

Your bag has 2 different colors of connecting cubes. Take out a handful of cubes. Make sure to get some cubes of each color.

How can you use numbers to show how many cubes you picked in all? Show how.

# Lesson 1-5

## Introducing Addition Expressions and Number Sentences

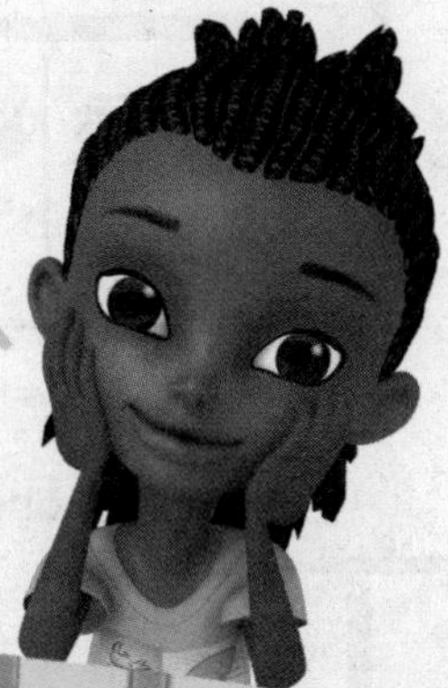

**TEKS 1.3B** Use objects and pictorial models to solve word problems involving joining, ... within 20 and unknowns as any one of the terms in the problem … . Also, 1.5D, 1.5E. **Mathematical Process Standards** 1.1B, 1.1C, 1.1D, 1.1F, 1.1G.

Digital Resources at PearsonTexas.com

Solve Learn Glossary Check Tools Games

Kenny picked 4 red cubes. Then he picked 2 blue cubes.

You can describe the parts as 4 and 2 and write 4 + 2.

**plus**

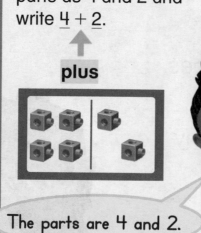

The parts are 4 and 2.

6 is the sum of 4 and 2.

You can **add** the parts to find the **sum**. 4 and 2 is 6 in all.

You can write an **addition sentence** to show the parts and the whole.

4 + 2 = 6

4 plus 2 **equals** 6.

## Do You Understand?

**Show Me!** What can you do to find how many there are in all?

**Guided Practice** Use the model. Write the parts. Then write an addition sentence.

1.

3 + 5

3 + 5 = 8

2.

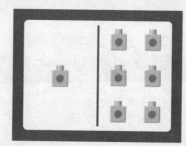

___ + ___

___ = ___ + ___

© Pearson Education, Inc. 1

Name _____

Use the model. Write the parts. Then write an addition sentence.

3.

___ + ___

___ + ___ = ___

4.

___ + ___

___ + ___ = ___

5.

___ + ___

___ = ___ + ___

6. **Extend Your Thinking**  Marco picked up 9 rocks. He picked up 2 of them on his way to school. He picked up the rest on his way home. How many rocks did Marco pick up on his way home?

Draw a picture to solve.
Then write an addition sentence.

___ + ___ = ___

7. Jen found 2 orange leaves.
Then she found 5 yellow leaves.
How many leaves did Jen
find in all?

Draw a picture to show the story.
Then write an addition sentence.

_____ + _____ = _____

8. Tim drew 9 apples. 4 of them are
green. The others are red.
How many red apples did he draw?

Which addition sentence matches
this story?

○  9 + 4 = 13

○  4 + 5 = 9

○  3 + 6 = 9

○  4 + 4 = 8

9. **Extend Your Thinking** Draw a
picture to show an addition story
about red worms and brown worms.
Write an addition sentence to tell
how many worms there are in all.

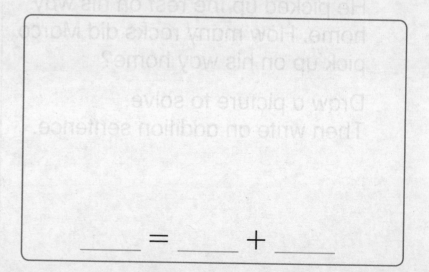

_____ = _____ + _____

Name _____

**Another Look** Use the parts to write an addition sentence.

There are 2 red circles and 3 yellow circles These are the parts.

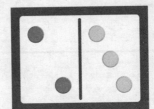

2 + 3
2 + 3 = 5

_3_ + _5_
_3_ + _5_ = _8_

**HOME CONNECTION** Your child used part-part mats to write addition sentences.

**HOME ACTIVITY** Give your child 2 groups of small objects to count (e.g., one group of 3 buttons and one group of 4 buttons). Together, find the total number of objects and say the corresponding addition sentence (e.g., "3 plus 4 equals 7."). Repeat the activity several times with different groupings.

Use the model. Write the parts. Then write an addition sentence.

1.

___ + ___
___ + ___ = ___

2.

___ + ___
___ + ___ = ___

3.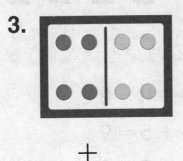

___ + ___
___ + ___ = ___

Use the model. Write the parts. Then write an addition sentence.

**4.**

_____ + _____

_____ + _____ = _____

**5.**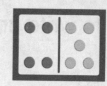

_____ + _____

_____ + _____ = _____

Write an addition sentence for each story.

**6.** Ian picked 3 apples on Monday.
Ian picked 5 apples on Tuesday.
How many apples did he pick in all?

_____ + _____ = _____

**7.** Sara has 2 rocks.
Jake has 4 rocks.
How many rocks do they have in all?

_____ + _____ = _____

**8.** ⭐ Which addition sentence goes with the picture?

○ $4 + 4 = 8$

○ $4 + 5 = 9$

○ $2 + 7 = 9$

○ $4 + 6 = 10$

**9. Extend Your Thinking** Circle 2 groups of fruit. Write an addition sentence to tell how many pieces of fruit there are in your 2 groups.

_____ + _____ = _____ + _____

Name _____

**Solve & Share**

You see 2 train cars on the track. Then 1 more train car joins them. How can you use connecting cubes to show this story? What addition sentence can you write?

**TEKS 1.3B** Use objects and pictorial models to solve word problems involving joining, ... within 20 and unknowns as any one of the terms in the problem ... . Also, 1.3, 1.5D, 1.5F. **Mathematical Process Standards 1.1A, 1.1C, 1.1D, 1.1F.**

**Digital Resources at PearsonTexas.com**

 Solve  Learn  Glossary  Check  Tools  Games

_____ + _____ = _____

5 train cars stop at the red light. Then 2 more train cars stop. How many train cars are there now?

You can join the groups to find the sum.

The first group is 5. The second group is 2 more.

5 + 2
5 plus 2 more

Add to find how many in all.

Write an addition sentence.

$$\underline{5} + \underline{2} = \underline{7}$$

There are 7 train cars in all.

## Do You Understand?

**Show Me!** How can you tell if a story is about joining?

☆ **Guided Practice** ☆  Write an addition sentence to solve each problem.

1. 3 trucks are stopped. 3 more trucks stop. How many trucks are there in all?

$$\underline{3} + \underline{3} = \underline{6}$$

2. Anna has 2 oranges. She buys 6 more. How many oranges does Anna have in all?

$$\underline{\phantom{0}} + \underline{\phantom{0}} = \underline{\phantom{0}}$$

**38** thirty-eight

© Pearson Education, Inc. 1

**Topic 1** | Lesson 6

**Independent ☆ Practice**  Write an addition sentence to solve each problem.

3. 4 students ride bikes to the park. Then 4 more students join them. How many students are riding bikes to the park now?

___ + ___ = ___

4. 3 students wait for the bus. Then 6 more students join them. How many students are waiting for the bus in all?

___ + ___ = ___

 Draw a picture to solve the story problem. Then write an addition sentence.

5. **Extend Your Thinking** There are 8 ducks swimming in the pond. 2 of the ducks are brown. The rest are white. How many ducks are white?

___ = ___ + ___

**6.** Ben saw 3 big dogs.
Then he saw 4 small dogs.
How many dogs did Ben see in all?

Write an addition sentence.

_____ + _____ = _____

**7.** 8 friends play ball.
1 more friend joins them.
How many friends play ball in all?

Write an addition sentence.

_____ + _____ = _____

**8.** Lisa has 8 beads.
3 of her beads are blue.
The rest are red.

Which addition sentence shows
how many red beads Lisa has?

○ $5 + 1 = 6$

○ $5 + 2 = 7$

○ $5 + 3 = 8$

○ $5 + 4 = 9$

**9. Extend Your Thinking** Write a
joining story about the birds.

Use pictures,
numbers, or
words.

Name _____

## Another Look

5 students are reading books.
Then 3 more students join them.
How many students are reading books now?

 $5 + 3 = 8$

7 students are running.
Then 2 more students start running.
How many students are running now?

Use color tiles to find the sum.

🏠 **HOME CONNECTION**
Your child used connecting cubes and drew pictures to solve stories about joining.

**HOME ACTIVITY** Write an addition sentence for your child. Have him or her tell you a number story to match the addition sentence. Then gather 9 pennies. Tell him or her this story: "I found 9 pennies. 3 of them were in my pocket. I found the rest on the ground. How many did I find on the ground?" Have your child use the pennies to solve the number story.

$\underline{\phantom{7}} + \underline{\phantom{2}} = \underline{\phantom{9}}$  (filled in: $7 + 2 = 9$)

Write an addition sentence to solve each problem.

1. 3 frogs are in the pond.
   Then 3 frogs join them.
   How many frogs are in the pond now?

    ___ + ___ = ___

2. 2 bugs are on a rock.
   3 bugs are on a leaf.
   How many bugs are there in all?

    ___ + ___ = ___

Write an addition sentence to solve each problem.

**3.**

2 puppies are sleeping.
4 puppies are playing.
How many puppies are there in all?

_____ + _____ = _____

**4.**

The team has 10 soccer balls.
5 balls are on the field. The rest are in
the bag. How many balls are in the bag?

_____ + _____ = _____

**5.** Which addition sentence
⭐ describes the picture?

○   3 + 0 = 3
○   2 + 2 = 4
○   3 + 1 = 4
○   3 + 2 = 5

**6.** Read the story. Which number is
⭐ missing from the addition sentence?

Grant has 5 jars. 3 are glass. The rest
are metal. How many jars are metal?

3 + _?_ = 5

3          5          2          |
○          ○          ○          ○

**7. Extend Your Thinking** Tell a joining story about
the frogs. Then write an addition sentence to
show how many in all.

_____ + _____ = _____

Name _____

**Solve & Share**

There are 5 train cars on the track.
3 of them are red. The rest are yellow.
How many yellow trains are on the track?
Use connecting cubes to model this story.
Write an addition sentence.

TEKS 1.3B Use objects
and pictorial models to solve
word problems involving
joining, ... within 20 and
unknowns as any one of the
terms in the problem ... .
TEKS 1.5D Represent word
problems involving addition ... .
Also, 1.3, 1.5F. Mathematical
Process Standards 1.1B,
1.1D, 1.1E.

Digital Resources at PearsonTexas.com

Solve   Learn   Glossary   Check   Tools   Games

____ + ____ = ____

_____ train cars are yellow.

The station has 7 train cars. Some more train cars roll into the station. Now the station has 9 train cars. How many train cars rolled in?

The first group has 7. We don't know how many the second group has. The total is 9.

7 plus what is 9?

Use cubes and a model to help find the answer.

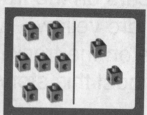

Write an addition sentence.

$$\underline{7} + \underline{2} = \underline{9}$$

addends        sum

2 train cars rolled in.

---

## ☆ Guided Practice ☆
Complete the models to solve each addition story.

## Do You Understand?

**Show Me!** How do you solve an addition problem if you know only one part and the sum?

1. Bobby had 7 fish in the bowl. 4 fish were blue. The rest were orange. How many fish were orange?

7

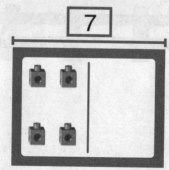

$4 + \underline{3} = 7$ fish

2. The team scored 5 points their first game. They scored 4 points their next game. How many points did the team score in all?

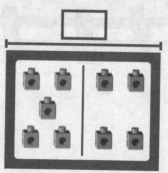

$5 + 4 = \underline{\phantom{0}}$ points

---

Name _____

Complete the models to solve each addition story.

3. Ted needs onions for a recipe. He has 3 onions. He needs 2 more. How many onions does he need in all?

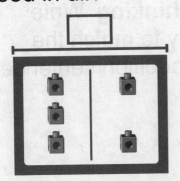

$3 + 2 =$ _____ onions

4. Mary needs 8 stickers for her book. She has 4 stickers. How many more stickers does Mary need?

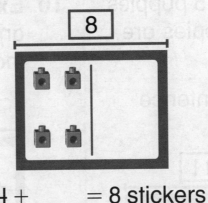

$4 +$ _____ $= 8$ stickers

5. Billy has 10 pages to read. He read 4 pages on Monday. How many pages does he have left to read?

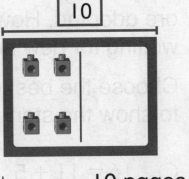

$4 +$ _____ $= 10$ pages

6. **Extend Your Thinking**
Megan has some shoes on the mat. She has 8 in the box. There are 12 shoes in all. How many shoes are on the mat?

Draw a picture to solve. Then write an addition sentence.

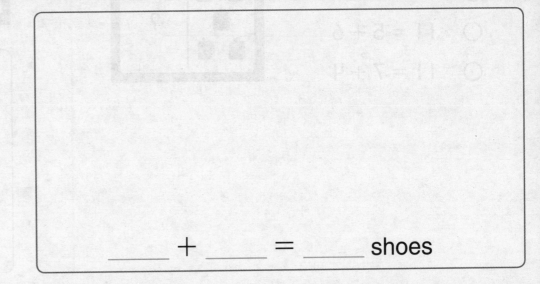

_____ $+$ _____ $=$ _____ shoes

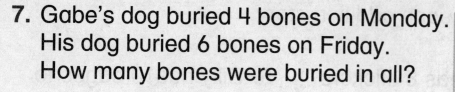

**Problem Solving** Write an addition sentence to solve each problem below.

**7.** Gabe's dog buried 4 bones on Monday. His dog buried 6 bones on Friday. How many bones were buried in all?

_____ + _____ = _____

_____ bones

**8.** The cage holds 9 hamsters. There are 2 hamsters in the cage. How many more hamsters can fit in the cage?

_____ + _____ = _____

_____ more hamsters

**9.** Anita's dog had 11 puppies. 5 puppies are adopted. How many puppies are waiting for new homes?

Choose the best addition sentence to show the story.

○  16 = 11 + 5

○  12 = 5 + 7

○  11 = 5 + 6

○  11 = 7 + 4

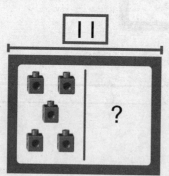

**10.** **Extend Your Thinking** Write an addition story to match the model and the addition sentence.

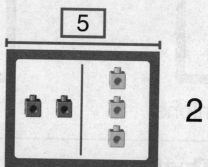

$$2 + 3 = 5$$

_____

_____

_____

_____

Name _____

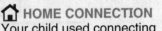

**Another Look** You can use a model to solve an addition story.

Max had 6 golf balls in his bag. He found 2 more golf balls. How many golf balls does he have now?

Jim had 4 golf balls in his bag. He found 3 more golf balls. How many golf balls does he have now?

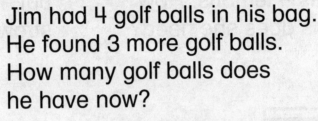

🏠 **HOME CONNECTION** Your child used connecting cubes, counters, and models to solve addition stories.

**HOME ACTIVITY** Give your child a collection of small objects to use as counters. Tell your child this story: "There are 9 ants on the ground. 4 ants are brown. The rest are red. How many ants are red?" Have your child use the small objects to solve the addition story.

$6 + 2 = 8$ golf balls

$\underline{4} + \underline{3} = \underline{7}$

 Complete the models to solve each addition story.

1. 2 cats are playing with a ball of yarn. 5 cats are napping. How many cats are there in all?

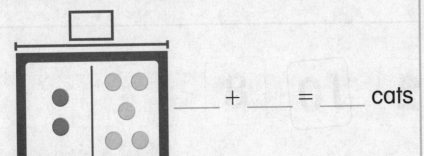

___ + ___ = ___ cats

2. 8 friends are playing a game. There is room for 13 friends to play. How many more friends can join the game?

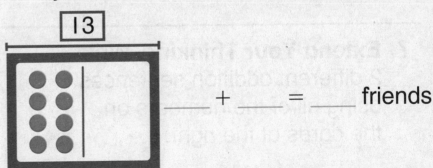

___ + ___ = ___ friends

Digital Resources at PearsonTexas.com

Write an addition sentence to solve each addition story.

3. Linda needs 8 lemons to make lemonade. She has 4 lemons. How many more lemons does she need?

8

?

____ + ____ = ____ lemons

4. Tia put 5 strawberries in a basket. Brad put 4 more in the basket. How many strawberries are in the basket?

?

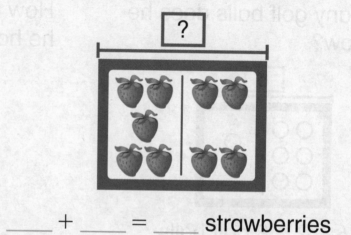

____ + ____ = ____ strawberries

Find the missing number for each problem.

5. Algebra ____ $+ 3 = 4$
   ○ 1    ○ 2    ○ 7    ○ 3

6. Algebra $12 = 7 +$ ____
   ○ 4    ○ 5    ○ 6    ○ 7

7. **Extend Your Thinking** Write 2 different addition sentences using all of the numbers on the cards at the right.

2   10   8

____ + ____ = ____

____ + ____ = ____

Name _____

**Solve & Share**

Write an addition sentence for each cube tower. How are the addition sentences the same? How are they different?

⭐ TEKS 1.5G Apply properties of operations to add and subtract two or three numbers. **Mathematical Process Standards 1.1C, 1.1D, 1.1F, 1.1G.**

**Digital Resources at PearsonTexas.com**

Solve  Learn  Glossary  Check  Tools  Games

**1.**

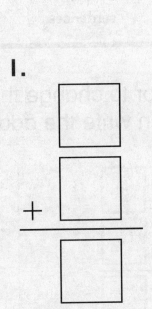

$$+ \frac{\boxed{\phantom{0}}}{\boxed{\phantom{0}}}$$

**2.**

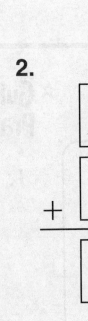

$$+ \frac{\boxed{\phantom{0}}}{\boxed{\phantom{0}}}$$

4 and 2 is 6.

2 and 4 is 6.

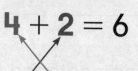
$$4 + 2 = 6$$
$$2 + 4 = 6$$

4 plus 2 equals 6.

2 plus 4 equals 6.

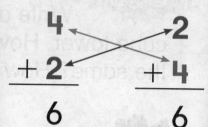

You can change the order of the addends. You will see that the sum is the same.

You can write 2 addition sentences.

## Do You Understand?

**Show Me!** How can you use cubes to show that 5 + 3 is the same as 3 + 5?

☆ **Guided Practice** ☆   Color to change the order of the addends. Then write the addition sentences.

**I.**

$$\begin{array}{r} 3 \\ + 4 \\ \hline 7 \end{array}$$

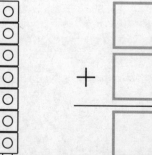

$$+ \underline{\phantom{0}}$$

**2.**

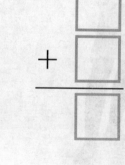

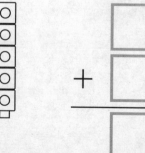

$$+ \underline{\phantom{0}}$$

© Pearson Education, Inc. I

Name _____

**Independent Practice**    Write the sum. Then change the order of the addends. Write the new addition sentence.

3.

2 + 3 = ____

____ + ____ = ____

4.

1 + 6 = ____

____ + ____ = ____

5.

____ = 3 + 6

____ = ____ + ____

6.
```
   5
 + 2
 ____
 [ ]
```
[ ] + [ ]
____

7.
```
   4
 + 5
 ____
 [ ]
```
[ ] + [ ]
____

8.
```
   6
 + 2
 ____
 [ ]
```
[ ] + [ ]
____

**Extend Your Thinking** Use the numbers on the cards to write 2 addition sentences.

9.   **3**  **8**  **5**

____ + ____ = ____

____ + ____ = ____

10.  **4**  **6**  **2**

____ = ____ + ____

____ = ____ + ____

## Problem Solving    Solve each problem below.

**11.** Liza and Anna collected 6 cans on Monday. On Tuesday, they collected 4 more. How many cans did they collect in all?

Draw a picture. Then write 2 different addition sentences.

\_\_\_\_ + \_\_\_\_ = \_\_\_\_

\_\_\_\_ + \_\_\_\_ = \_\_\_\_

**12.** Look at the 2 addition sentences. ⭐ Which is the missing addend?

9 = \_?\_ + 2

9 = 2 + \_?\_

Both addition sentences have a 2 and a 9.

○ 6

○ 7

○ 8

○ 9

**13. Extend Your Thinking**
Draw a picture of 5 birds.
Make some blue.
Make the rest red.

Write 2 addition sentences to tell about the picture.

\_\_\_\_ + \_\_\_\_ = \_\_\_\_

\_\_\_\_ + \_\_\_\_ = \_\_\_\_

Name _____

**Another Look** When you change the order of addends, the sum is the same.

$4 + 2 = 6$

$2 + 4 = 6$

🏠 **HOME CONNECTION**
Your child learned that if the order of addends is changed, the sum is the same.

**HOME ACTIVITY** Write several addition sentences for your child. Have him or her change the order of addends and write the new addition sentence. Ask, "How are the addition sentences the same? How are they different?"

$5 + 2 = 7$

$2 + 5 = 7$

Add. Write an addition sentence with addends in a different order.

1.

___ + ___ = ___

___ + ___ = ___

Write 2 addition sentences for each cube train.

**2.**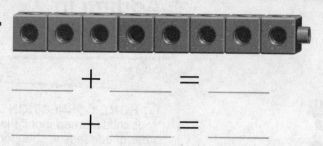

___ + ___ = ___

___ + ___ = ___

**3.**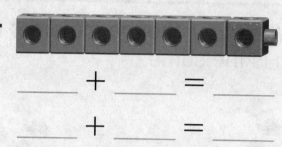

___ + ___ = ___

___ + ___ = ___

**4.** Which is the same as 5 + 1?

○ 1 + 2

○ 5 + 3

○ 2 + 6

○ 1 + 5

**5.** Which shows 2 ways to add the cubes in the cube train?

○ 4 + 3, 3 + 4

○ 2 + 6, 6 + 2

○ 2 + 7, 7 + 2

○ 5 + 2, 2 + 5

**6. Extend Your Thinking** Use the cubes below. Pick 2 colors of cubes. Write an addition story. Then write 2 addition sentences for your story.

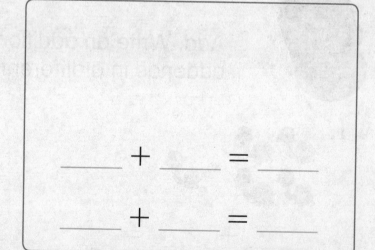

___ + ___ = ___

___ + ___ = ___

© Pearson Education, Inc. 1

**Solve & Share**

Mia needs 8 movie tickets. She buys 5 tickets online. Her mom buys her 3 more tickets. Does she have enough tickets? Show how you know with pictures, numbers, or words.

TEKS 1.1G Display, explain, and justify mathematical ideas and arguments using precise mathematical language in written or oral communication. Also, 1.3B, 1.3E. **Mathematical Process Standards** 1.1A, 1.1B, 1.1D, 1.1E.

Digital Resources at PearsonTexas.com

Solve   Learn   Glossary   Check   Tools   Games

add   +   plus   =   in all

## Analyze

Jon has 4 tickets to the go-kart track. He buys 3 more tickets. He wants to go with 6 of his friends. Will Jon have enough tickets? Explain.

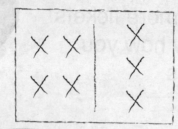

## Plan

You can draw a model to find out how many tickets Jon has.

$4 + 3 = 7$ tickets.

## Solve, Justify, and Evaluate

You can use a different model to show the tickets Jon and his 6 friends need.

$1 + 6 = 7$ people

7 people. 7 tickets. Jon has enough tickets.

## Do You Understand?

**Show Me!** Show 2 ways to explain why $2 + 4$ is the same as $3 + 3$.

## ☆ Guided Practice ☆

Solve. Use words, addition sentences, models, or pictures to explain.

1. Gina has 6 stickers. Her sister gives her 2 more stickers. She wants to put two rows of 4 stickers in her album.

Stickers Gina Has

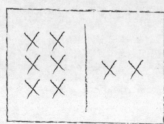

$6 + 2 = \underline{8}$

Stickers Gina Needs

$4 + 4 = \underline{8}$

Will Gina have enough stickers?

**Yes**                    **No**

**Topic 1** | Lesson 9

Name _____

Solve. Use words, addition sentences, models, or pictures to explain.

2. Max has 3 apples. He buys 2 more apples. He wants to keep 1 apple for himself and give apples to 5 of his friends.

Will Max have enough apples?

**Yes**      **No**

3. Kim has 8 flowers. She picks 1 more flower. She wants to put 2 flowers in a small vase and 7 flowers in a large vase.

Will Kim have enough flowers?

**Yes**      **No**

4. **Extend Your Thinking** Solve. Use words, addition sentences, models, or pictures to explain.

Jan has 7 pennies. She wants to buy a toy car for 3 pennies and a toy plane for 5 pennies. How many more pennies does Jan need? Explain.

**5.** Brad has 5 tickets to the school play. He buys 1 more ticket. Will Brad have enough tickets to go to the play with 6 of his friends?

**6.** Jen has 3 muffins. She buys 1 more muffin. She wants to keep 1 muffin for herself and give muffins to 2 of her friends. Will Jen have enough muffins?

**Yes**          **No**

**Yes**          **No**

**7.** Beth has 4 crayons. She wants to give crayons to 8 of her friends. She wants to keep 1 crayon for herself. How many more crayons does Beth need to buy?

○ 5

○ 6

○ 7

○ 8

**8. Extend Your Thinking** Pretend you have 6 marbles. You want to keep some and give some to your friends. Use addition sentences, pictures, models, or your own words to write and solve a story problem.

Name _____

## Homework 1-9
## Writing to Explain

**Another Look** Bill has 3 bananas. He buys 3 more. He wants to keep 1 banana for himself and give bananas to 5 of his friends.

First, find how many bananas Bill will have.

Next, find how many people there are.

🏠 **HOME CONNECTION** Your child used words, addition sentences, models, or pictures to explain answers to word problems.

**HOME ACTIVITY** Tell your child the following story: "Jack has 2 marbles. He buys 1 more. He wants to keep 1 marble and give marbles to 3 of his friends. Will he have enough marbles?" Have your child use number sentences, pictures, models, and his or her own words to explain whether or not Jack has enough marbles.

$3 + 3 = \underline{6}$ bananas

$1 + 5 = \underline{6}$ people

Will Bill have enough bananas?

(**Yes**)　　　　**No**

Solve. Use words, addition sentences, models, or pictures to explain.

1. Tim has 7 toy cars. He buys 2 more. He wants to keep 1 toy car for himself and give toy cars to 8 of his friends. Will Tim have enough toy cars?

**Yes**　　　　**No**

Topic 1 | Lesson 9

Digital Resources at **PearsonTexas.com**

Solve. Use words, addition sentences, models, or pictures to explain.

2. Nita has 2 bottles of water. She buys 2 more. She wants to keep 1 bottle for herself and give bottles to 3 of her friends. Will Nita have enough bottles of water?

3. Dan has 5 oranges. He buys 3 more. He wants to keep 1 orange for himself and give oranges to 7 of his friends. Will Dan have enough oranges?

**Yes**　　　　**No**

**Yes**　　　　**No**

4. **Algebra** Write the missing number.
⭐ $3 + 4$ is the same as $5 + \underline{\ ?\ }$.

4 ○　　3 ○　　2 ○　　1 ○

5. **Algebra** Write the missing number.
⭐ $6 + 2$ is the same as $7 + \underline{\ ?\ }$.

0 ○　　1 ○　　5 ○　　6 ○

6. **Extend Your Thinking** Solve. Use words, addition sentences, models, or pictures to explain.

Jake has 3 tickets to the skating rink.
He buys 2 more tickets.
He wants to go with some of his friends.
How many friends can go with Jake? _____

Name _____

Think about how you can **analyze** information as you solve this problem.

1. Tina has 5 fish.
   Some fish are orange.
   The rest of the fish are yellow.

   Draw a picture to show the problem.
   Write an addition sentence.

   ____ + ____ = ____

2. Tina has 5 fish in all. 3 fish are orange. The rest of the fish are yellow. Circle the model that shows how many yellow fish Tina has.

3. Write 2 different addition sentences for Tina's fish story.

   ____ + ____ = ____

   ____ + ____ = ____

## Number Sense

## Make a List

1. Sasha shows all the ways to make 6 using red and yellow counters. She shows the ways in a list. Find the pattern to write the missing numbers.

| ● | ● |
|---|---|
| 6 | 0 |
|   |   |
| 4 |   |
|   |   |
|   | 4 |
|   |   |
| 0 |   |

## What's Wrong?

2. 5 pink flowers bloomed yesterday. 3 more pink flowers bloomed today.

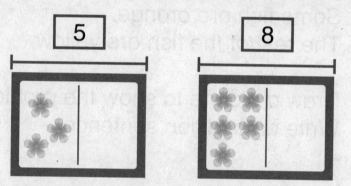

Cross out the model that does **not** go with the story. Then complete the model that matches the story.

## Complete It!

3. Fill in the missing numbers.

$8 = \boxed{\phantom{0}} + 5$

$4 + \boxed{\phantom{0}} = 6$

$7 = 3 + \boxed{\phantom{0}}$

Name _____

Set A

You can use patterns to see numbers.

This pattern shows 4.

Write the number of dots.

1.  _____

2.  _____

Set B

You can look for patterns to count.

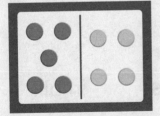 

One side has 5.
One side has 4.
There are 9 counters in all.

Write the number that tells how many.

3. 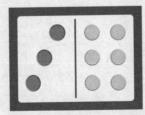 _____

4.  _____

Topic 1

You can write the number
inside and outside.

You can write the number in all.

__3__    __4__    __7__

inside    outside    in all

Write the number inside and outside.
Then write the number in all.

**5.**

_____    _____    _____

inside    outside    in all

**Set D**

You can write numbers to
show parts of 9.

The whole set is 9 in all.

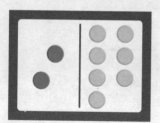

__2__ ● and __7__ ○ is __9__ in all.

Write the numbers to show parts of 9.

**6.**

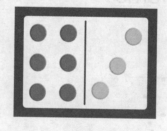

_____ ● and _____ ○ is _____ in all.

**7.**

_____ ● and _____ ○ is _____ in all.

**Set E**

You can write an
addition sentence
to show how
many in all.

The parts are 3 and 2.

_3_ + _2_

3 and 2 is 5 in all.
3 plus 2 equals 5.

_3_ + _2_ = _5_

Use the model. Write the parts.
Then write an addition sentence.

8.

_____ + _____

_____ + _____ = _____

**Set F**

You can write an addition
sentence to solve a joining story.

Cindy has 3 shells. She finds
I more. How many shells
does Cindy have in all?

**3** plus **I** more
equals **4**.

_3_ + _1_ = _4_

Write an addition sentence to solve.

9. Ethan plants 5 flowers.
Then he plants 2 more.
How many flowers does
Ethan plant in all?

_____ + _____ = _____

You can use a model to help you
solve an addition story.

Ty has 9 grapes in a bag. He ate
some grapes. There are 4 grapes left.
How many grapes did Ty eat?

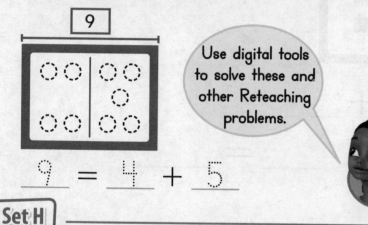

Use digital tools
to solve these and
other Reteaching
problems.

$\underline{9} = \underline{4} + \underline{5}$

Complete the model to solve the
addition story.

10. Ivy has 5 fish. She fed them after
school. 2 fish did not eat.
How many fish ate?

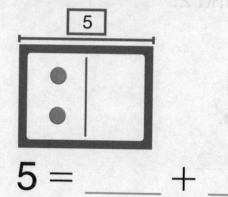

$5 = \underline{\phantom{0}} + \underline{\phantom{0}}$

Find the sum.

$$2 + 5 = \underline{7}$$
sum

You can change the order
of the addends.

Write the new addition sentence.

$$\underline{5} + \underline{2} = \underline{7}$$
sum

The sum is the same.

Write the sum. Then change the order
of the addend and write the new
addition sentence.

11. $1 + 4 = \underline{\phantom{0}}$

$\underline{\phantom{0}} + \underline{\phantom{0}} = \underline{\phantom{0}}$

12. $6 + 3 = \underline{\phantom{0}}$

$\underline{\phantom{0}} + \underline{\phantom{0}} = \underline{\phantom{0}}$

**1.** Chuck made a dot pattern to show the number 8.
   Which is **not** a pattern for 8?

○        ○        ○        ○

---

**2.** There are 3 peppers inside.
   4 peppers are outside.
   How many are there in all?

4

○ 4        ○ 6

○ 5        ○ 7

**3.** Which shows parts of 8?

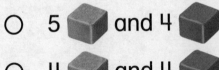

○ 5 ▢ and 4 ▢

○ 4 ▢ and 4 ▢

○ 4 ▢ and 3 ▢

○ 3 ▢ and 4 ▢

**4.** Trina has 4 markers. Her mother gives her 5 more markers.

Which addition sentence shows how many markers Trina has in all?

- ○ $5 + 2 = 7$
- ○ $4 + 3 = 7$
- ○ $4 + 4 = 8$
- ○ $4 + 5 = 9$

**5.** George had 7 postcards. Now he has 9 postcards.

How many new postcards did George get?

- ○ 1
- ○ 2
- ○ 3
- ○ 4

**6.** Dante has 5 books. He buys 2 more books. Now he can keep 1 book and give 1 book to each of his cousins. How many cousins does Dante have?

2      4      5      6
○      ○      ○      ○

**7.** Which addition sentence tells about the balls?

   ○  $2 + 1 = 3$

   ○  $2 + 2 = 4$

   ○  $3 + 1 = 4$

   ○  $4 + 1 = 5$

$1 + 4 = 5$

$\underline{?} + \underline{?} = \underline{?}$

**8.** Trina has 6 ribbons. Julie has 2 ribbons.
Which addition sentence shows how many ribbons they have in all?

   ○  $7 = 5 + 2$

   ○  $8 = 5 + 3$

   ○  $8 = 6 + 2$

   ○  $9 = 6 + 3$

**9.** 5 penguins are inside. There are 7 penguins in all.
How many penguins are outside?

   ○  1

   ○  2

   ○  4

   ○  5

 ?

**10.** Rita ate 5 crackers. Then she ate some more.
Rita made a pattern to show the 10 crackers she ate in all.
Which could be her pattern?

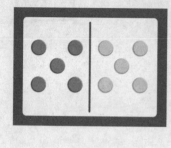  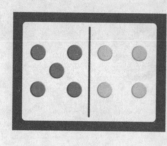    

      ○

---

**11.** Complete the model to solve.
Write the parts.
Then write an addition sentence.

4 students wash the dog.
2 more students come to help them.
How many students are washing the dog now?

_____ + _____

_____ + _____ = _____

---

**12.** Color the cubes to solve.

☐☐☐☐☐☐☐☐

Write the missing addend to
complete the addition sentences.

$3 + \underline{\quad} = 8$

$\underline{\quad} + 3 = 8$

# Understanding Subtraction

**Essential Question:** What are ways to think about subtraction?

Weather happens all around us.

The weather can affect what we do every day.

Wow! Let's do this project and learn more.

## Math and Science Project: Track the Weather

**Find Out** Talk to friends and relatives about the weather. Ask how the weather can affect what they plan for the day.

**Journal: Make a Book** Show what you found out. In your book, also:

• Keep track of the weather for a week.

• Make up and solve subtraction problems about the weather.

Name _____

# Review What You Know

## Vocabulary

1. Circle the numbers that are the **parts**.

$3 + 5 = 8$

2. Circle the number that is the **whole**.

$3 + 5 = 8$

3. Circle the symbol for **equals**.

$+$    $-$    $=$

## Understanding Addition

4. Write an addition sentence to match the picture.

___ $+$ ___ $=$ ___

5. Bob sees 5 bees. Ella sees some bees. They see 9 bees in all. How many bees did Ella see?

   Write an addition sentence to solve.

___ $+$ ___ $=$ ___

## Making Numbers

6. Draw counters to show one way to make 8.

**My Word Cards** Study the words on the front of the card.
Complete the activity on the back.

A-Z

## minus

5     —     3

5 **minus** 3

This means 3 is taken away from 5.

## subtract

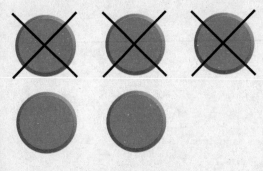

5 − 3 = 2

## difference

4 − 1 = 3

**difference**

## subtraction sentence

12 − 4 = 8

This is a **subtraction sentence**.

## take away

4 **take away** 1 is 3.

## separate

# My Word Cards

Use what you know to complete the sentences.
Extend learning by writing your own sentence using each word.

The answer to a subtraction sentence is called the

_____.

I use a minus sign to

_____.

5 _____

3 equals 2.

When you subtract, you

can _____

one group from another.

To _____

_____

means to remove or subtract.

I can write a

_____

_____

to subtract.

© Pearson Education, Inc. 1

Name _____

**Solve & Share**

There are 7 dog bones in all. You see 4 bones. The rest are hidden inside the bowl. How can you find how many bones are inside the bowl?

⊙ TEKS 1.3B Use objects and pictorial models to solve word problems involving ... separating, ... within 20 and unknowns as any one of the terms in the problem ... . **Mathematical Process Standards 1.1B, 1.1C, 1.1D, 1.1F.**

Digital Resources at PearsonTexas.com

Solve  Learn  Glossary  Check  Tools  Games

?

_____       _____       _____
 whole       part I know    missing part

There are 6 bones in all.

"How many bones are inside the bowl?"

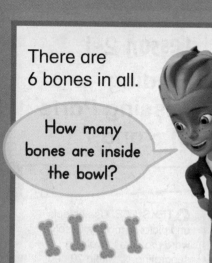

Since there are 6 bones in all, the whole is 6.

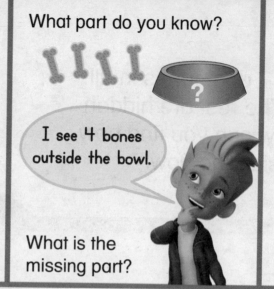

What part do you know?

"I see 4 bones outside the bowl."

What is the missing part?

part I know

missing part

"There are 2 bones inside the bowl."

The other bones show the missing part.

---

## Do You Understand?

**Show Me!** You have 7 counters. You know that 3 of them are red. How could you find how many are **not** red?

---

☆ **Guided Practice** ☆  Find the missing part. Write the numbers. Draw bones in the bowl to help you.

**1.** 6 bones in all.

5

1

part I know     missing part

**2.** 7 bones in all.

____     ____

part I know     missing part

**3.** 7 bones in all.

____     ____

part I know     missing part

**4.** 7 bones in all.

____     ____

part I know     missing part

---

**76** seventy-six

© Pearson Education, Inc. 1

Name _____

Find the missing part. Write the numbers.
Draw bones in the bowl to help you.

**5.** 6 bones in all.

_____     _____
part I know   missing part

**6.** 6 bones in all.

_____     _____
part I know   missing part

**7.** 7 bones in all.

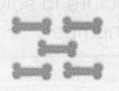 

_____     _____
part I know   missing part

Find the missing part. Complete the addition sentence.

**8.** Jenna has 6 beans in all. 3 beans
are in the bowl. How many beans
are outside the bowl?

$3 + \underline{\quad} = 6$

**9.** Luke has 7 cats in all. Some
cats are gray. 5 cats are black.
How many cats are gray?

$\underline{\quad} + 5 = 7$

**10. Extend Your Thinking**
Write a story to match
the picture. Complete
the addition sentence.

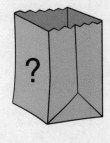 

$\underline{\quad} + \underline{\quad} = \underline{\quad}$

Topic 2 | Lesson 1

seventy-seven **77**

# Problem Solving — Solve each problem below.

**11.** There are 7 pens in all. 5 pens are red. The rest are blue. How many pens are blue?

Draw a picture to solve. Then write the number.

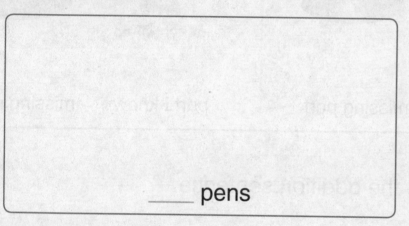

_____ pens

**12.** Grace has 6 ribbons in all. 2 ribbons are purple. The rest are green. How many ribbons are green?

Draw a picture to solve. Then write the number.

_____ ribbons

**13.** 6 eggs are in the carton.
Emma cooks 2 eggs.
How many eggs are left in the carton?

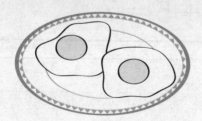

3      4      5      8
○      ○      ○      ○

**14. Extend Your Thinking** Write a number story about a toy box and 6 toys. Draw counters to show the number story.

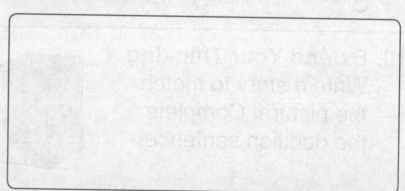

Name _____

**Another Look** You can use a picture to find the missing parts of 6 or 7.

6 apples in all.

| 6 | 1 | 5 |
|---|---|---|
| whole | part I know | missing part |

7 apples in all.

| 7 | 5 | 2 |
|---|---|---|
| whole | part I know | missing part |

🏠 **HOME CONNECTION**
Your child used pictures to find missing parts of 6 and 7.

**HOME ACTIVITY** Have your child set 7 small objects on a table. Then take turns covering some of the objects with a piece of paper. Have your child answer the following questions each time: "How many are missing? How many in all?"

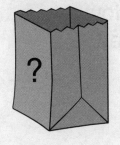

Find the missing part. Write the numbers.

1. 6 bananas in all.

_____ _____ _____
whole      part I know      missing part

2. 7 balls of yarn in all.

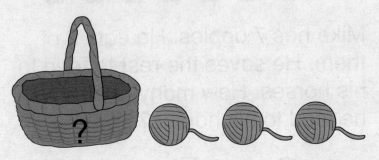

_____ _____ _____
whole      part I know      missing part

**3.** ⭐ There are 7 fish.
2 fish are blue.
The rest are yellow.
How many yellow fish
are there?

$2 + \underline{\phantom{?}} = 7$

| 2 | 3 | 4 | 5 |
|---|---|---|---|
| ○ | ○ | ○ | ○ |

**4.** ⭐ There are 6 cups.
4 cups are empty.
The rest are full.
How many full cups
are there?

$4 + \underline{\phantom{?}} = 6$

| 1 | 2 | 3 | 4 |
|---|---|---|---|
| ○ | ○ | ○ | ○ |

**5. Extend Your Thinking** Write
an addition sentence to solve
for the missing part.

Mike has 7 apples. He eats 2 of
them. He saves the rest to feed to
his horses. How many apples will
he feed to his horses?

$\underline{\phantom{xx}} + \underline{\phantom{xx}} = \underline{\phantom{xx}}$

$\underline{\phantom{xx}}$ apples

**6. Extend Your Thinking** Write
an addition sentence to solve
for the missing part.

Leo has 6 goats. 1 of them
is spotted black and white.
The rest are all white. How
many goats are all white?

$\underline{\phantom{xx}} + \underline{\phantom{xx}} = \underline{\phantom{xx}}$

$\underline{\phantom{xx}}$ white goats

Name _____

 Solve & Share

Beth has 9 dogs. 5 are outside the doghouse. The rest are inside. How can you find out how many dogs are inside?

⊕ TEKS 1.3B Use objects and pictorial models to solve word problems involving ... separating, ... within 20 and unknowns as any one of the terms in the problem ... . **Mathematical Process Standards 1.1A, 1.1B, 1.1C, 1.1D.**

**Digital Resources at PearsonTexas.com**

Solve   Learn   Glossary   Check   Tools   Games

There are 8 counters in all.

**8**

There are 6 counters in the part you know.

**8**

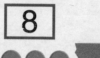

How many counters are in the missing part?

**8**

I know that 6 and 2 are parts of 8.

**8**

6
part
I know

2
missing
part

## Do You Understand?

**Show Me!** There are 8 counters. 3 are **not** covered. How can you find the number of covered counters?

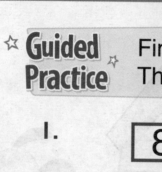
**1.**

**8**

3
part I know

5
missing part

**2.**

**9**

4 ○ ○ ○ ○

_____
part I know

_____
missing part

**3.**

**9**

_____
part I know

_____
missing part

**4.**

**8**

_____
part I know

_____
missing part

© Pearson Education, Inc. I

**Topic 2** | Lesson 2

Name _____

Find the missing parts of 8 and 9. Then write the numbers.

5.

___ ___

part I know    missing part

6.

___ ___

part I know    missing part

7.

___ ___

part I know    missing part

Find the missing part. Complete the addition sentence.

8. Mark has 9 bagels. He cooks 4 of them. How many bagels are **not** cooked?

$4 + \underline{\quad} = 9$

9. Hanna has 7 eggs. 5 eggs hatched. How many eggs are **not** hatched?

$5 + \underline{\quad} = 7$

10. **Extend Your Thinking** There are 9 dogs. There are 3 more small dogs than big dogs. Draw a picture to find the missing part. Then write the numbers.

_____ small dogs and _____ big dogs

11. Jill has 8 blocks. 6 blocks are green. The rest are pink. How many blocks are pink?

_____ blocks

12. José sees 9 frogs. Some of the frogs are in the pond. 6 frogs are on the grass. How many frogs are in the pond?

_____ frogs

13. There are 8 mice in all. 3 mice are on the cheese. The rest are not. How many mice are **not** on the cheese?

3     4     5     8
○     ○     ○     ○

14. **Extend Your Thinking** There are 8 marbles in all. There is 1 inside the jar. The rest are outside. Draw a picture to match the story, and then write how many are inside and outside.

_____ inside _____ outside

Name _____

**Another Look** You can draw a picture to help you find missing parts of 8.

$7 + \underline{\ ?\ } = 8$

First, color the part you know.

Then, count the circles you did **not** color.
Write the numbers.

$7 + 1 = 8$

$5 + \underline{\ ?\ } = 8$

$5 + \underline{\ 3\ } = 8$

 Color the part you know. Count the circles you did **not** color. Write the number.

1.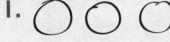

$6 + \underline{\quad} = 9$

2. ○ ○ ○ ○
○ ○ ○ ○

$4 + \underline{\quad} = 8$

3. ○ ○ ○ ○
○ ○ ○

$3 + \underline{\quad} = 8$

Use counters to solve each problem below.

**4.** ⭐ Felix sees 8 lions at the zoo. Some lions are babies. 2 lions are adults. How many lions are babies?

| 10 | 8 | 6 | 4 |
|----|---|---|---|
| ○ | ○ | ○ | ○ |

**5.** ⭐ Andre has 9 plants. Some plants are inside the house. 5 plants are outside. How many plants are inside?

| 4 | 5 | 7 | 9 |
|---|---|---|---|
| ○ | ○ | ○ | ○ |

**6.** ⭐ Tam has 8 grapes. Some grapes are green. 3 of the grapes are purple. How many grapes are green?

| 8 | 5 | 3 | 1 |
|---|---|---|---|
| ○ | ○ | ○ | ○ |

Find the missing parts of 8 and 9. Write the numbers.

**7.**

8

_____  _____
part I know    missing part

**8.**

9

_____  _____
part I know    missing part

**9. Extend Your Thinking** There are 8 books in all. Some books are in the bag. Others are on the floor.

Draw a picture to show the story. Then write numbers to tell about the story.

_____ in the bag

_____ on the floor

© Pearson Education, Inc. 1

Name _____

**Solve & Share**

Alex has 5 connecting cubes on the table. He hides some cubes. How can you use numbers to show how many cubes are hidden?

⭐ **TEKS 1.3B** Use objects and pictorial models to solve word problems involving ... separating, ... within 20 and unknowns as any one of the terms in the problem ... . Also, 1.5D, 1.5E. **Mathematical Process Standards** 1.1B, 1.1C, 1.1E, 1.1F.

Digital Resources at PearsonTexas.com

| Solve | Learn | Glossary | Check | Tools | Games |

Mike has 8 cubes.
He hides some cubes.

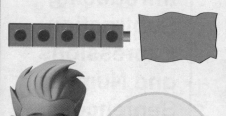

5 is the part you see. What is the hidden part?

You can describe the whole as 8 and one of the parts as 5. Find the hidden part by writing 8 − 5.

8

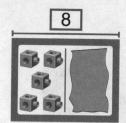

You can **subtract** to find the **difference**. 8 − 5 is 3.

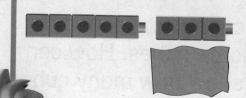

3 is the hidden part. It is the difference.

You can write a **subtraction sentence**.

$$8 - 5 = 3$$

8

8 minus 5 equals 3.

## Do You Understand?

**Show Me!** The whole is 9. One of the parts is 3. How can you find the difference?

 **Guided Practice** Complete the model. Write the parts. Then write a subtraction sentence.

1.

8

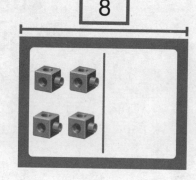

8 − 4

8 − 4 = 4

2.

6

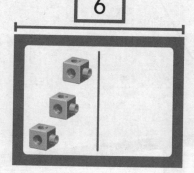

___ − ___

___ = ___ − ___

© Pearson Education, Inc. 1

**Topic 2** | Lesson 3

Name _____

Complete the model. Write the parts.
Then write a subtraction sentence.

3.

| 7 |

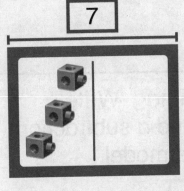

\_\_\_ \_\_\_

\_\_\_ \_\_\_ = \_\_\_

4.

| 9 |

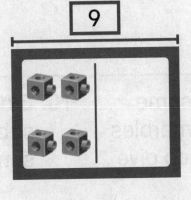

\_\_\_ \_\_\_

\_\_\_ \_\_\_ = \_\_\_

5.

| 6 |

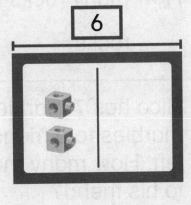

\_\_\_ \_\_\_

\_\_\_ \_\_\_ = \_\_\_

6. **Extend Your Thinking** There are 5 kittens in all. I is inside a basket. The rest are outside. How many kittens are outside the basket?

Draw a picture to show the story. Then write the missing part.

5 − \_\_\_ = I

**7.** Liz has 8 rocks.
She drops 3 of the rocks into a pond.
How many rocks does Liz have now?

_____ rocks

**8.** Troy picks 9 flowers.
He gives 5 flowers to his sister.
How many flowers does Troy still have?

_____ flowers

**9.** Rico has 7 marbles. He gave some
marbles to a friend. He has 2 marbles
left. How many marbles did Rico give
to his friend?

Choose the subtraction sentence
that matches the story.

7

?

○ $9 - 7 = 2$

○ $9 - 2 = 7$

○ $7 - 3 = 4$

○ $7 - 2 = 5$

**10. Extend Your Thinking** Write a
subtraction story and a subtraction
sentence about the model.

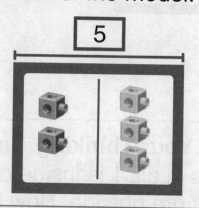

5

_____

_____

_____

_____

_____ − _____ = _____

Name _____

**Another Look** Write the parts. Then you can write a subtraction sentence to find how many are left.

$5 - 2$

5 minus 2 equals 3.

$5 - 2 = 3$

$6 - 4$

6 minus 4 equals _2_ .

$6 - 4 = 2$

🏠 **HOME CONNECTION**
Your child used connecting cubes, part-part-whole mats, and pictures to write subtraction sentences.

**HOME ACTIVITY** Place a group of 5 or 6 pennies on the table. Take away some pennies. Ask your child, "How many are left?" Have your child answer the question and write a subtraction sentence. For example, show 6 pennies. Take away 4. Write $6 - 4 = 2$.

Use the picture. Write the parts. Then write a subtraction sentence.

1.

___ − ___

4 minus 1 equals ___ .

___ − ___ = ___

2.

___ − ___

7 minus 4 equals ___ .

___ − ___ = ___

3.

___ − ___

5 minus 1 equals ___ .

___ − ___ = ___

Write a subtraction sentence for each story.

4. There are 6 butterflies in a tree. 2 butterflies fly away. How many butterflies are left?

_____ − _____ = _____

5. There are 8 oranges on a branch. 2 oranges fall off. How many oranges are still on the branch?

_____ − _____ = _____

Write the missing number for each problem.

6. Algebra

$7 - \underline{\hspace{1cm}} = 4$

7. Algebra

$\underline{\hspace{1cm}} - 4 = 4$

8. Algebra

$5 = 6 - \underline{\hspace{1cm}}$

9. Which subtraction sentence tells about the model?

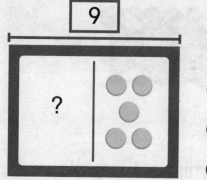

○ $9 - 2 = 7$

○ $9 - 4 = 5$

○ $9 - 6 = 3$

○ $5 - 4 = 1$

10. Extend Your Thinking Draw a picture that shows subtraction. Write a subtraction sentence that tells about your picture.

_____ − _____ = _____

Name _____

**Solve & Share**

6 ducks swim in a pond. 2 ducks fly away. How can you use connecting cubes to show how many ducks are left? What subtraction sentence can you write?

⭐ TEKS 1.3B Use objects and pictorial models to solve word problems involving … separating, … within 20 and unknowns as any one of the terms in the problem … . Also, 1.3, 1.5D, 1.5F. Mathematical Process Standards 1.1C, 1.1D, 1.1E, 1.1F.

Digital Resources at PearsonTexas.com

Solve   Learn   Glossary   Check   Tools   Games

_____ − _____ = _____

7 ducks are in a pond. 3 fly away. How many are still in the pond?

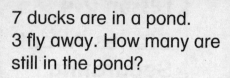

You can use cubes to show the story.

7 is the whole.

3 is the part that you **take away** or **separate**.

So, 4 is the difference.

You can write a subtraction sentence.
$$7 - 3 = 4$$

There are 4 ducks still in the pond.

## Do You Understand?

**Show Me!** There are 6 bees in a yard. 2 bees fly away. How would you find the difference in this subtraction story?

☆ **Guided Practice** ☆ Complete the model. Then write a subtraction sentence.

1. Dan has 6 pens. He gives 2 pens away. How many pens does Dan have left?

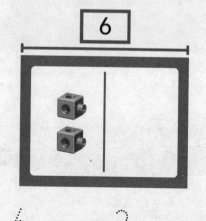

6

$$6 - 2 = 4$$

2. 7 students are playing. Then 1 student leaves. How many students are still playing?

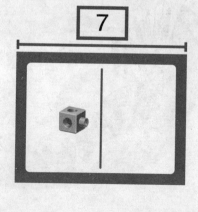

7

$$\_\_ - \_\_ = \_\_$$

Name _____

Complete the model. Then write a subtraction sentence.

**3.** 8 frogs sit on a log. Then 4 frogs jump away. How many frogs are still on the log?

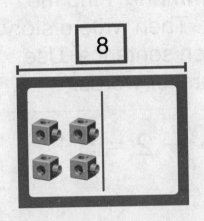

8

___ − ___ = ___

**4.** Some kittens are playing on a rug. 6 kittens walk away. There are 3 kittens left. How many kittens were playing on the rug?

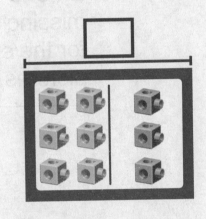

___ − ___ = ___

**5.** 7 students are in the pool. Then 2 students leave. How many students are still in the pool?

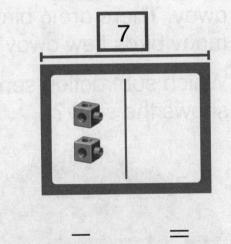

7

___ − ___ = ___

Use cubes to solve. Draw a picture and write a subtraction sentence.

**6. Extend Your Thinking** There are 8 students in a reading group. Some of the students leave. 2 students are left. How many students left the group?

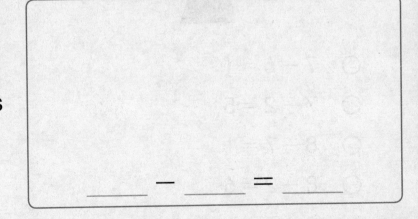

___ − ___ = ___

7. Lin has 9 stamps. She gives some to Tom. Now she has 4. How many stamps did Lin give away?

_____ − _____ = _____

8. Gloria has 8 flowers. She gives 5 flowers to her mother. How many flowers does Gloria have now?

_____ − _____ = _____

9. ⭐ 8 birds were in a tree. Some flew away. There are 6 birds left. How many birds flew away?

Which subtraction sentence shows the story?

○ 7 − 6 = 1

○ 7 − 2 = 5

○ 8 − 7 = 1

○ 8 − 2 = 6

10. **Extend Your Thinking** Find the missing number. Then write a story for the subtraction sentence. Use pictures, numbers, or words.

_____ − 2 = 5

Name _____

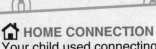

**Another Look** You can write a subtraction sentence to tell what happens in the story.

There are 6 cats on a fence.
3 cats jump off the fence.
How many cats are left?

$$6 - 3 = 3$$

There are 5 cats on a fence.
2 cats jump off.
How many cats are left?

$$5 - 2 = 3$$

🏠 **HOME CONNECTION**
Your child used connecting cubes and drew pictures to solve stories about subtraction, or taking away.

**HOME ACTIVITY** Place 8 small objects, such as buttons, on the table. Take away several of the buttons. Ask your child to tell a subtraction story. Then have your child write a subtraction sentence, such as $8 - 2 = 6$. Have your child count the buttons that are left to check if his or her answer is correct.

Write a subtraction sentence to solve each problem.

1. There are 9 apples in a bag. 7 apples roll out. How many apples are left in the bag?

____ − ____ = ____

2. There are 10 crayons in a box. 7 of the crayons spill out of the box. How many crayons are still in the box?

____ − ____ = ____

Find the missing number for each problem.

**3. Algebra** ⭐

$7 = 8 - $ _____ ?

1 ○  2 ○  7 ○  8 ○

**4. Algebra** ⭐

_____ ? $- 4 = 5$

4 ○  5 ○  8 ○  9 ○

**5. Algebra** ⭐

$10 - 2 = $ _____ ?

2 ○  5 ○  8 ○  9 ○

Write a subtraction sentence for each story.

**6.** There are 6 bees on a flower.
4 bees fly away. How many
bees are still on the flower?

_____ $-$ _____ $=$ _____

**7.** 8 ducks are in the pond.
4 ducks get out. How many
ducks are still in the pond?

_____ $-$ _____ $=$ _____

**8. Extend Your Thinking**

9 boys are playing baseball.
Some boys leave to go home.
How many boys are still playing baseball?

Draw a picture to match the story.
Then write a subtraction sentence
to solve.

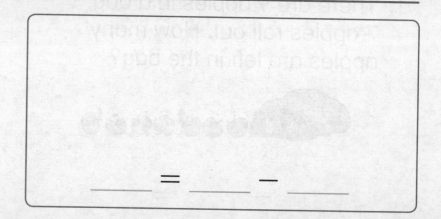

_____ $=$ _____ $-$ _____

© Pearson Education, Inc. 1

Name _____

**Solve & Share**

Lori sees 5 red cars and 3 blue cars drive by. Did she see more red cars or blue cars? How many more? How can you tell?

**TEKS 1.3B** Use objects and pictorial models to solve word problems involving ... comparing within 20 and unknowns as any one of the terms in the problem ... . Also, 1.3, 1.5D, 1.5F. **Mathematical Process Standards** 1.1B, 1.1C, 1.1D, 1.1E.

**Digital Resources at PearsonTexas.com**

Solve   Learn   Glossary   Check   Tools   Games

5 cats have blue hats.
2 cats have orange hats.
How many more blue hats
than orange hats are there?

You can use cubes
to compare.

You can write a subtraction
sentence to compare.

$$5 - 2 = 3$$

There are 3 more
blue hats than
orange hats.

## Do You Understand?

**Show Me!** If you have 2 groups of objects, how can you tell which has more?

★ **Guided Practice** ★ Use cubes to write a subtraction sentence. Then write how many more or fewer.

1. Peggy draws 6 frogs. Mike draws 3 frogs. How many more frogs does Peggy draw than Mike?

$$\underline{6} - \underline{3} = \underline{3}$$

$\underline{3}$ more frogs

© Pearson Education, Inc. 1

Name _____

☆ **Independent**
☆ **Practice**

Use cubes to write a subtraction sentence.
Then write how many more or fewer.

**2.** Sue walks her dog 3 times.
Julio walks his dog 1 time.
How many fewer walks does
Julio take than Sue?

____ − ____ = ____

____ fewer walks

**3.** Tony counts 7 mice. Marie
counts 5 fewer mice than
Tony. How many mice
does Marie count?

____ − ____ = ____

____ mice

**Extend Your Thinking**  Use the picture.
Find the missing number for each problem.

**4.**

____ − 3 = 1

**5.**

6 − ____ = 1

**Topic 2** | Lesson 5

one hundred one  **101**

## Problem Solving · Write a subtraction sentence to solve each problem below.

**6.** The pond has 4 fish.
The fish tank has 2 fish.
How many more fish does the
pond have than the fish tank?

_____ − _____ = _____

**7.** Luis sees 5 green frogs.
He sees 4 fewer red frogs than
green frogs. How many red frogs
does Luis see?

_____ − _____ = _____

**8.** Bill counts 6 grey cats.
He counts some white cats.
He counts 4 more grey cats
than white cats.

How many white cats did Bill count?

○  2

○  4

○  6

○  10

You can draw a picture to help.

**9. Extend Your Thinking**
Draw some yellow flowers. Draw more
red flowers than yellow flowers. Write
a subtraction sentence that tells how
many more red flowers than yellow
flowers there are.

_____ − _____ = _____

Name _____

**Another Look** Match the red cubes with the blue cubes.
Then count how many more or fewer.

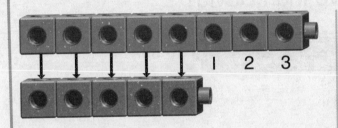

How many more red cubes?

___3___ more red cubes

How many fewer blue cubes?

___3___ fewer blue cubes

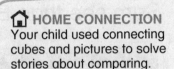

🏠 **HOME CONNECTION**
Your child used connecting cubes and pictures to solve stories about comparing.

**HOME ACTIVITY** Give your child 5 pennies and 2 nickels. Have your child tell how many more pennies than nickels he or she has. Then have your child tell how many fewer nickels than pennies he or she has. Repeat with up to 10 pennies and 10 nickels.

Write how many red cubes and blue cubes.
Then write how many more or fewer.

1.

_____ red cubes

_____ blue cubes

_____ more red cubes

2.

_____ red cubes

_____ blue cubes

_____ more red cubes

3.

_____ red cubes

_____ blue cubes

_____ fewer blue cubes

## Write a subtraction sentence. Then write how many more or fewer.

4. Sam sees 5 dogs.
Beth sees 3 dogs.
How many more dogs does
Sam see than Beth?

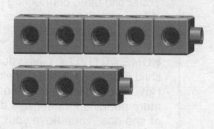

___ − ___ = ___

___ more dogs

5. David has 6 tickets.
Mimi has 2 tickets.
How many fewer tickets does
Mimi have than David?

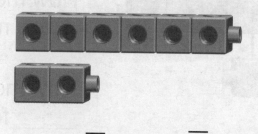

___ − ___ = ___

___ fewer tickets

6. **Algebra**  Use the picture.
   Find the missing number.

$$\underline{\;?\;} - 6 = 1$$

6        7        8        9
○        ○        ○        ○

7. **Extend Your Thinking**  Draw some
red cubes. Draw fewer blue cubes
than red cubes. Write a subtraction
sentence that shows how many
fewer blue cubes than red cubes
you drew.

___ − ___ = ___

© Pearson Education, Inc. 1

**Topic 2** | Lesson 5

Name _____

**Solve & Share**

Sofie found 5 pebbles by the lake. Now she has 7 pebbles. How many pebbles did Sofie already have? Use cubes to show how you know.

**TEKS 1.3B** Use objects and pictorial models to solve word problems involving … separating, … within 20 and unknowns as any one of the terms in the problem … . Also, 1.5D, 1.5F. **Mathematical Process Standards** 1.1B, 1.1C, 1.1D, 1.1G.

Digital Resources at PearsonTexas.com

Solve    Learn    Glossary    Check    Tools    Games

There are 8 cats and dogs on the dance floor. 5 dogs are dancing. How many cats are dancing?

Think about the whole in the story.

| 8 |

There are 8 cats and dogs.

Now think about the part you know from the story.

| 8 |

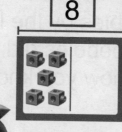

There are 5 dogs dancing.

The part you want to know is the missing part.

| 8 |

Subtract to find the missing part.
$8 - 5 = 3$

There are 3 cats dancing.

## Guided Practice
Complete the model. Then write a subtraction sentence.

## Do You Understand?

**Show Me!** If you know the whole and one of the parts, how can you find the missing part?

1. Nick and Roger have 9 robots in all. Nick has 3 robots. How many robots does Roger have?

| 9 |

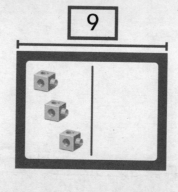

____ = ____ − ____

2. Gail has 6 kites. Some kites are red and some kites are blue. If 2 kites are red, how many kites are blue?

| 6 |

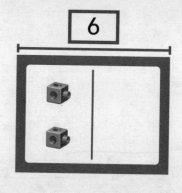

____ − ____ = ____

Name _____

☆ **Independent**
☆ **Practice**

Complete the model. Then write a subtraction sentence.

**3.** Carlos buys 1 toy car. Now he has 6 toy cars. How many toy cars did Carlos have before?

6

_____ − _____ = _____

**4.** Jill wants to walk her dog 9 blocks. She has walked 5 blocks. How many more blocks does Jill need to walk?

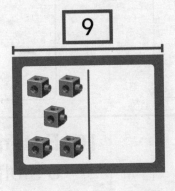

9

_____ − _____ = _____

**5.** Rita makes 3 new friends. Now she has 7 friends. How many friends did Rita have before?

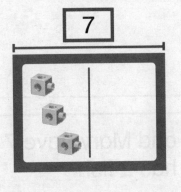

7

_____ − _____ = _____

**6. Extend Your Thinking** Henry has 8 shells in all. 3 shells are big and some are small.

Draw a picture to solve. Then write a subtraction sentence.

_____ − _____ = _____

**7.** Joe has 2 red fish. He buys some blue fish. Now he has 9 fish in all. How many blue fish does Joe have?

_____ blue fish

**8.** Rachel needs 8 nickels. She has 4 nickels. How many more nickels does Rachel need?

_____ nickels

**9.** Liz and Mary have 7 fish in all. Liz has 2 fish.

Which subtraction sentence shows how many fish Mary has?

○ $7 = 9 - 2$

○ $5 = 6 - 1$

○ $5 = 7 - 2$

○ $1 = 8 - 7$

The number of fish Mary has is the difference.

**10. Extend Your Thinking** Nina has 8 stuffed bears and tigers. She has more bears than tigers. Draw a picture to show how many of each animal Nina could have. Then write the numbers.

_____ bears and _____ tigers

Name _____

**Another Look** The dog has 8 spots on its back. It has 6 brown spots. The rest of the spots are black. How many spots are black?

There are 8 spots in all. Subtract 6 to find the number of black spots.

$$8 - 6 = 2$$

| spots in all | brown spots | black spots |

🏠 **HOME CONNECTION**
Your child used connecting cubes and pictures to solve problems with missing parts.

**HOME ACTIVITY** Place 6 to 9 small objects in a paper cup. Have your child pour some of the objects onto the table. Ask, "How many are still in the cup?" Have your child subtract the number of objects on the table from the number he or she started with. Then have your child count the objects that are left to check if his or her answer is correct.

Draw the missing number of spots. Then write a subtraction sentence.

**1.** 6 spots in all

___ − ___ = ___

**2.** 9 spots in all

___ − ___ = ___

**3.** 7 spots in all

___ − ___ = ___

Solve each problem below.

4. Juan has 9 shirts. 6 of his shirts are white. The rest are **not** white.

Draw a picture and write a subtraction sentence to show how many of his shirts are **not** white.

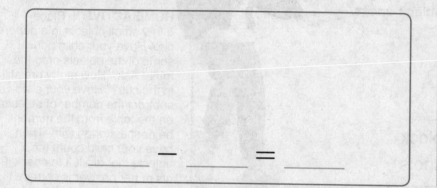

_____ − _____ = _____

5. Pedro had some baseball cards. He gave a friend 1 baseball card. Now Pedro has 8 baseball cards.

Which subtraction sentence matches the story?

○  9 − 1 = 8

○  8 − 1 = 7

○  8 − 7 = 1

○  7 − 1 = 6

6. **Extend Your Thinking** Draw a picture to show how many there are of each fruit. Write the numbers to complete the chart.

| | Bananas | Oranges | Drawings |
|---|---|---|---|
| Amy has 8 in all. | 4 | | |
| Joe has 6 in all. | | 2 | |

© Pearson Education, Inc. 1

Name _____

**Solve & Share**

There are 7 flowers in Maya's garden. Some are roses. Some are daisies.

If 4 are roses, how many flowers are daisies? Write a subtraction sentence to help solve the problem.

⭐ TEKS 1.3B Use objects and pictorial models to solve word problems involving … separating, and comparing within 20 and unknowns as any one of the terms in the problem … . TEKS 1.5D Represent word problems involving … subtraction … . Also, 1.3, 1.5F. Mathematical Process Standards 1.1C, 1.1D, 1.1F.

Digital Resources at PearsonTexas.com

Solve    Learn    Glossary    Check    Tools    Games

_____ – _____ = _____

Tom had 5 toys.
He gave some to his brother.
Now Tom has 3 toys.
How many toys did Tom
give to his brother?

5

$5 - 3 = 2$

Juan has 5 apples.
Sue has 3 apples.
How many more
apples does Juan
have than Sue?

$5 - 3 = 2$

Dan has 5 bow ties.
Some are blue and
some are orange.
If 3 bow ties are blue,
how many are orange?

5

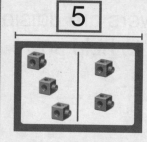

$5 - 3 = 2$

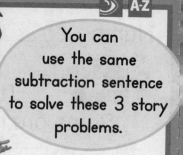

You can use the same subtraction sentence to solve these 3 story problems.

$5 - 3 = 2$

## Do You Understand?

**Show Me!** Can you tell more subtraction stories for $5 - 3 = 2$? Tell a friend a new story for $5 - 3 = 2$.

## ☆ Guided Practice ☆

Use cubes to solve. Complete the model. Then write a subtraction sentence.

1. 7 students are in the park. 5 students go home. How many students are left?

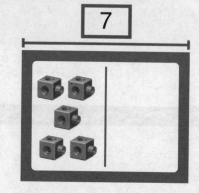

$7 - 5 = 2$

2. Kerry sees 4 dogs. Teo sees 1 dog. How many more dogs does Kerry see than Teo?

___ − ___ = ___

Name _____

Use cubes to solve. Complete the model.
Then write a subtraction sentence.

**3.** There are 8 squirrels.
4 squirrels are black.
The rest are gray.
How many squirrels
are gray?

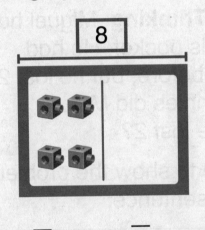

8

____ − ____ = ____

**4.** 9 swans are in the
pond. There are
6 geese in the pond.
How many fewer
geese than swans are
there in the pond?

____ − ____ = ____

**5.** Jan sees 7 birds in
the tree. 3 of the birds
fly away. How many
birds are left in the
tree?

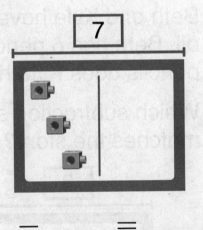

7

____ − ____ = ____

**6. Extend Your Thinking** Circle the
group that has more brown cats
than gray cats.

How many more brown cats than
gray cats are in that group?

Write a subtraction sentence.

____ − ____ = ____

____ more brown cats

# Problem Solving
Use cubes to solve each problem below.

**7.** Leo had some crayons.
He gave away 1 crayon.
Now he has 7 crayons.
How many crayons did
Leo have at the start?

_____ crayons

**8.** Dana has 4 dolls.
She has 2 more dolls
than Cindy. How many
dolls does Cindy have?

_____ dolls

**9.** Beth and Kyle have 8 pencils in all. Beth has 6 pencils. How many pencils does Kyle have?

Which subtraction sentence matches the story?

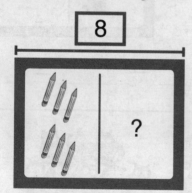

○ 8 − 7 = 1

○ 8 − 6 = 2

○ 8 − 5 = 3

○ 8 − 4 = 4

**10. Extend Your Thinking** Miguel has 7 pennies in his pocket. He had more pennies before, but he lost 2. How many pennies did Miguel have before he lost 2?

Draw a picture to show the problem. Complete the sentence.

Miguel had _____ pennies before he lost 2 pennies.

© Pearson Education, Inc. 1

Name _____

**Another Look** You can subtract to take away, compare, or find the missing parts.

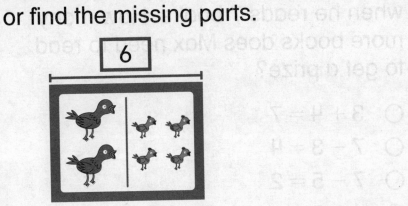

6

$6 - 2 = 4$

birds   blue birds   red birds

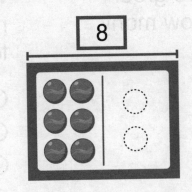

8

$8 - \underline{6} = \underline{2}$

balls   green balls   yellow balls

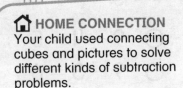
**HOME CONNECTION**
Your child used connecting cubes and pictures to solve different kinds of subtraction problems.

**HOME ACTIVITY** Have your child make up different subtraction stories for the problem $8 - 6 = 4$. Have him or her tell you different stories, show different stories with small objects, and draw pictures to show the stories.

Use cubes to solve. Complete the model.
Then write a subtraction sentence.

1. Lisa has 8 marbles. Some are blue and some are green. If 5 are green, how many are blue?

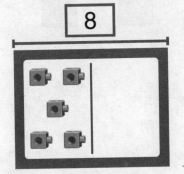

8

___ − ___ = ___

2. Seth has 9 stickers. He gives 3 stickers to a friend. How many stickers does Seth have now?

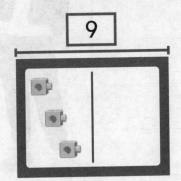

9

___ − ___ = ___

**Topic 2** | Lesson 7        Digital Resources at PearsonTexas.com        one hundred fifteen   **115**

Choose the subtraction sentence that matches each story.

**3.** Keri has 9 grapes. Some of the grapes are red and some are green. If 4 of the grapes are red, how many are green?

○ $9 - 4 = 5$
○ $9 - 3 = 6$
○ $9 - 1 = 8$
○ $4 + 5 = 9$

**4.** Max read 3 books. He gets a prize when he reads 7 books. How many more books does Max need to read to get a prize?

○ $3 + 4 = 7$
○ $7 - 3 = 4$
○ $7 - 5 = 2$
○ $4 - 3 = 1$

**5. Extend Your Thinking** Will the answer to $5 - 3 = \underline{\ ?\ }$ be more than 5 or less than 5?

Explain how you know.

**6. Extend Your Thinking** Circle 2 different colors of shirts. Write a subtraction sentence to match the shirts you chose.

_____ − _____ = _____

Name _____

**Solve & Share**

Use counters. How can you show parts of 5? How can you write addition and subtraction sentences for what you show?

5

★ TEKS I.5F Determine the unknown whole number in an addition or subtraction equation when the unknown may be any one of the three or four terms in the equation. **Mathematical Process Standards I.IC, I.ID, I.IF.**

Digital Resources at PearsonTexas.com

Solve  Learn  Glossary  Check  Tools  Games

5 − ___ = ___          ___ + ___ = 5

5 − ___ = ___          ___ + ___ = 5

You can use the whole and the parts to write number sentences.

6 is the whole.
You see 4.
So, 2 is the other part.

$6 - 4 = 2$

This is a subtraction sentence.

6 is the whole.
You see 2.
So, 4 is the other part.

$6 - 2 = 4$

This is another subtraction sentence.

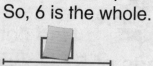

4 is one part.
2 is the other part.
So, 6 is the whole.

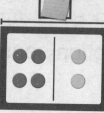

$4 + 2 = 6$

This is an addition sentence.

**Guided Practice** Write 2 subtraction sentences for each model. Then write an addition sentence.

## Do You Understand?

**Show Me!** How are these addition and subtraction sentences the same?

$$8 - 2 = 6$$
$$2 + 6 = 8$$

1. 6

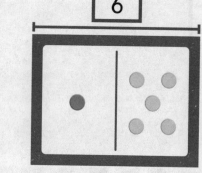

$6 - 1 = 5$

$6 - 5 = 1$

$1 + 5 = 6$

2. 7

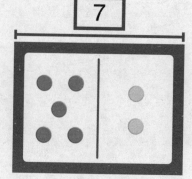

___ − ___ = ___

___ − ___ = ___

___ + ___ = ___

© Pearson Education, Inc. 1

Name _____

Write the subtraction sentences for each model.
Then write the addition sentences.

**3.**

8

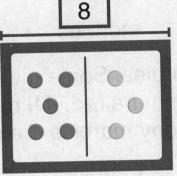

___ − ___ = ___

___ − ___ = ___

___ + ___ = ___

___ + ___ = ___

**4.**

9

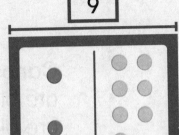
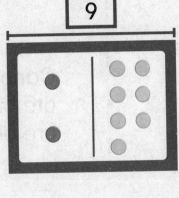

___ − ___ = ___

___ − ___ = ___

___ + ___ = ___

___ + ___ = ___

**5.**

7

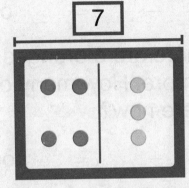

___ − ___ = ___

___ − ___ = ___

___ + ___ = ___

___ + ___ = ___

Draw counters to show the parts. Then write an addition sentence and a subtraction sentence.

**6. Extend Your Thinking** 5 friends are at a party. Some are girls and some are boys. How many girls and boys could there be?

5

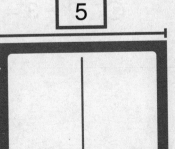

___ + ___ = ___

___ − ___ = ___

# Problem Solving    Use counters to solve each problem. Write the number sentences.

**7.** There are 7 oranges. Jessie eats 1 of them. How many oranges are left?

_____ − _____ = _____ oranges

There are 6 oranges. Jessie buys 1 more. How many oranges are there now?

_____ + _____ = _____ oranges

**8.** Carlos has 5 red marbles and 4 blue marbles. How many marbles does Carlos have in all?

_____ + _____ = _____ marbles

Carlos has 9 marbles. Some marbles are blue and some are red. If 4 marbles are blue, how many marbles are red?

_____ − _____ = _____ marbles

**9.** Which subtraction sentence does **not** match the model?

○  6 + 3 = 9

○  6 − 3 = 3

○  9 − 6 = 3

○  9 − 3 = 6

**10. Extend Your Thinking** Rae and Nikki combined their blue stickers. Write an addition sentence to show the stickers they combined.

| Stickers | | | |
| --- | --- | --- | --- |
| | **Pink** | **Blue** | **Orange** |
| Rae | 2 | 2 | 7 |
| Nikki | 3 | 4 | 2 |
| Anna | 5 | 3 | 6 |

_____ + _____ = _____

Name _____

**Another Look** The addition sentence and the
subtraction sentence use the same numbers.

$$4 + 3 = 7$$

$$7 - 3 = 4$$

$$6 + 2 = 8$$

$$8 - 2 = 6$$

Write a subtraction sentence
for each model. Then write
an addition sentence.

🏠 **HOME CONNECTION**
Your child wrote addition
and subtraction sentences
using the same numbers to
show the inverse relationship
between addition and
subtraction.

**HOME ACTIVITY** Have your
child use small objects, such
as pennies or paper clips,
to model 5 − 3. Ask your
child to write a subtraction
sentence. [5 − 3 = 2] Then
have your child use objects to
show 3 + 2. Have him or her
write the addition sentence.
[3 + 2 = 5]

**I.**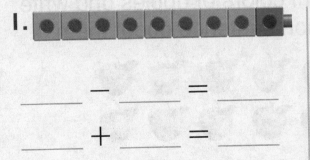

___ − ___ = ___

___ + ___ = ___

**2.**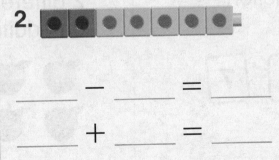

___ − ___ = ___

___ + ___ = ___

**3.**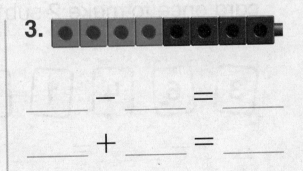

___ − ___ = ___

___ + ___ = ___

Find the missing number for each problem.

**4. Algebra** $9 = 2 + $ ___

&#9733;

6    7    8    9
○    ○    ○    ○

**5. Algebra** ___ $- 2 = 7$

&#9733;

9    8    6    5
○    ○    ○    ○

**6. Algebra** $2 + 7 = $ ___

&#9733;

5    7    8    9
○    ○    ○    ○

Write an addition sentence and a subtraction sentence for each story.

**7.** There are 6 bottles of water.
Students drink 4 of them.
How many bottles are left?

___ − ___ = ___

___ + ___ = ___

**8.** Mike has 8 baseballs. He sells 5 of them. How many baseballs does Mike have now?

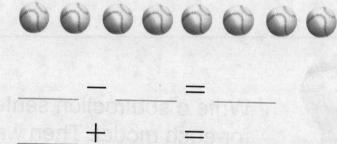

___ − ___ = ___

___ + ___ = ___

**9. Extend Your Thinking** Use each card once to make 2 subtraction sentences.

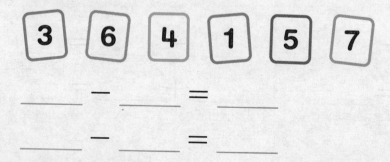

3   6   4   1   5   7

___ − ___ = ___

___ − ___ = ___

**10. Extend Your Thinking** Circle 2 different colors of apples and write an addition sentence about them.

___ + ___ = ___

© Pearson Education, Inc. 1

Name _____

**Solve & Share**

There are 9 students playing inside. Some of them go outside. If 6 students stay inside, how many students go outside? Use counters to show how you know. Then write a subtraction sentence.

⭐ **TEKS 1.1C** Select tools, including ... manipulatives, paper and pencil, ... and techniques, including ... number sense, ... to solve problems. Also, 1.3B, 1.5E. **Mathematical Process Standards 1.1A, 1.1B, 1.1D, 1.1G.**

Digital Resources at PearsonTexas.com

Solve   Learn   Glossary   Check   Tools   Games

_____ − _____ = _____

## Analyze

There are 8 apples on the tree. 3 apples fall off. How many are left?

## Plan

8 is the whole.
3 is one part.

I can use counters to act out the story.

## Solve and Justify

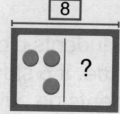

8

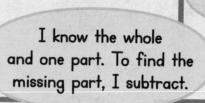

$8 - 3 = 5$

There are 5 apples left.

I know the whole and one part. To find the missing part, I subtract.

## Evaluate

I can write an addition sentence that uses the same numbers.

$5 + 3 = 8$

My answer makes sense.

---

## Do You Understand?

**Show Me!** How can you use addition to help you subtract?

---

☆ **Guided Practice** ☆   Use counters to act out each story.
Write a subtraction sentence.
Write an addition sentence to check.

1. Kia has 7 balloons.
   4 fly away.
   How many are left?

   $7 - 4 = 3$

   Check:

   __ + __ = __

2. 5 bugs are on a leaf.
   2 crawl away.
   How many are left?

   __ − __ = __

   Check:

   __ + __ = __

---

© Pearson Education, Inc. 1

Name _____

Use counters to act out each story. Write a subtraction sentence. Write an addition sentence to check.

3. 9 apples are in a bowl.
   Tina eats 1 apple.
   How many are left?

   ___ − ___ = ___

   Check:

   ___ + ___ = ___

4. The farmer has 7 flowers.
   The farmer sells 5.
   How many are left?

   ___ − ___ = ___

   Check:

   ___ + ___ = ___

5. 4 chicks are in a nest.
   4 chicks jump out.
   How many are left?

   ___ − ___ = ___

   Check:

   ___ + ___ = ___

6. **Extend Your Thinking**  Fran said that
   8 minus 5 equals 4. Is Fran right or wrong?
   Draw a picture and explain how you know.

   Fran is _____.

7. Flora has 8 seeds. 4 of the seeds are for green beans. The rest are for carrots. How many seeds are for carrots?

____ are carrot seeds.

8. There are 9 bees in the garden. 6 bees fly away. How many bees are left in the garden?

____ bees are left.

9. Bree has some flowers. She gives 3 flowers to her mother. Now Bree has 3 flowers.

Choose the subtraction sentence that shows the story.

○ $6 - 6 = 0$

○ $6 - 3 = 3$

○ $3 + 3 = 6$

○ $9 - 3 = 6$

10. **Extend Your Thinking** Use the numbers 9, 5, and 4 to write 2 different subtraction sentences.

____ − ____ = ____

____ − ____ = ____

Make sure you use all 3 numbers in each subtraction sentence.

Name _____

**Another Look** You can use counters to show a story and to help write a subtraction sentence.

Ben has 7 tennis balls.
He gives 3 of them to Ava.
How many tennis balls does
Ben have left?

7 is the whole.
3 is the part
we know.

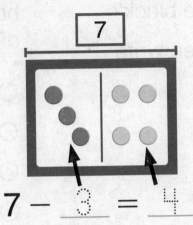

$7 - 3 = 4$

Ben has _4_ tennis balls left.

🏠 HOME CONNECTION
Your child used counters to act out subtraction problems, and then wrote subtraction sentences.

HOME ACTIVITY Have your child use small objects, such as pennies, to act out the following problem: "Carla owns 8 books. She wants to read all of her books by the end of the month. So far, Carla has read 5 of her books. How many more books does Carla need to read?" [3] Repeat the activity using other numbers through 9.

Use counters to show each story.
Then write a subtraction sentence.

1. There are 8 students in the park. 6 are boys. How many are girls?

___ = ___ − ___

2. Dan has 9 toy trucks. 3 trucks are large and the rest are small. How many trucks are small?

___ − ___ = ___

3. Zoey has 6 puppets. She gives 4 puppets to her sister. How many puppets does Zoey have now?

___ − ___ = ___

Topic 2 | Lesson 9
Digital Resources at PearsonTexas.com
one hundred twenty-seven 127

Use counters to act out each story.

4. There are 7 cats in the yard. 4 of the cats are gray. The rest are black. How many cats are black?

Complete the model. Then write a subtraction sentence.

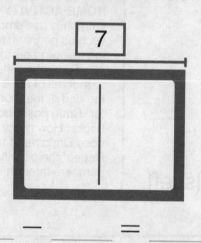

7

\_\_\_ \_\_\_ = \_\_\_

5. ⭐ Joy has 6 shirts and 3 pairs of pants. Which subtraction sentence shows how many more shirts than pairs of pants Joy has?

○  $6 + 3 = 9$

○  $9 - 3 = 6$

○  $8 - 5 = 3$

○  $6 - 3 = 3$

6. **Extend Your Thinking** Theo has 5 trading cards. He gives away some trading cards, but he keeps more than he gives away. How many trading cards did Theo give away? Explain how you know.

\_\_\_ trading cards

© Pearson Education, Inc. 1

Think about how addition and subtraction are **related** as you solve this soccer problem.

**1.** Cross out the model that does **not** match the problem.

Two teams score 7 goals.
The Spurs score some goals.
The Wolves score 2 goals.
How many goals do the
Spurs score?

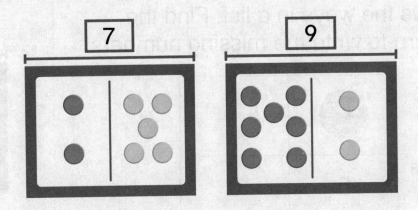

**2.** Write an addition sentence or a subtraction sentence for the soccer problem in Exercise 1.

____ ◯ ____ = ____

**3.** Tell why you can write an addition sentence or a subtraction sentence for the soccer problem.

_____

_____

_____

_____

## Make a List

1. Lucia shows all the ways to make 5 using yellow and red counters. She shows the ways in a list. Find the pattern to write the missing numbers.

| | |
|---|---|
| ⬤ | ⬤ |
| 5 | 0 |
| | |
| 3 | |
| | |
| | 4 |
| 0 | |

## What's Wrong?

2. Cross out the model that **can't** be right. Complete the model that is right.

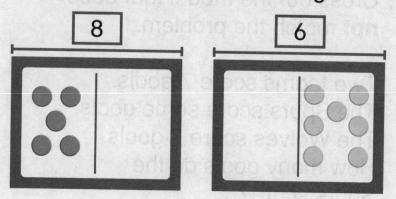

---

## Complete It!

3. Fill in the missing numbers.

$$3 + \boxed{\phantom{0}} = 9$$

$$\boxed{\phantom{0}} - 4 = 4$$

$$7 = \boxed{\phantom{0}} + 5$$

$$5 = 8 - \boxed{\phantom{0}}$$

Name _____

**Set A**

6 bones in all

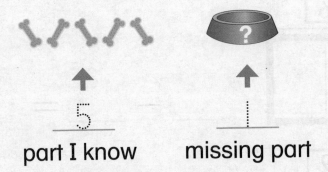

5
part I know     missing part

The part I know is 5 bones.
The I bone in the bowl is
the missing part.

Find the missing part.
Then write the numbers.

1. 6 bones in all

_____     _____
part I know     missing part

2. 7 bones in all

_____     _____
part I know     missing part

**Set B**

You can find the missing part.
Then write the numbers.

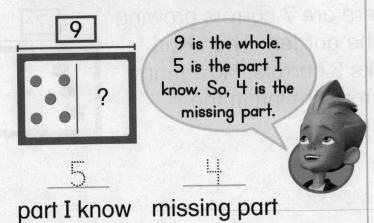

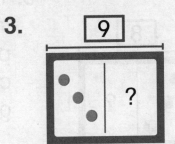
9 is the whole.
5 is the part I
know. So, 4 is the
missing part.

5     4
part I know    missing part

Find the missing part.
Then write the numbers.

3.

9

?

_____
part I know

_____
missing part

You can write a subtraction
sentence about the whole
and the parts.

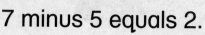

7 is the whole.
5 is the part I know.
2 is the missing part.

7 minus 5 equals 2.

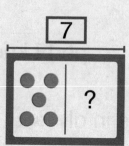

Draw the missing counters.
Then write a subtraction sentence.

4.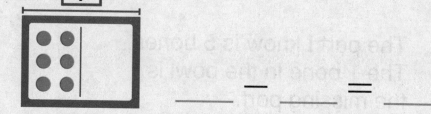

_____ — _____ = _____

5.

_____ — _____ = _____

You can use cubes to show a
separating story. Then you can
write a subtraction sentence.

Rob has 8 pears. Then
he gives 3 pears to Sal.
How many pears does
Rob have left?

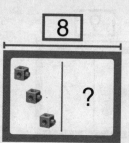

8 — 3 = 5

Complete the model. Use cubes to help
you. Then write a subtraction sentence.

6. There are 7 carrots growing
in the garden. Then Karl
picks 3 carrots. How many
carrots are left in the
garden?

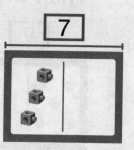

_____ — _____ = _____

Name _____

**Set E**

You can use cubes to compare and write a subtraction sentence.

Carla has 4 blue pencils. She has 3 yellow pencils. How many more blue pencils than yellow pencils does Carla have?

$4 - 3 = 1$

Use cubes to solve.

7. Mosi has 4 pens. Holly has 1 pen. How many more pens does Mosi have than Holly?

___ — ___ = ___

8. Martin has 7 baseballs and 3 soccer balls. How many more baseballs than soccer balls does he have?

___ — ___ = ___

**Set F**

You can find missing parts.

Tom had 9 books. He lost 4 books. How many does he have left?

$9 - 4 = 5$

Complete the model. Then write a subtraction sentence.

9. John and Jenny have 8 pairs of shoes in all. Jenny has 4 pairs of shoes. How many pairs of shoes does John have?

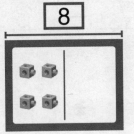

___ — ___ = ___

You can use the whole and
the parts to write addition
and subtraction sentences.

A group of birds sits on a fence.
There are 4 bluebirds. 3 birds
are red cardinals.

How many birds are on the fence?

$$4 + 3 = 7$$

There are 7 birds on a fence.
Some are blue and some are red.

If 3 are red, how many are blue?

$$7 - 3 = 4$$

Solve. Write the number sentences.

10. Ricky has 9 balloons.
Some of the balloons are yellow.
5 balloons are green.

How many balloons are yellow?

_____ — _____ = _____

Ricky gave his sister 5 balloons.
He gave his brother 4 balloons.

How many balloons did Ricky
give away?

_____ + _____ = _____

© Pearson Education, Inc. 1

Topic 2

Name _____

**1.** Which is the missing part?
6 bones in all

$\underline{\quad 3 \quad}$
part I know

$\underline{\quad ? \quad}$
missing part

3          4          6          10
○          ○          ○          ○

**2.** There are 8 plates.
4 plates have pasta.
The rest have salad.

Which subtraction sentence shows
how many plates have salad?

○   $12 - 8 = 4$

○   $12 - 4 = 8$

○   $8 - 3 = 5$

○   $8 - 4 = 4$

**3.** Which is the missing part?
9 owls in all

$\underline{\quad 6 \quad}$
part I know

$\underline{\quad ? \quad}$
missing part

2          3          4          5
○          ○          ○          ○

**4.** There are 7 bowls.
5 bowls have cereal.
The rest are empty.

Which subtraction sentence
matches the story?

○   $7 - 6 = 1$

○   $7 - 5 = 2$

○   $7 - 4 = 3$

○   $7 - 3 = 4$

**5.** Choose the number sentence that shows the story.

Owen has 5 blocks. He gives 1 to Jordan. How many blocks does Owen have left?

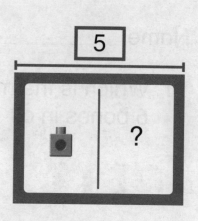

5 + 1 = 6          5 − 5 = 0          5 − 1 = 4          6 − 5 = 1
   ○                  ○                  ○                  ○

---

**6.** Hannah sees 7 flowers. Carrie sees 6 flowers. How many more flowers does Hannah see than Carrie?

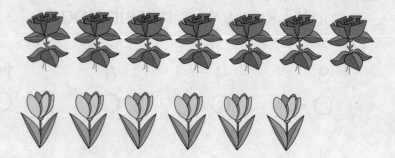

7 − 7 = 0          7 − 6 = 1          7 + 1 = 8          7 + 2 = 9
   ○                  ○                  ○                  ○

---

**7.** Choose the number sentence that shows the story.

Lucy and Ellie have 6 cubes in all. Ellie has 5 cubes. How many cubes does Lucy have?

6 + 1 = 7          7 − 6 = 1          6 − 5 = 1          6 − 6 = 0
   ○                  ○                  ○                  ○

8. Nikki has 8 tennis balls. Thomas has 6 tennis balls. How many more tennis balls does Nikki have than Thomas?

$4 + 4 = 8$ ○

$8 - 3 = 5$ ○

$2 - 0 = 2$ ○

$8 - 6 = 2$ ○

9. Find the missing part.

○ 4

○ 5

○ 8

○ 9

$\boxed{9}$

$\underline{4}$
part I know

$\underline{?}$
missing part

10. Roma has 8 stamps. She uses 7 stamps to send letters. How many stamps are left?

Which number sentence tells about the story?

$\boxed{8}$

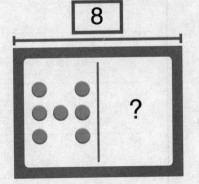

$1 = 8 - 7$ ○

$7 = 6 + 1$ ○

$6 = 7 - 1$ ○

$9 = 8 + 1$ ○

**11.** Which number sentence does **not** match the model?

5

- ○ $5 - 3 = 2$
- ○ $5 - 2 = 3$
- ○ $3 - 2 = 1$
- ○ $2 + 3 = 5$

**12.** Draw the missing counters. Write the numbers.

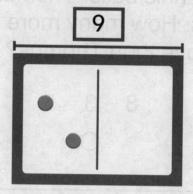

9

$9 - \underline{\hspace{1.5cm}} = \underline{\hspace{1.5cm}}$

$9 - \underline{\hspace{1.5cm}} = \underline{\hspace{1.5cm}}$

$\underline{\hspace{1.5cm}} + \underline{\hspace{1.5cm}} = 9$

**13.** Solve. $6 - \underline{\hspace{1.5cm}} = 2$

Write a subtraction story for the number sentence. Draw a picture.

© Pearson Education, Inc. 1

# Five and Ten Relationships

**Essential Question:** How can you show numbers up to 10?

Look! 2 groups of marbles.

The marbles are different colors, but they are all round.

Wow! Let's do this project and learn more.

## Math and Science Project: Sorting Objects

**Find Out** Talk to friends and relatives about sorting groups of objects. Ask them to help you find 10 objects that can be sorted into 2 groups by color, shape, or size.

**Journal: Make a Book** Show what you found out. In your book, also:

• Draw your 2 different groups of objects. Write how many are in each group.

• Write an addition sentence for your 2 groups of objects.

Name _____

# Review What You Know

## Vocabulary

**1.** Write a **subtraction sentence**.

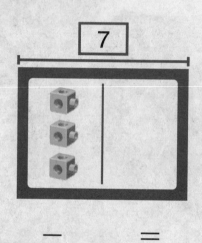

7

___ − ___ = ___

**2.** Circle the sign for **plus**.

$+$

$-$

$=$

**3.** Write the **parts** shown in the model.

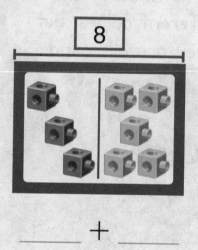

8

___ + ___

---

## Stories about Joining

Write an addition sentence to solve the problem.

**4.** Yao has 5 fish. He buys 4 more fish. How many fish are in Yao's tank now?

___ + ___ = ___

## Subtraction Stories

Use cubes to solve. Write the subtraction sentence.

**5.** 8 squirrels are on the ground. 5 are eating acorns. How many squirrels are **not** eating acorns?

___ − ___ = ___

**6.** Brett has 5 markers. Pablo has 3 markers. How many more markers does Brett have than Pablo?

___ − ___ = ___

Name _____

☆ **Solve & Share** ☆

How can you show 6 counters on the ten-frame so they are easy to count? Draw your counters.

TEKS 1.2A Recognize instantly the quantity of structured arrangements. **Mathematical Process Standards** 1.1C, 1.1D, 1.1E.

Digital Resources at PearsonTexas.com

Solve   Learn   Glossary   Check   Tools   Games

You can show numbers up to 10 on a ten-frame.

Let's show 7.

Start at the top left box.

I have 1 so far.

Fill the top row first.

I have 5 so far.

Then fill the bottom row as you need to.

7

Now I have 7. 7 is 2 more than 5.

## Do You Understand?

**Show Me!** How can you use a ten-frame to show the number 8?

☆ **Guided Practice** ☆ Draw counters in the ten-frame to show each number.

1. 3

2. 2

3. 5

4. 6

© Pearson Education, Inc. 1

**Topic 3** | Lesson 1

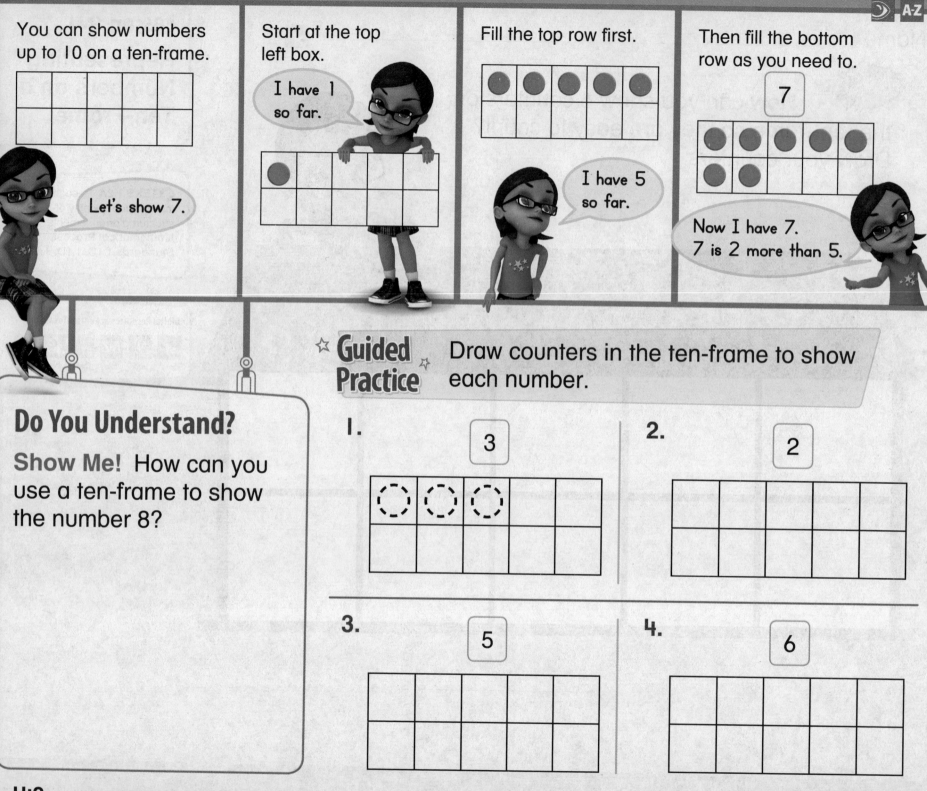

Name _____

Draw counters in the ten-frame to show each number.

5.  | 9 |

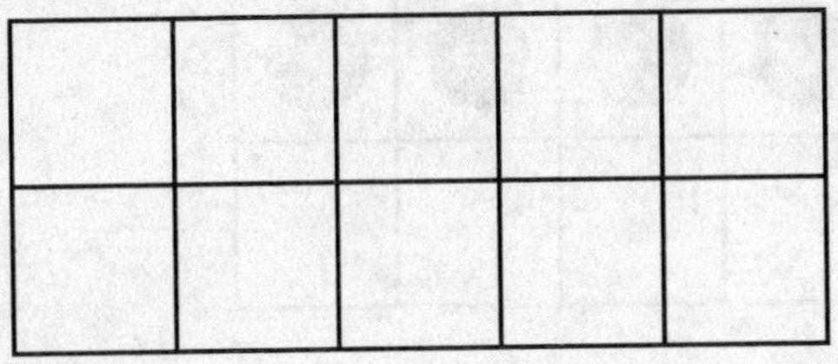

6.  | 4 |

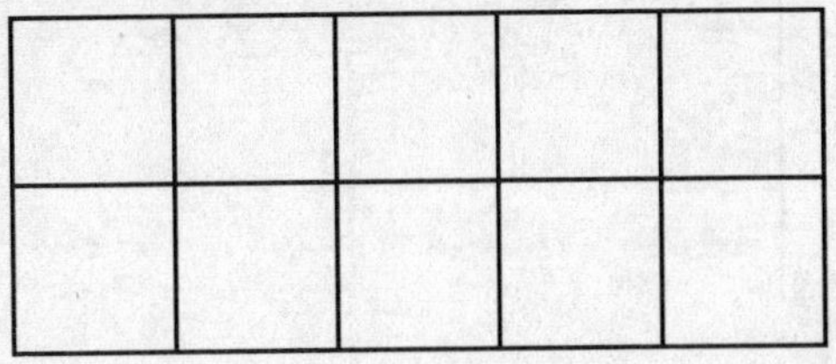

7.  | 1 |

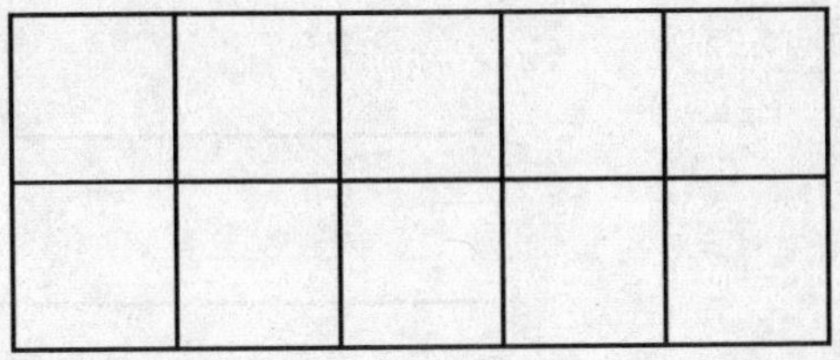

8.  | 10 |

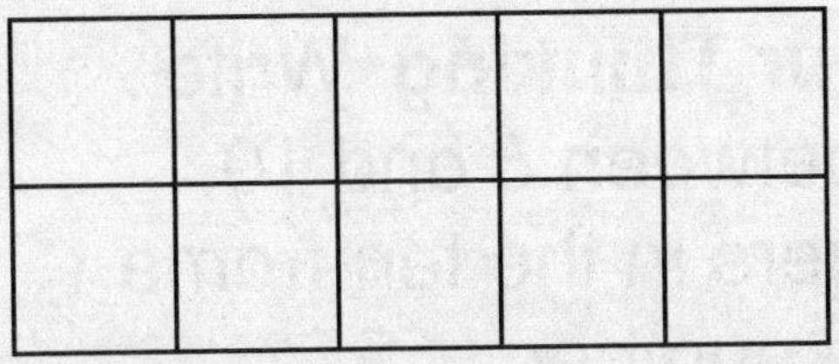

9.  | 7 |

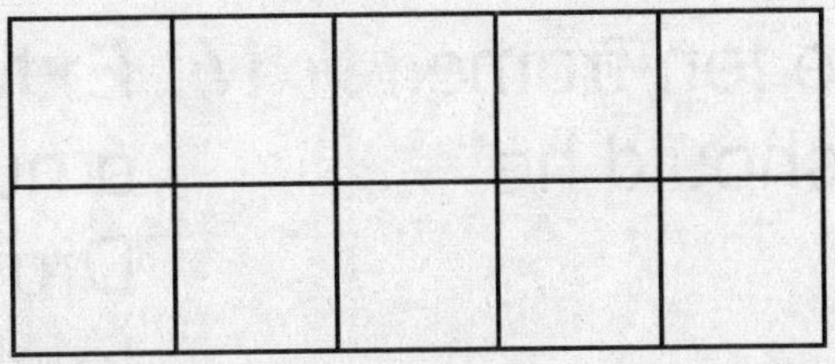

10.  | 3 |

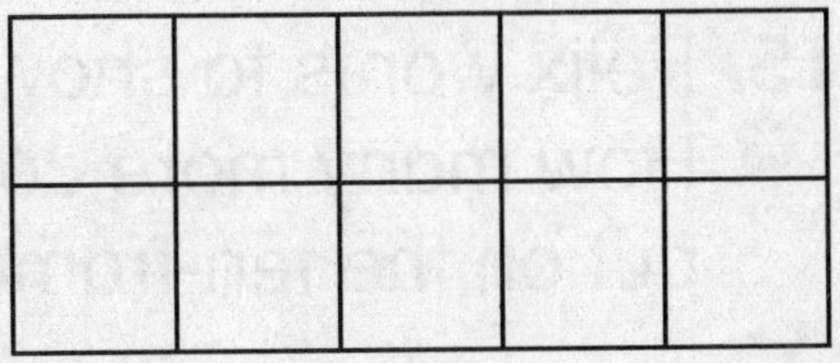

**Extend Your Thinking** Draw counters. Write the number.

11. Show how 8 is 5 and _____ more.

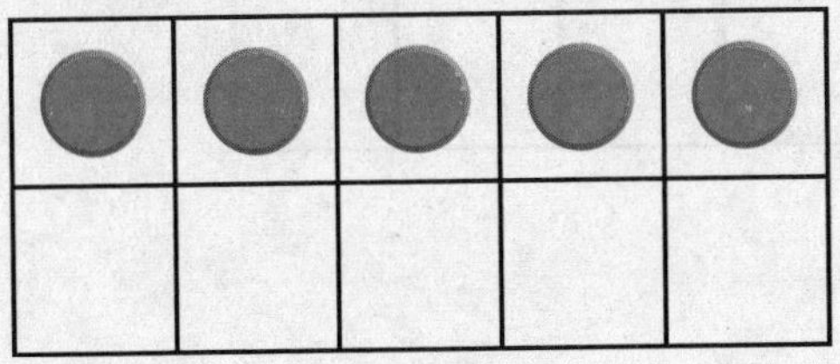

12. Show how 6 is 4 and _____ more.

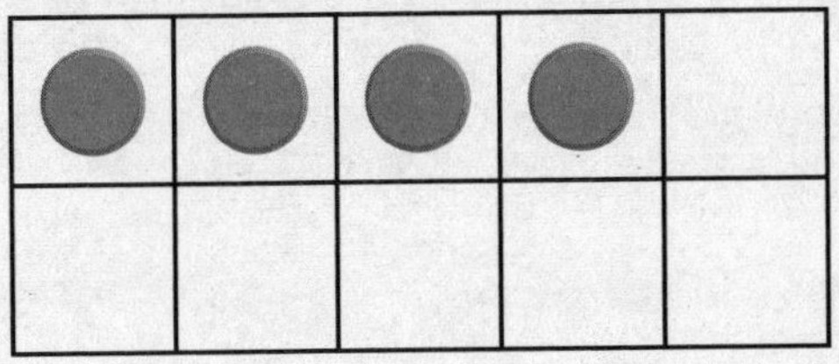

**13.** Nita shows 9 on a ten-frame.
Draw the counters Nita put in each row.
Then write the numbers.

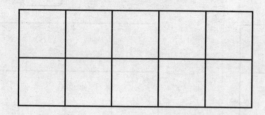

9 is ____ and ____ more.

**14.** Steve put 5 counters in a ten-frame.
How many more counters does
Steve need to show 10?

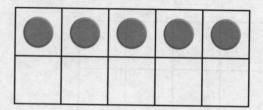

| 1 | 5 | 6 | 10 |
| ○ | ○ | ○ | ○ |

**15.** Felix wants to show 6 in the ten-frame.
How many more counters should he
put on the ten-frame?

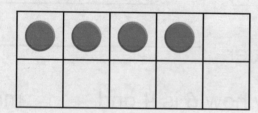

○ 4
○ 3
○ 2
○ 1

**16. Extend Your Thinking** Write
a number between 6 and 10.
Draw counters in the ten-frame
to show the number.

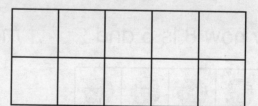

Name _____

**Another Look** You can use a ten-frame to show numbers up to 10.

To show 7, start at the top left box. When the top row is filled, continue counting in the bottom row.

Count as you draw a counter for each number.

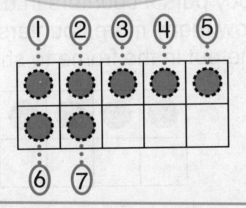

Draw counters in the ten-frame to show 10.

Remember, to show 10, start at the top left box. When the top row is filled, continue counting in the bottom row.

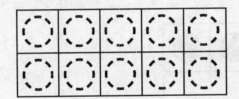

🏠 HOME CONNECTION
Your child used counters to show the numbers 1 to 10 on a ten-frame.

HOME ACTIVITY Sketch a ten-frame. Say a number between 6 and 10. Have your child use pennies to fill in the ten-frame. Ask, "How many boxes have you filled in?" Repeat with other numbers.

Draw counters in the ten-frame to show each number.

1. 6

2. 8

3. 5

4. 9

**5. Algebra** Draw counters to show how 7 is 5 and 2.

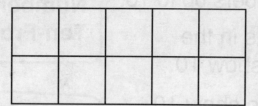

**6. Algebra** Draw counters to show how 9 is 5 and 4.

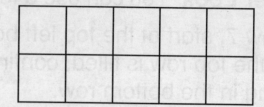

**7.** ✪ Juan wants to show 9 in the ten-frame. How many more counters does he need to add?

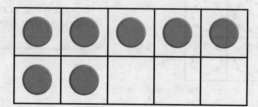

2 ○     3 ○     6 ○     7 ○

**8.** ✪ Lucy puts 4 counters in a ten-frame. How many more counters should she put in the frame to show 10?

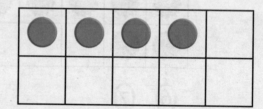

7 ○     6 ○     5 ○     4 ○

**9. Extend Your Thinking** Pick a number greater than 5 and less than 10.

Write the number. Draw counters in the ten-frame to show your number.

© Pearson Education, Inc. 1

**Lesson 3-2**
**Recognizing Numbers on a Ten-Frame**

⭐ TEKS 1.2A Recognize instantly the quantity of structured arrangements. **Mathematical Process Standards 1.1C, 1.1D, 1.1E, 1.1G.**

Digital Resources at PearsonTexas.com

Solve    Learn    Glossary    Check    Tools    Games

**Solve & Share**

Use counters to show a number on the ten-frame. Have a partner tell the number and explain how the number was easy to count.

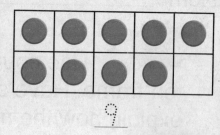

What number is shown on the ten-frame?

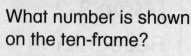

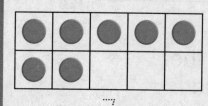

7

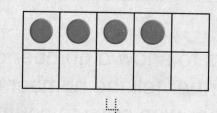

4

9

The number is more than 5.

5 and 2 more is 7.

The number is less than 5. It is 1 away from 5.

The number is less than 10. It is 1 away from 10.

## Do You Understand?

**Show Me!** Chris says 5 and 3 is 8. Maya says 2 away from 10 is 8. Who is correct? Explain.

## Guided Practice

Write the number shown on each ten-frame.

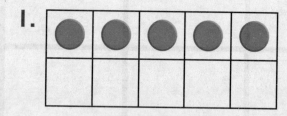

1.

5

2. _____

3. _____

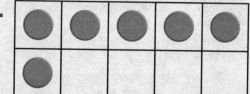

4. _____

© Pearson Education, Inc. 1

Name _____

Write the number shown on each ten-frame.

5.

_____

6.

_____

7.

_____

8.

_____

9.

_____

10.

_____

Draw counters to solve. Write the number.

11. **Extend Your Thinking**

Carrie uses a ten-frame.
She shows 5 and 1 more.
What number does she show?

**12.** Alex wrote a sentence about the ten-frame.

Circle the sentence Alex should have written.

2 away from 10 is 7.

5 and 2 is 7.

**13.** Wendy says a ten-frame shows 5 and 4 more.

Stan says it shows 1 away from 10.

If both Wendy and Stan are correct, what number is shown on the ten-frame?

9      8      6      4
○      ○      ○      ○

---

**14. Extend Your Thinking** Write a number between 6 and 10.

Draw counters in the ten-frame to show your number. Complete the sentence to describe your number.

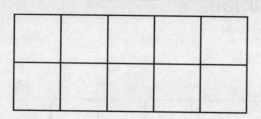

5 and ____ is ____.

The ten-frame can help you complete the sentence.

© Pearson Education, Inc. 1

Name _____

**Another Look** You can put counters on a ten-frame to show numbers.

The number 8 is more than 5.
5 and __3__ more is 8.

The number 8 is less than 10.
It is __2__ away from 10.

The number 9 is more than 5.
5 and __4__ more is 9.

The number 9 is less than 10.
It is __1__ away from 10.

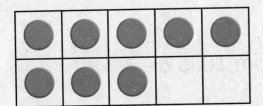

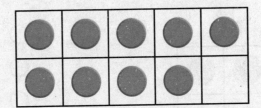

🏠 **HOME CONNECTION**
Your child used counters to recognize the numbers 1 to 10 on a ten-frame.

**HOME ACTIVITY** Sketch a ten-frame with 5 boxes in the top row and 5 boxes in the bottom row. Put pennies in some of the boxes, starting with the top left box. Ask, "How many boxes have pennies in them?" Repeat using different numbers to 10.

Write the number shown on each ten-frame.

1.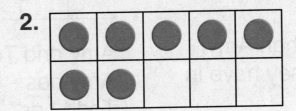
_____

2. _____

3. _____

## Which number is shown on each ten-frame?

**4.**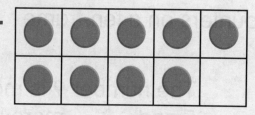

**5.** 

**6.**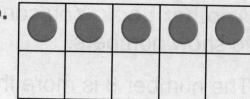

_____     _____     _____

**7.** Nick wrote a sentence about the ten-frame.

Which sentence did Nick write?

○ 5 and 5 is 10.

○ 4 away from 10 is 6.

○ 5 and 2 is 7.

○ 3 away from 10 is 7.

**8. Extend Your Thinking** Draw counters in the ten-frame to solve the problem. Write the numbers.

Amy has some counters.
Todd has more counters than Amy.
The number of counters they have in all is 2 away from 10.

Amy and Todd have ____ counters in all.
Amy has ____ counters.
Todd has ____ counters.

Name _____

**Solve & Share**

Jackson and I bought 10 hats. How can you use counters and a ten-frame to show the number of hats we bought? Draw your counters in the ten-frame and write the numbers.

⭐ TEKS 1.3C Compose 10 with two or more addends with and without concrete objects. Mathematical Process Standards 1.1C, 1.1E.

Digital Resources at PearsonTexas.com

Solve  Learn  Glossary  Check  Tools  Games

| | | | | |
|---|---|---|---|---|
| | | | | |
| | | | | |

_____ and _____

Topic 3 | Lesson 3

Digital Resources at PearsonTexas.com

one hundred fifty-three **153**

You can use a ten-frame to show parts of 10.

6 is one part.

4 is the other part.

10 is 6 and 4.

↑ whole   ↑ part   ↑ part

10 is the whole.

6 red and 4 yellow

## Do You Understand?

**Show Me!** How many more counters do you need to make 10? How do you know?

1.

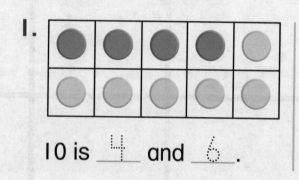

10 is _4_ and _6_.

2.

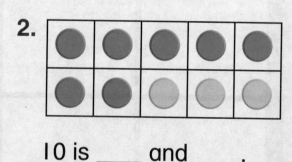

10 is ___ and ___.

3.

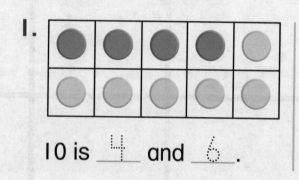

10 is ___ and ___.

4.

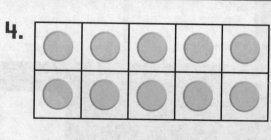

10 is ___ and ___.

**Topic 3** | Lesson 3

Name _____

Write the numbers that show ways to make 10.

5.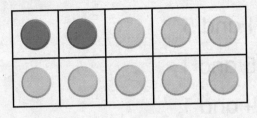

10 is ____ and ____ .

6.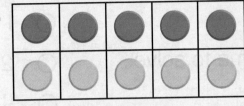

10 is ____ and ____ .

7.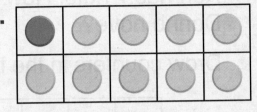

10 is ____ and ____ .

8.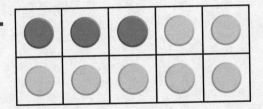

10 is ____ and ____ .

9.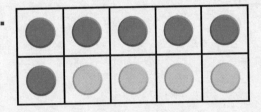

10 is ____ and ____ .

10.

10 is ____ and ____ .

11. **Extend Your Thinking**

Barb has some purple grapes.
Gail has some green grapes.
Will has the same number of red
grapes as Gail's green grapes.
They have 10 grapes in all.

Draw counters to show the number
of grapes Barb, Gail, and Will have.
Write the numbers.

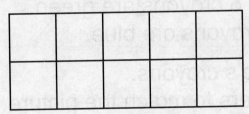

10 is ____ and ____ and ____ .
**Barb      Gail      Will**

# Problem Solving Solve each problem below.

12. Ken and Donna have 10 hats in all. Ken has 7 hats. How many hats does Donna have?

Draw counters in the ten-frame to solve.

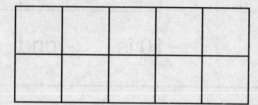

10 is 7 and ____.

____ hats

13. ⭐ Which numbers are parts of 10?

○ 1 and 4 and 5

○ 2 and 5 and 1

○ 4 and 4 and 1

○ 6 and 3 and 2

14. **Extend Your Thinking** Shane has 10 crayons. 6 crayons are green. The other crayons are blue.

Draw Shane's crayons.
Write numbers to match the picture.

10 is ____ and ____.

© Pearson Education, Inc. 1

Name _____

## Another Look

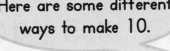
Here are some different ways to make 10.

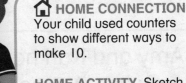
🏠 **HOME CONNECTION**
Your child used counters to show different ways to make 10.

**HOME ACTIVITY** Sketch a ten-frame. Have your child put pennies in some of the boxes and nickels in the remaining boxes. Ask, "How many pennies are there? How many nickels?" Then have your child complete the following statement by giving the number of each type of coin: "10 coins is ____ pennies and ____ nickels." Repeat with other combinations of pennies and nickels.

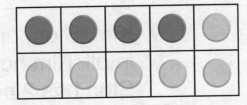

10 is 7 and 3.

10 is __4__ and __6__.

Write the numbers that show ways to make 10.

1.
10 is ___ and ___.

2.
10 is ___ and ___.

3.
10 is ___ and ___.

4.
10 is ___ and ___.

Write the missing number for each problem.

**5. Algebra**

$4 + \underline{\hspace{1cm}} = 10$

**6. Algebra**

$\underline{\hspace{1cm}} + 5 = 10$

**7. Algebra**

$1 + 9 = \underline{\hspace{1cm}}$

**8.** ✪ Amy and Karl have 10 cups in all. Amy has 2 cups.

How many cups does Karl have?

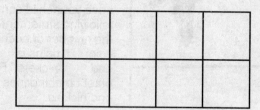

| 10 | 9 | 8 | 2 |
|----|---|---|---|
| ○ | ○ | ○ | ○ |

**9.** ✪ Kim, Stan, and Alan have 10 pennies in all. Kim has 3 pennies. Stan has 2 pennies.

How many pennies does Alan have?

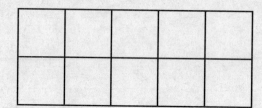

| 5 | 4 | 3 | 1 |
|---|---|---|---|
| ○ | ○ | ○ | ○ |

**10. Extend Your Thinking**

Draw counters to solve the problem.
Write the numbers.

Pedro has 10 beads. Some beads are round and some are square. He has more than 3 square beads.

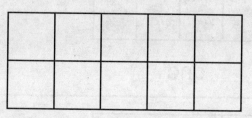

10 is _____ round beads and _____ square beads.

Name ______________________

**Solve & Share**

Tracy collected 10 shells. Some shells are hidden in the sand. Tracy can only see 8 shells. How many shells are hidden? Use counters to show the story problem.

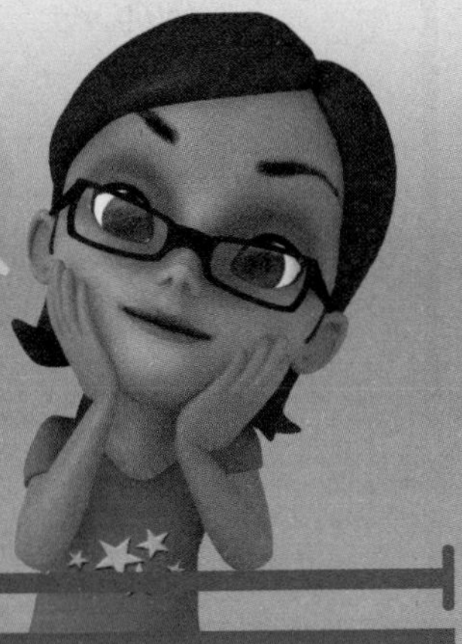

# Lesson 3-4
## Finding Missing Parts of 10

**TEKS 1.3C** Compose 10 with two or more addends with and without concrete objects. **Mathematical Process Standards** 1.1A, 1.1C, 1.1E, 1.1F.

**Digital Resources at PearsonTexas.com**

Solve Learn Glossary Check Tools Games

10

_____ part I know

_____ missing part

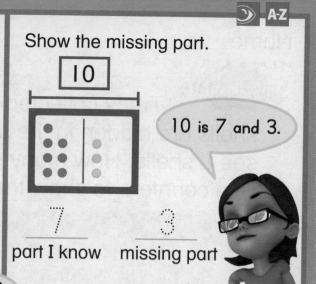
There are 10 balls. Some are hidden inside the box.

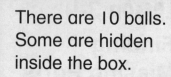

You know the whole.

| 10 |
whole

There are 10 balls in all.

You know one part.

| 10 |

?

7
part I know

What is the missing part?

Show the missing part.

| 10 |

10 is 7 and 3.

7              3
part I know   missing part

---

**Guided Practice**   Draw the missing part. Then write the numbers.

## Do You Understand?

**Show Me!** What is the missing part? How do you know?

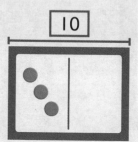

| 10 |

1.
| 10 |

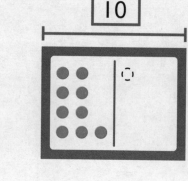

9              1
part I know   missing part

2.
| 10 |

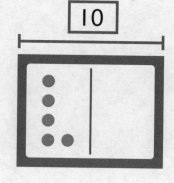

_____          _____
part I know   missing part

---

**160** one hundred sixty

**Topic 3** | **Lesson 4**

Name _____

Draw the missing part. Then write the numbers.

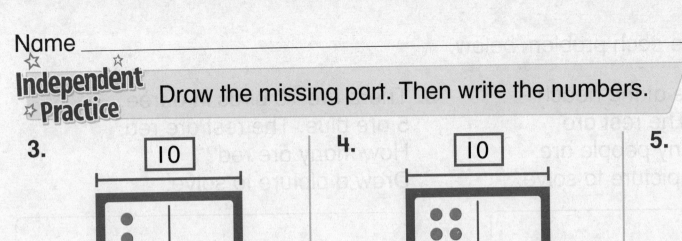

3. | 10 |

_____     _____
part I know     missing part

4. | 10 |

_____     _____
part I know     missing part

5. | 10 |

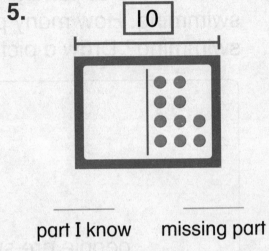

_____     _____
part I know     missing part

Use the part-part-whole mat to solve.

6. **Extend Your Thinking**
Bob has some red crayons.
Jan has some blue crayons.
Alex has some purple crayons.
Alex has more crayons than Jan.
They have 10 crayons in all.

Draw counters to show the number of
crayons Bob, Jan, and Alex could have.

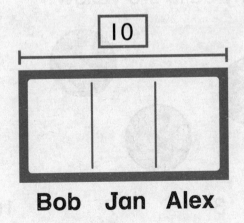

| 10 |

**Bob   Jan   Alex**

**7.** There are 10 people at the beach. 8 are on the sand. The rest are swimming. How many people are swimming? Draw a picture to solve.

_____ people are swimming.

**8.** There are 10 birds in a tree. 5 are blue. The rest are red. How many are red? Draw a picture to solve.

_____ birds are red.

**9.** Helen sees 10 balls. Some are yellow. 3 are red. How many balls are yellow?

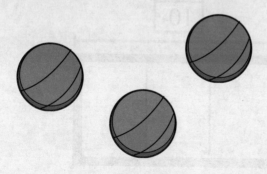

2          3          7          10
○          ○          ○          ○

**10. Extend Your Thinking** There are 10 shells. Some shells are inside the pail. Some shells are outside the pail. Draw the shells. Write the parts.

_____          _____
part I know    missing part

© Pearson Education, Inc. 1

Name _____

**Another Look** You can use a ten-frame to help find missing parts of 10.

You know one part. 4 is one part of 10.

To find the missing part, draw counters to fill the frame.

Write the missing part.

4        6
part I know    missing part

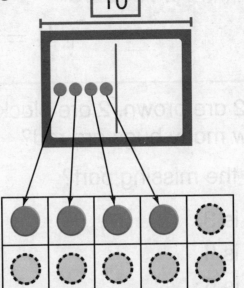

🏠 **HOME CONNECTION**
Your child used counters to find the missing parts of 10.

**HOME ACTIVITY** Draw 2 large circles. Put some pennies in the circle on the left. Say, "I have 10 pennies. How many pennies are missing?" Have your child put pennies in the circle on the right until the total in both circles is 10 pennies. Have your child tell you how many pennies are missing. Repeat with other numbers to 10.

Look at the model. Draw the missing part in the model and ten-frame. Write the numbers.

**1.**
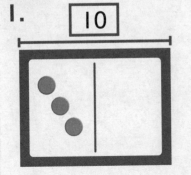
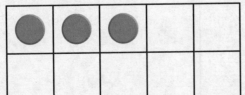

part I know    missing part

**2.**
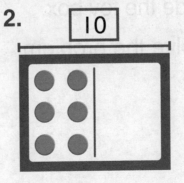
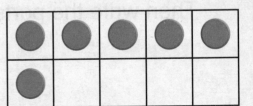

part I know    missing part

Write the missing part for each problem.

**3. Algebra**

$8 +$ ____ $= 10$

**4. Algebra**

____ $+ 4 = 10$

**5. Algebra**

$3 +$ ____ $= 10$

**6.** Kami sees 10 bugs. 2 are brown. 2 are black. The rest are red. How many bugs are red?

Which sentence tells the missing part?

○ The missing part is 3.

○ The missing part is 4.

○ The missing part is 5.

○ The missing part is 6.

**7. Extend Your Thinking** Ned has 10 toy cars.
Some cars are inside the toy box.
Some cars are outside the toy box.

Draw a picture to solve the problem.
Then write the parts.

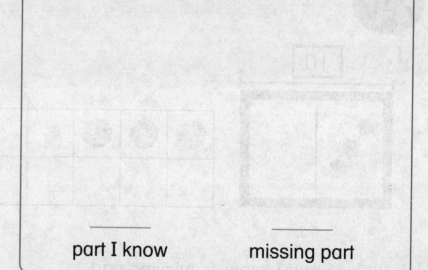

____        ____

part I know       missing part

Name _____

**Solve & Share**

Use counters and the part-part-whole mat to show different ways to make 10. Write the different ways in the table.

10

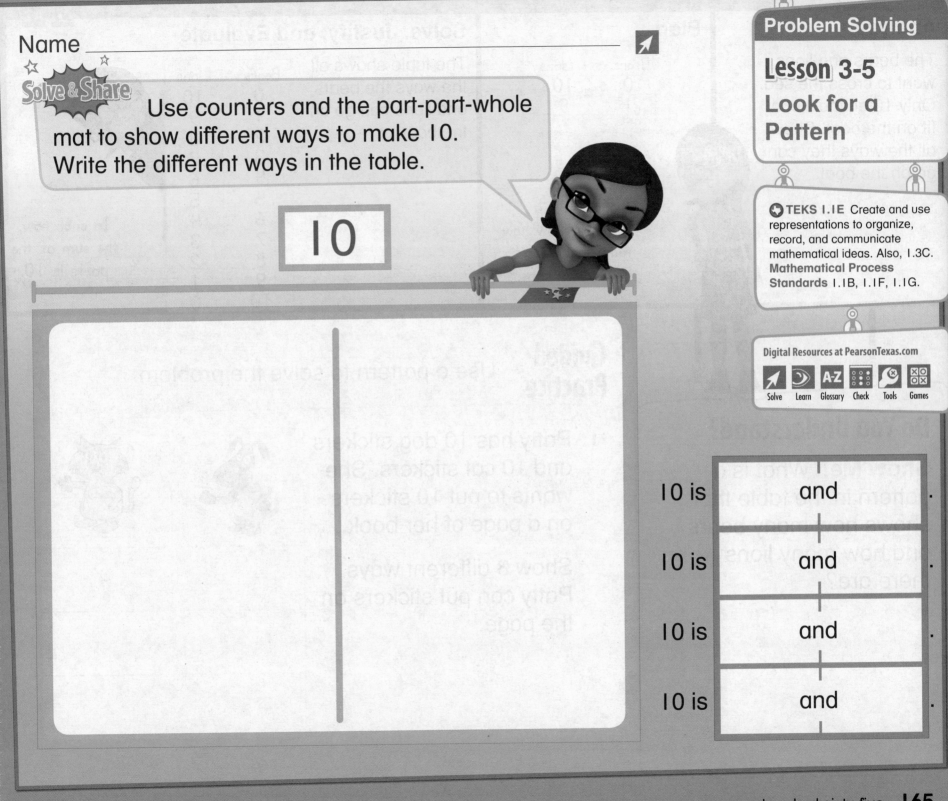

TEKS 1.1E Create and use representations to organize, record, and communicate mathematical ideas. Also, 1.3C. **Mathematical Process Standards 1.1B, 1.1F, 1.1G.**

Digital Resources at PearsonTexas.com

| Solve | Learn | Glossary | Check | Tools | Games |

10 is _____ and _____ .

10 is _____ and _____ .

10 is _____ and _____ .

10 is _____ and _____ .

## Analyze

The bears and lions want to cross the sea. Only 10 animals can fit on the boat. Show all the ways they can go on the boat.

## Plan

| Bears | Lions |
|-------|-------|
| 0 | 10 |
| 1 | 9 |

I can make a table to show how many bears and how many lions.

## Solve, Justify, and Evaluate

The table shows all the ways the bears and lions can go on the boat.

| Bears | Lions |
|-------|-------|
| 0 | 10 |
| 1 | 9 |
| 2 | 8 |
| 3 | 7 |
| 4 | 6 |
| 5 | 5 |
| 6 | 4 |
| 7 | 3 |
| 8 | 2 |
| 9 | 1 |
| 10 | 0 |

In each row, the sum of the parts is 10.

## Do You Understand?

**Show Me!** What is a pattern in the table that shows how many bears and how many lions there are?

## ☆ Guided Practice ☆   Use a pattern to solve the problem.

1. Patty has 10 dog stickers and 10 cat stickers. She wants to put 10 stickers on a page of her book.

Show 3 different ways Patty can put stickers on the page.

| | |
|---|---|
| 1 | 9 |
| | |
| | |

© Pearson Education, Inc. 1

**Topic 3** | Lesson 5

## ☆ Independent ☆ Practice

Use a pattern to solve each problem.

**2.** Max has 5 blue markers and 5 yellow markers. He wants to put 5 markers in his bag for art class.

Complete the table to show 3 different ways Max can put markers in his bag.

| | |
|---|---|
| 3 | |
| | 1 |
| | |

**3.** ⭐ Mrs. Davis fills a box with prizes. She has 10 balls and 10 balloons. She wants to put 10 prizes in the box.

Find the missing number.

| 10 | 0 |
|---|---|
| 8 | 2 |
| 6 | ? |

3 ○　　4 ○　　5 ○　　6 ○

Use a pattern to solve.

**4. Extend Your Thinking** Julie is planting 10 flowers. She has tulips and roses. Write 3 different ways Julie can plant 10 flowers.

_____ tulips and _____ roses

_____ tulips and _____ roses

_____ tulips and _____ roses

5. Manuel wants to buy 10 balloons. He can pick green and orange balloons. If he buys 2 green balloons, how many orange balloons should he buy?

_____ orange balloons

If he buys 3 green balloons, how many orange balloons should he buy?

_____ orange balloons

6. Jen draws 5 cows. She draws some standing up and some lying down. If she draws 3 cows standing up, how many cows does she draw lying down?

_____ cows

If she draws 2 cows standing up, how many cows does she draw lying down?

_____ cows

7. Rosa buys 10 stickers. She can pick from butterflies and horses.

What is one way Rosa can **not** buy the stickers?

○ 5 butterfly stickers, 5 horse stickers

○ 1 butterfly sticker, 9 horse stickers

○ 6 butterfly stickers, 6 horse stickers

○ 2 butterfly stickers, 8 horse stickers

8. **Extend Your Thinking** Bill has 10 apples and 10 bananas. He always puts 10 pieces of fruit in a bowl. He always puts more apples than bananas in the bowl. Show 3 different ways Bill can put the fruit in the bowl.

|  |  |
|---|---|
|  |  |
|  |  |
|  |  |

**Topic 3** | Lesson 5

Name _____

**Another Look** Karen has purple marbles and yellow marbles. She can only fit 5 marbles in her pocket.

Complete the table to show different ways Karen can solve this problem.

The sum of each row is __5__.

| ⬤ | ⬤ |
|---|---|
| 5 | 0 |
| 4 | 1 |
| 3 | 2 |
| 2 | 3 |
| 1 | 4 |

🏠 **HOME CONNECTION**
Your child used tables to find patterns.

**HOME ACTIVITY** Have your child place 5 pennies in a row. Ask, "How many pennies? How many nickels?" Then replace I penny with a nickel and ask the questions again. Continue replacing pennies with nickels one at a time, asking the questions after each turn. Then ask, "What is the sum each time?"

Use a pattern to solve each problem below.

1. Tom has 5 red toy cars and 5 blue toy cars. He wants to put 5 toy cars in his toy box. Complete the table to show 3 different ways Tom can put his toy cars in the box.

| 🚗 | 🚗 |
|---|---|
| 5 | |
| | 1 |
| | |
| 2 | |

2. Kathy has 5 tulips and 5 roses. She wants to plant 5 flowers in her garden. Complete the table to show 3 different ways Kathy can plant the flowers in her garden.

| 🌷 | 🌹 |
|---|---|
| | 3 |
| 3 | |
| | 1 |

Find the missing number for each problem.

**3. Algebra**

$1 + 9 = 10$

$2 + \underline{\phantom{00}} = 10$

**4. Algebra**

$6 + 4 = 10$

$7 + \underline{\phantom{00}} = 10$

**5. Algebra**

$10 = 9 + 1$

$10 = \underline{\phantom{00}} + 0$

**6.** A store sells 5 party hats for $1. The hats have stripes or spots. The table shows the different ways you can pick 5 party hats.

Which numbers are missing from the table?

| 5 | 0 |
|---|---|
| 4 | 1 |
| 3 | 2 |
| 2 | 3 |
| 1 | 4 |
| ? | ? |

○ 1, 3

○ 1, 5

○ 0, 4

○ 0, 5

**7. Extend Your Thinking** Use a pattern to solve the problem.

Ed eats 10 pieces of fruit. He can eat strawberries or grapes. Fill in the table to show how many different ways Ed can pick which fruit to eat.

How many different ways are there?

_____

What is the sum of each row in the table?

_____

Think about the different **representations** used in these turtle problems.

**1.** Cross out the model that does **not** match the problem.

A zookeeper has 8 turtles.
Some turtles are buried in the sand. 6 turtles are eating.

How many turtles are buried in the sand?

| 8 |
|---|

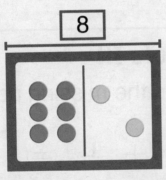

part I know       missing part

| 6 |
|---|

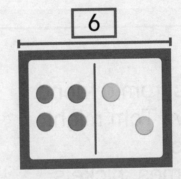

part I know       missing part

**2.** Write an addition sentence and a subtraction sentence for the turtle problem in Exercise 1.

____ + ____ = ____

____ − ____ = ____

**3.** Draw counters in the ten-frame to show the zookeeper's turtles.

## Make a List

1. Ray shows all the ways to make 10 using red and yellow counters. He shows the ways to make 10 in a list. Use the pattern to find the missing numbers.

| ⬤ | 0 | ___ | 2 | ___ | ___ | 5 | ___ | ___ | 9 | ___ |
| ⬤ | 10 | ___ | ___ | ___ | ___ | ___ | 3 | ___ | ___ | 0 |

## What's the Gift?

2. Tom received 10 cents from a friend. Show the different ways Tom might have received 10 cents.
Write the number of dimes, nickels, and pennies for each way.

| | (dime) | (nickel) | (penny) |
|---|---|---|---|
| **Way 1** | | | |
| **Way 2** | | | |
| **Way 3** | | | |

## Complete It!

3. Fill in the missing parts of 10.

$$6 + 4 = \boxed{\phantom{0}}$$

$$\boxed{\phantom{0}} + 7 = 10$$

$$9 + \boxed{\phantom{0}} = 10$$

$$\boxed{\phantom{0}} + \boxed{\phantom{0}} = 10$$

Name ______________________________

**TOPIC 3**

**Reteaching**

**Set A**

You can use a ten-frame to show numbers.

Draw counters to show 9.

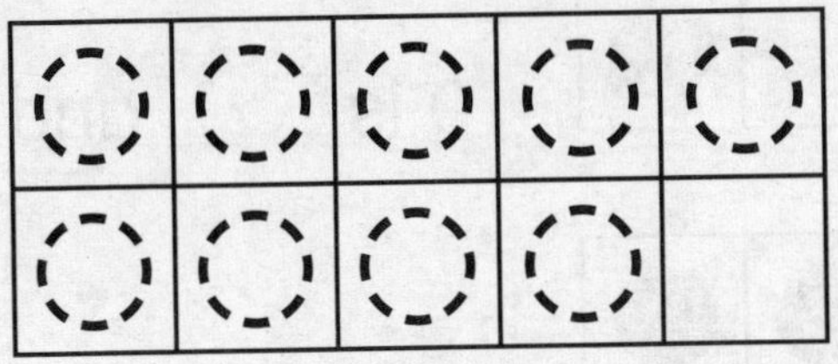

Draw counters in the ten-frame to show each number.

1. 6

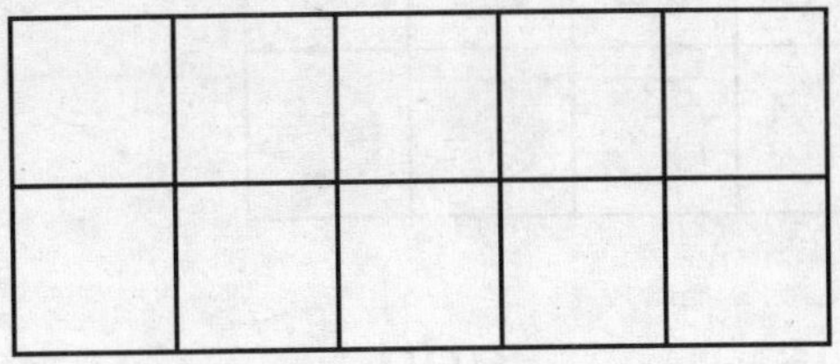

2. 10

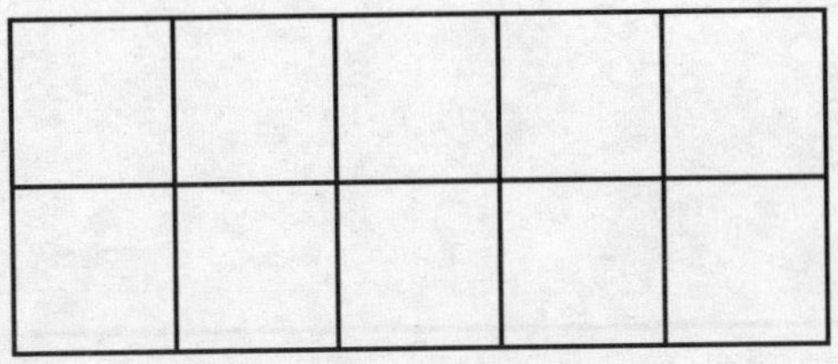

**Set B**

What number is shown on the ten-frame?

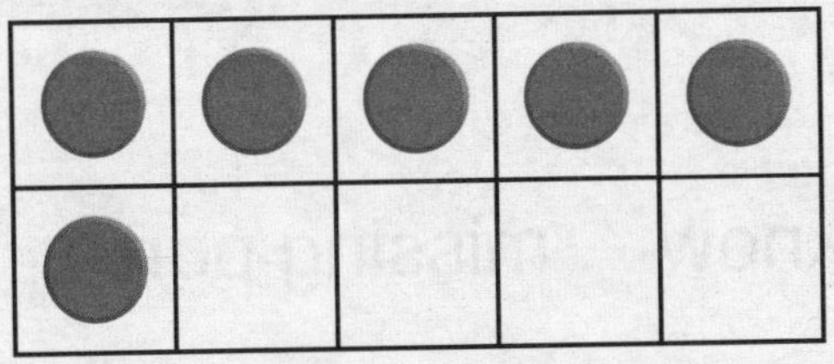

6

5 and 1 more is 6.

Write the number shown on each ten-frame.

3.

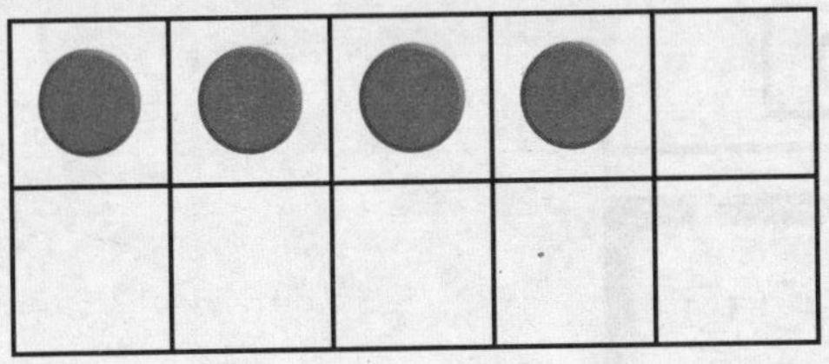

______

4.

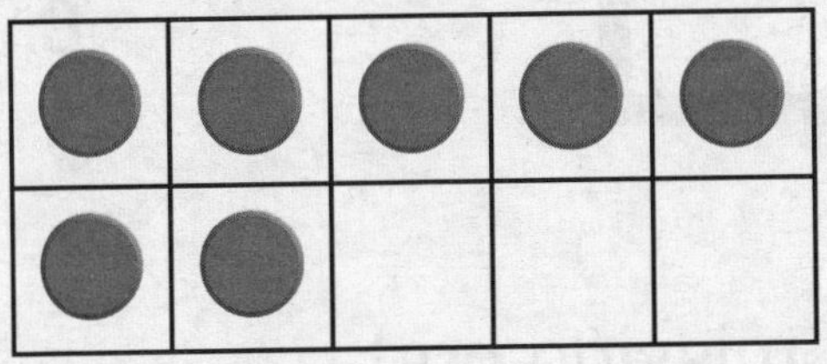

______

You can use a ten-frame to show ways to make 10.

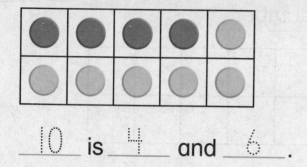

____10____ is ___4___ and ___6___.

Write the numbers that show ways to make 10.

5.
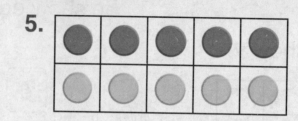

10 is ____ and ____.

6.
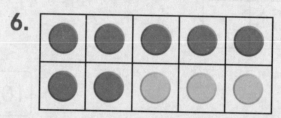

10 is ____ and ____.

You can use counters and a model to show the part you know. This helps you find the missing part.

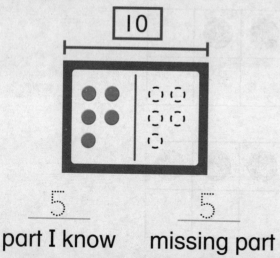

___5___          ___5___

part I know    missing part

Use counters to model the problem. Then draw the missing counters and write the numbers.

7.
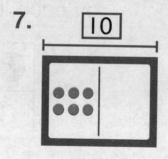

____          ____

part I know    missing part

8.
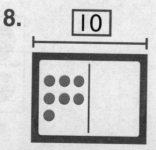

____          ____

part I know    missing part

© Pearson Education, Inc. 1

Name _____

1. Noah drew 3 counters in a ten-frame. How many more counters does he need to draw to make 10?

○ 10

○ 8

○ 7

○ 2

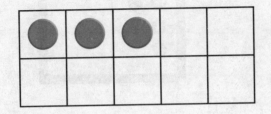

___

2. Which sentence describes the ten-frame?

○ 1 away from 10 is 8.

○ 5 and 2 is 8.

○ 3 away from 10 is 8.

○ 5 and 3 is 8.

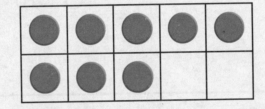

___

3. Which number is shown?

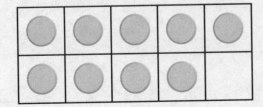

○ 4          ○ 9

○ 8          ○ 10

4. Which is a way to make 10?

○ 10 is 8 and 1.     ○ 10 is 2 and 7.

○ 10 is 8 and 3.     ○ 10 is 2 and 8.

**5.** A store has 10 hats.
Some are green. 4 are red.
How many hats are green?

○ 2

○ 3

○ 6

○ 10

**6.** Which shows the missing part?

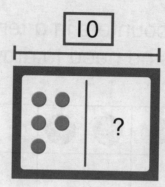

○ 4

○ 5

○ 6

○ 10

**7.** Tina wants to buy 6 beads. She can buy red or blue
beads. Show the different ways she can buy beads.
Write the numbers in the table.

| Red | | ___ | ___ | ___ | 3 | ___ | 5 | ___ |
|---|---|---|---|---|---|---|---|---|
| Blue | | ___ | 5 | ___ | ___ | ___ | ___ | 0 |

# Addition and Subtraction Facts to 12

**Essential Question:** What strategies can you use while adding and subtracting?

A habitat is the natural home for an animal.

Each animal lives in a habitat that meets its needs.

Wow! Let's do this project and learn more.

## Math and Science Project: Animal Habitats

**Find Out** Talk to friends and relatives about animal habitats. Ask them to help you look at animal habitats on a computer.

**Journal: Make a Book** Show what you found out. In your book, also:

- Draw a picture of one of the habitats you found.
- Make up and solve addition and subtraction problems about the animals in your habitat.

Name _____

# Review What You Know

## Vocabulary

**1.** Circle the numbers that are the **parts**.

$5 - 3 = 2$

**2.** Circle the number that is the **whole**.

$9 - 2 = 7$

**3.** Circle the **addition fact**.

$10 - 4 = 6$

$4 + 6 = 10$

---

## Addition and Subtraction Stories

**4.** Write the subtraction problem to match the picture.

____ − ____ = ____

**5.** There are 6 frogs in a pond. 4 frogs hop out.

How many frogs are left?

____ frogs

## Parts of 10

**6.** Write the numbers to show this way to make 10.

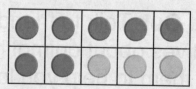

10 is ____ and ____.

## My Word Cards

Study the words on the front of the card.
Complete the activity on the back.

---

### addition fact

$$9 + 8 = 17$$

This is an **addition fact**.

---

### near double

$$4 + 5 = 9$$

This is a **near double**.

---

### number sentence

$$6 + 4 = 10 \quad 6 - 2 = 4$$

$$10 = 6 + 4 \quad 4 = 6 - 2$$

These are **number sentences**.

---

### double

$$4 + 4 = 8$$

This is a **double**.

---

# My Word Cards

Use what you know to complete the sentences.
Extend learning by writing your own sentence using each word.

I can solve a word problem by writing a

_____

_____ .

If I have an addend that is 1 more than the other addend, the sum would be a

_____

_____ .

$2 + 2 = 4$ is an example of an

_____

_____ .

If I have an addend that is the same as the other addend, the sum would be a

_____ .

© Pearson Education, Inc. 1

Name _____

**Solve & Share**

The rabbit put 5 carrots in a pot. He needs to add 1 more. Can you find how many there will be in all without counting all the carrots?

⊕ **TEKS 1.3D** Apply basic fact strategies to add and subtract within 20, including making 10 and decomposing a number leading to a 10. Also, 1.3, 1.5G. **Mathematical Process Standards** 1.1C, 1.1D, 1.1F.

**Digital Resources at PearsonTexas.com**

Solve   Learn   Glossary   Check   Tools   Games

___ + ___ = ___

**Topic 4** | Lesson 1
Digital Resources at PearsonTexas.com
one hundred eighty-one   181

There are 3 carrots in the pot. Add 1 more. How many in all?

 $3 + 1 = 4$

1 more than 3 is 4. 4 carrots in all!

There are 6 tomatoes in the pot. Add 2 more. How many in all?

 $6 + 2 = 8$

2 more than 6 is 8. 8 tomatoes in all!

There are 5 peppers in the pot. Add 0 more. How many in all?

 $5 + 0 = 5$

0 more than 5 is 5. 5 peppers in all!

Each one is an **addition fact!**

$$\begin{array}{r} 3 \\ +1 \\ \hline 4 \end{array} \qquad \begin{array}{r} 6 \\ +2 \\ \hline 8 \end{array} \qquad \begin{array}{r} 5 \\ +0 \\ \hline 5 \end{array}$$

I can add with 1, 2, or 0.

## Do You Understand?

**Show Me!** How do you add 1 to any number? How do you add 2 to any number?

**☆ Guided Practice ☆** Add 1, 2, or 0 to find the sum. Write the addition fact.

1.

$\underline{4} + \underline{1} = \underline{5}$

2.

$\underline{\phantom{0}} + \underline{\phantom{0}} = \underline{\phantom{0}}$

3.

$\underline{\phantom{0}} = \underline{\phantom{0}} + \underline{\phantom{0}}$

4.

$\underline{\phantom{0}} + \underline{\phantom{0}} = \underline{\phantom{0}}$

Name _____

☆ ☆
**Independent**
☆ **Practice**
Add 1, 2, or 0. Complete the addition fact.

5.

$3 + 2 =$ _____

6.

$8 +$ _____ $= 9$

7.

$7 + 0 =$ _____

8. $9 +$ _____ $= 10$

9. $4 + 2 =$ _____

10. $9 = 9 +$ _____

11. $2 + 6 =$ _____

12. $7 =$ _____ $+ 2$

13. $5 +$ _____ $= 10$

14. **Extend Your Thinking** Circle **true** or **false**.

$8 + 0 = 0 + 8$     True     False

$7 + 1 = 0 + 7$     True     False

$6 + 2 = 2 + 6$     True     False

$3 + 1 = 3 + 2$     True     False

$4 + 0 = 4 + 1$     True     False

$5 + 2 = 2 + 5$     True     False

15. Anna fills some bowls with soup. Jason fills 1 more. Now there are 8 bowls of soup. How many bowls did Anna fill?

Anna filled _____ bowls of soup.

16. Dana has 8 grapes in a bag. Her sister gives her 2 more. How many grapes does Dana have now?

_____ grapes

17. Maria is 2 years older than Tim. She is 7 years old.

    Which addition sentence helps you find Tim's age?

    ○ $2 + 7 = 9$

    ○ $5 + 1 = 6$

    ○ $5 - 2 = 3$

    ○ $5 + 2 = 7$

18. **Extend Your Thinking** Max has 1 more carrot than Jena. Jena has 2 more carrots than Sal. Sal has 4 carrots.

    Write how many carrots each person has.

    _____        _____        _____
    Max          Jena          Sal

© Pearson Education, Inc. 1

**Another Look** These addition facts follow a pattern.

| Add 0 and the sum stays the same. | Add 1 and the sum is 1 more. | Add 2 and the sum is 2 more. |
|---|---|---|

$$3 + 0 = \mathbf{3}$$

$$\begin{array}{r} 3 \\ +0 \\ \hline 3 \end{array}$$

$$3 + 1 = \mathbf{4}$$

$$\begin{array}{r} 3 \\ +1 \\ \hline \boxed{4} \end{array}$$

$$3 + 2 = \underline{5}$$

$$\begin{array}{r} 3 \\ +2 \\ \hline 5 \end{array}$$

🏠 **HOME CONNECTION**
Your child learned how to add 0, 1, or 2 more to a number.

**HOME ACTIVITY** Place a number of small objects on a table. Have your child count the objects. Then add 0, 1, or 2 more. Ask your child to add the objects. Have your child write an addition sentence on a piece of paper to correspond with the objects on the table. Repeat several times with a different number of objects.

Add 1, 2, or 0. Complete the addition facts.

**1.**

$$\begin{array}{r} 6 \\ +1 \\ \hline \square \end{array}$$

$$6 + 1 = \underline{\hphantom{0}}$$

**2.**

$$\begin{array}{r} 8 \\ +0 \\ \hline \square \end{array}$$

$$8 + 0 = \underline{\hphantom{0}}$$

**3.**

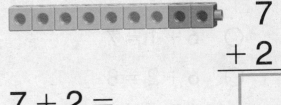

$$\begin{array}{r} 7 \\ +2 \\ \hline \square \end{array}$$

$$7 + 2 = \underline{\hphantom{0}}$$

Solve each problem below.

**4.** Max earned 5 dollars for washing dishes. Then he earned more dollars for walking the dog. In all, Max earned 7 dollars. How many dollars did Max earn for walking the dog?

Draw a picture. Write the number.

_____ dollars

**5.** Emma read 9 books in one week. Then she read 2 more books. How many books did Emma read in all?

Draw a picture. Write the number.

_____ books

**6.** There are 6 bees in a hive. Some more fly in. Now there are 8 bees in the hive. How many bees flew in?

Which addition fact matches the story?

○   6 + 1 = 7

○   6 + 2 = 8

○   6 + 0 = 6

○   8 + 0 = 8

**7. Extend Your Thinking** Write the missing number.

$$3 + 2 = 2 + \underline{\quad}$$

© Pearson Education, Inc. 1

Name _____

**Solve & Share**

Emily and I have the same number of toys. If we each have 3 toys, how many do we have in all? Use cubes to find the answer. Write a number sentence.

⭐ TEKS 1.3D Apply basic fact strategies to add and subtract within 20, including making 10 and decomposing a number leading to a 10. Also, 1.3. Mathematical Process Standards 1.1D, 1.1F, 1.1G.

Digital Resources at PearsonTexas.com

Solve  Learn  Glossary  Check  Tools  Games

_____ + _____ = _____

This is a **double**.
2 + 2 = 4

The addends are the same.

This is also a double.
5 + 5 = 10

---

This is not a double.
2 + 1 = 3

The addends are not the same.

This is not a double.
3 + 5 = 8

---

I know that double 3 is 6.

$$\begin{array}{r} 3 \\ + 3 \\ \hline 6 \end{array}$$

So, 3 + 3 = 6.

---

Think of doubles when both addends are the same.

2 + 2 = 4

5 + 5 = 10

3 + 3 = 6

---

## Do You Understand?

**Show Me!** Is 6 + 4 a double? Explain.

---

☆ **Guided Practice** ☆   Write the addition sentence for each double.

1.

4 + 4 = 8

2.

___ + ___ = ___

3.

___ = ___ + ___

4.

___ + ___ = ___

© Pearson Education, Inc. 1

Name _____

Write the addition sentence for each double.

5.

_____ + _____ = _____

6.

_____ + _____ = _____

7.

_____ + _____ = _____

8.
$$\begin{array}{r} 2 \\ +\ 2 \\ \hline \square \end{array}$$

9.
$$\begin{array}{r} 4 \\ +\ 4 \\ \hline \square \end{array}$$

10.
$$\begin{array}{r} 3 \\ +\ 3 \\ \hline \square \end{array}$$

11. **Extend Your Thinking** Draw a picture to show a double.
Write the addition sentence to match your drawing.

_____ + _____ = _____

**12.** Neela made 4 pies. John made the same number of pies.

How many pies did Neela and John make in all?

_____ pies

**13.** Kim has 2 pockets. She has 5 pennies in each pocket.

How many pennies does Kim have in all?

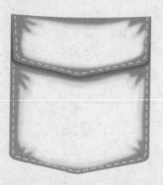 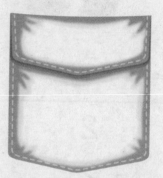

_____ pennies

**14.** Danny has 2 baskets. He has the same number of pencils in each basket. He has 12 pencils in all.

How many pencils does Danny have in each basket?

6    8    10    12
○    ○    ○    ○

**15.** **Extend Your Thinking** Is there a doubles fact that has a sum of 9? Draw a picture to find out. Circle **yes** or **no**.

**Yes**        **No**

Name _____

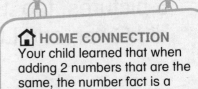

**Another Look** When the addends are the same, it is a double. Here are some doubles.

$$2 + 2 = 4$$

$$\begin{array}{r} 2 \\ +2 \\ \hline 4 \end{array}$$

addend    addend    sum

$$\begin{array}{r} 3 \\ +3 \\ \hline 6 \end{array}$$

$$3 + 3 = 6$$

addend    addend    sum

> **HOME CONNECTION**
> Your child learned that when adding 2 numbers that are the same, the number fact is a double.
>
> **HOME ACTIVITY** Have your child use small objects to show 2 groups of 4. Then ask your child to write an addition sentence to show the double (4 + 4 = 8). Repeat for other doubles of 1 + 1 through 6 + 6.

 Write the sum for each double.

1.
$$\begin{array}{r} 6 \\ +6 \\ \hline \square \end{array}$$

2.
$$\begin{array}{r} 4 \\ +4 \\ \hline \square \end{array}$$

3.
$$\begin{array}{r} 5 \\ +5 \\ \hline \square \end{array}$$

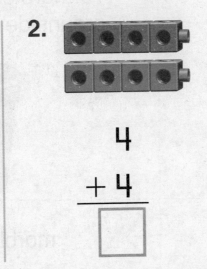

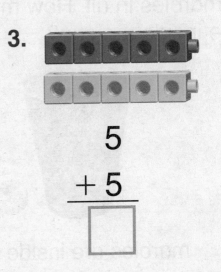

Write an addition sentence to solve each problem.

4. Owen painted 5 pictures. Luis painted 5 pictures, too. How many pictures did Owen and Luis paint in all?

___ + ___ = ___

5. Tess and Maya grew 12 flowers. Tess grew 6 flowers. How many flowers did Maya grow?

___ = ___ + ___

Write the missing number for each problem.

6. Algebra

$4 = 2 + \underline{\,?\,}$

2 ○   4 ○   6 ○   8 ○

7. Algebra

$\underline{\,?\,} + 4 = 8$

8 ○   6 ○   5 ○   4 ○

8. Algebra

$6 + \underline{\,?\,} = 12$

4 ○   6 ○   7 ○   8 ○

9. Extend Your Thinking There are 6 marbles in all. How many marbles are inside the cup?

___ marbles are inside the cup.

10. Extend Your Thinking There are 10 marbles in all. How many marbles are inside the cup?

___ marbles are inside the cup.

© Pearson Education, Inc. 1

Name _____

**Solve & Share**

Emily and I each have 5 shells. If I find another shell, how many will I have? How can you use counters to show how many we would have in all? Write a number sentence.

★ TEKS 1.3D Apply basic fact strategies to add and subtract within 20, including making 10 and decomposing a number leading to a 10. Also, 1.3. Mathematical Process Standards 1.1C, 1.1F, 1.1G.

Digital Resources at PearsonTexas.com

| Solve | Learn | Glossary | Check | Tools | Games |

_____ + _____ = _____

You can use a double to add a near double.

$4 + 5 = ?$

First, double the 4.

$4 + 4 = 8$

$4 + 5$ is $4 + 4$ and 1 more.

$$\begin{array}{r} 4 \\ +5 \\ \hline \end{array}$$ Think → $$\begin{array}{r} 4 \\ +4 \\ \hline 8 \end{array}$$

and 1 more.

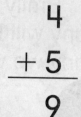

8 and 1 more is 9.

$$\begin{array}{r} 4 \\ +5 \\ \hline 9 \end{array}$$

## Do You Understand?

**Show Me!** How does knowing the sum of $3 + 3$ help you find the sum of $3 + 4$?

## ☆ Guided Practice ☆   Add the doubles and near doubles.

**1.**
$2 + 3$ →  and 1 more → $2 + 3 = \underline{5}$.

**2.**
$5 + 6$ → ☐ + ☐ and 1 more → $5 + 6 = \underline{\phantom{0}}$.

**3.**
$3 + 4$ → ☐ + ☐ and 1 more → $3 + 4 = \underline{\phantom{0}}$.

© Pearson Education, Inc. 1

# Independent Practice

Add the near doubles.

**4.**
$$\begin{array}{r} 3 \\ + 4 \\ \hline \square \end{array}$$

**5.**
$$\begin{array}{r} 5 \\ + 4 \\ \hline \square \end{array}$$

**6.**
$$\begin{array}{r} 5 \\ + 6 \\ \hline \square \end{array}$$

**7.**
$$\begin{array}{r} 4 \\ + 5 \\ \hline \square \end{array}$$

**8.**
$$\begin{array}{r} 2 \\ + 3 \\ \hline \square \end{array}$$

**9.**
$$\begin{array}{r} 2 \\ + 1 \\ \hline \square \end{array}$$

**10.**
$$\begin{array}{r} 3 \\ + 2 \\ \hline \square \end{array}$$

**11.**
$$\begin{array}{r} 4 \\ + 3 \\ \hline \square \end{array}$$

> Think of a double and add 1 more.

**Extend Your Thinking** Write the missing numbers.

**12.** If $2 + \underline{\quad} = 4$, then $2 + \underline{\quad} = 5$.

**13.** If $4 + \underline{\quad} = 8$, then $4 + \underline{\quad} = 9$.

Write an addition sentence to solve each problem.

**14.** Omar ate 5 pears. Jane ate 5 pears and then 1 more. How many pears did Omar and Jane eat in all?

_____ + _____ = _____

Omar and Jane ate _____ pears.

**15.** Sam and Jack found 7 shells. Sam found 3 shells. Jack found 1 more shell than Sam. How many shells did Jack find?

_____ + _____ = _____ shells

Jack found _____ shells.

**16.** Patty played 4 games of jump rope. Mary played 4 games of jump rope and then 1 more.

How many games of jump rope did Patty and Mary play in all?

○ 10

○ 9

○ 8

○ 7

You can use a near double to help solve the problem.

**17. Extend Your Thinking** Write a story problem about a near double. Then draw a picture to show the story.

_____

_____

_____

© Pearson Education, Inc. 1

Name _____

**Another Look** You can use doubles to add near doubles.

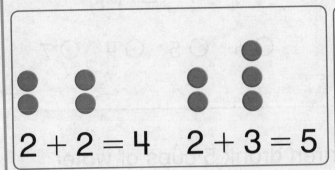

$2 + 2 = 4$    $2 + 3 = 5$

$3 + 3 = 6$    $3 + 4 = 7$

If $2 + 2 = 4$, then $2 + 3$ is 1 more.

$2 + 3 = 5$

🏠 **HOME CONNECTION**
Your child learned how to use doubles in order to add numbers that are near doubles.

**HOME ACTIVITY** Play a game with small objects, like pennies. First, use the pennies to represent numbers that are doubles. Ask your child to add the set of doubles. Then add another penny and ask your child to add the set of near doubles.

Add the doubles. Then add the near doubles.

1.

___ + ___ = ___    ___ + ___ = ___

2.

___ + ___ = ___    ___ + ___ = ___

Find the number to complete each near double.

**3. Algebra** ☆

$$3 + \underline{\ ?\ } = 7$$

○ 2  ○ 3  ○ 4  ○ 5

**4. Algebra** ☆

$$13 = 6 + \underline{\ ?\ }$$

○ 6  ○ 7  ○ 5  ○ 8

**5. Algebra** ☆

$$5 + \underline{\ ?\ } = 11$$

○ 6  ○ 5  ○ 4  ○ 7

Write an addition sentence to solve each problem.

**6.** Sandy played 3 games. Bill played 3 games and then 1 more. How many games did Sandy and Bill play in all?

$$\underline{\quad} + \underline{\quad} = \underline{\quad}$$

Sandy and Bill played _____ games.

**7.** Nina and Karen drank 5 cups of water in all. Nina drank 2 cups of water. Karen drank 1 more cup than Nina. How many cups did Karen drink?

$$\underline{\quad} + \underline{\quad} = \underline{\quad}$$

Karen drank _____ cups.

**8. Extend Your Thinking** Use each card once to write addition sentences using doubles and near doubles.

| 5 | 6 | 5 | 10 | 5 | 11 |

$$\underline{\quad} + \underline{\quad} = \underline{\quad}$$

$$\underline{\quad} + \underline{\quad} = \underline{\quad}$$

**9. Extend Your Thinking** How does knowing the double $6 + 6 = 12$ help you solve the near double $6 + 7 = 13$?

© Pearson Education, Inc. 1

Name ______________________________

# Lesson 4-4
## Facts with 5 on a Ten-Frame

**Solve & Share** Put some counters on the bottom row of the ten-frame. What addition sentence can you write to match the counters?

**TEKS 1.3C** Compose 10 with two or more addends with and without concrete objects. Also, 1.3, 1.3D. **Mathematical Process Standards** 1.1A, 1.1C, 1.1D.

**Digital Resources at PearsonTexas.com**

Solve | Learn | Glossary | Check | Tools | Games

____ + ____ = ____

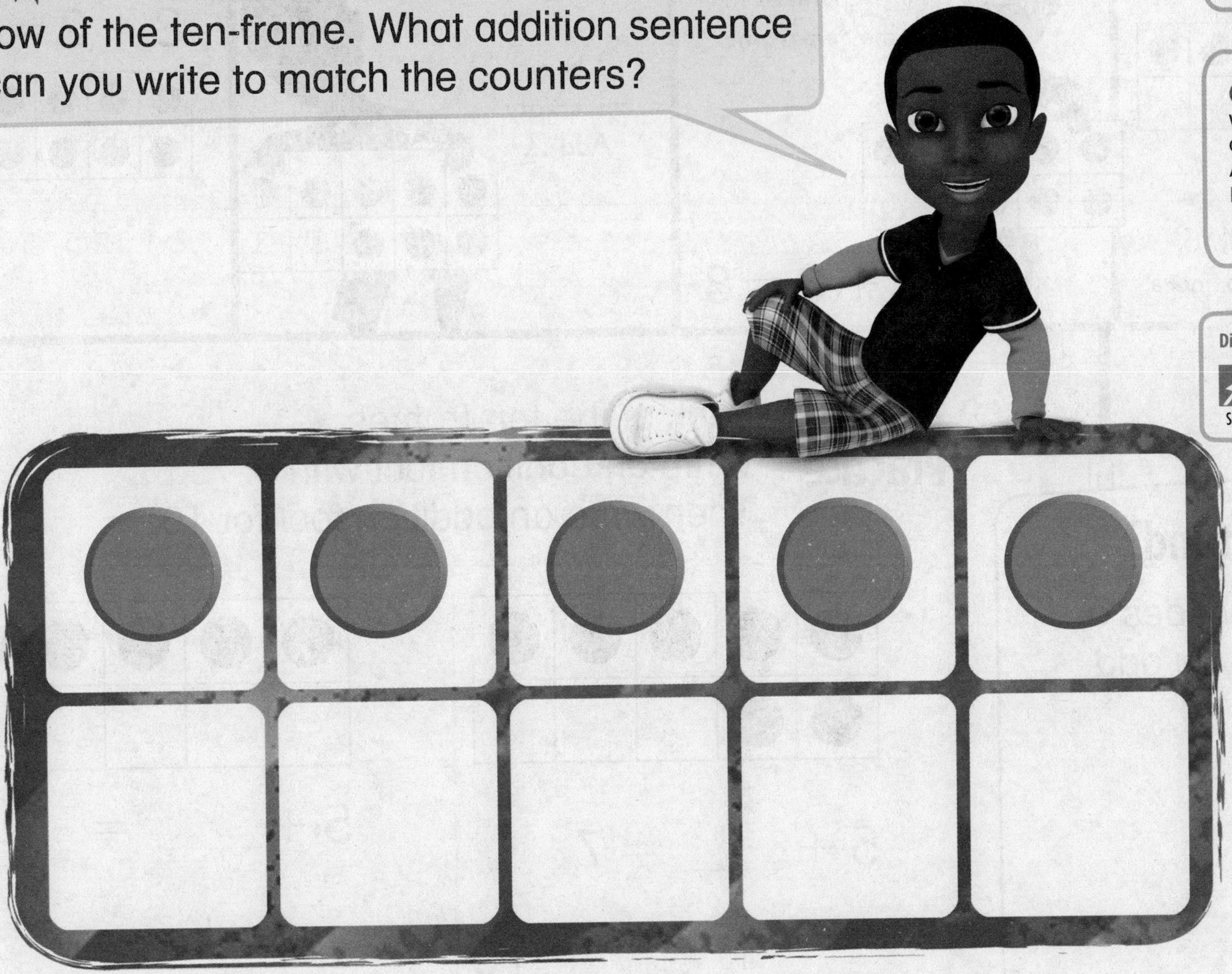

You can use a ten-frame to show an addition fact with 5.

$$5 + 3 = ?$$

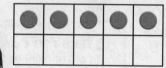

Start with 5. Then add 3 more.

5 and 3 more is 8.

There are 8 counters in the ten-frame.

$$5 + 3 = 8$$

The ten-frame shows another addition fact. You have 8. Make 10.

2 boxes are empty. Add 2.

8 plus 2 more is 10.

$$8 + 2 = 10$$

## Do You Understand?

**Show Me!** How does a ten-frame help you add $5 + 4$?

☆ **Guided Practice** ☆ Look at the ten-frames. Write an addition fact with 5. Then write an addition fact for 10.

1.
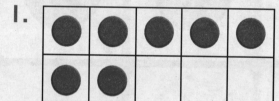

$$5 + \underline{\ 2\ } = 7$$

$$\underline{\ 7\ } + \underline{\ 3\ } = 10$$

2.
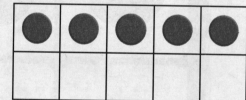

$$5 + \underline{\quad} = \underline{\quad}$$

$$\underline{\quad} + \underline{\quad} = 10$$

Name _____

**Independent Practice**

Look at the ten-frames.
Write an addition fact with 5.
Then write an addition fact for 10.

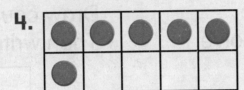

3.

5 + ____ = ____

____ + ____ = 10

4.

5 + ____ = ____

____ + ____ = 10

5.

5 + ____ = ____

____ + ____ = 10

6. **Extend Your Thinking** Using 2 colors, draw counters
in the ten-frames to match the addition sentences.
Then write the missing numbers.

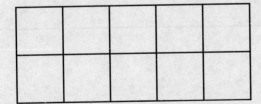

8 + ____ = 10

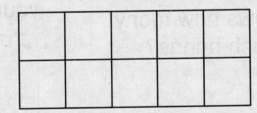

7 + ____ = 10

two hundred one **201**

**Topic 4** | Lesson 4

**7.** Maya's team has 5 softballs. Maya's coach brings 3 more. How many softballs does the team have now?

Draw counters in the ten-frame. Then write an addition fact to solve.

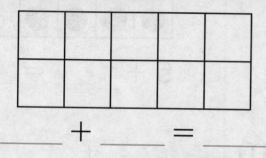

_____ + _____ = _____

_____ softballs

**8.** Kami read 5 books. Sue read 4 books. How many books did the girls read in all?

Draw counters in the ten-frame. Then write an addition fact to solve.

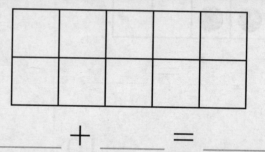

_____ + _____ = _____

_____ books

**9.** Todd's team has 5 soccer balls. Todd's coach brings some more. Todd's team now has 10 soccer balls.

Which addition fact shows how many soccer balls Todd's coach brings?

- ○  $5 + 5 = 10$
- ○  $10 + 3 = 13$
- ○  $7 + 3 = 10$
- ○  $10 + 7 = 17$

**10. Extend Your Thinking** Write a new story about the ten-frame in Exercise 7. Then write an addition sentence for your story.

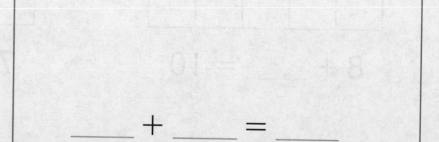

_____ + _____ = _____

Name _____

**Another Look** You can write an addition fact with 5 using a ten-frame. You can also write an addition fact for 10 using a ten-frame.

🏠 **HOME CONNECTION**
Your child learned how to use a ten-frame to help with addition facts with 5.

**HOME ACTIVITY** Play a game using ten-frames drawn on a sheet of paper. Draw circles on each ten-frame. Then ask your child to write an accompanying number sentence below each ten-frame.

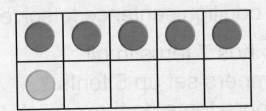

$5 + 1 = 6$

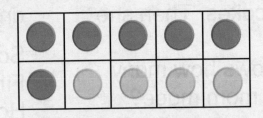

$6 + 4 = \underline{10}$

Look at the ten-frames.
Write an addition fact with 5.
Then write an addition fact for 10.

**1.**

$5 + 2 = \underline{\phantom{0}}$

$\underline{\phantom{0}} + \underline{\phantom{0}} = 10$

**2.**

$5 + 4 = \underline{\phantom{0}}$

$\underline{\phantom{0}} + \underline{\phantom{0}} = 10$

**3.**

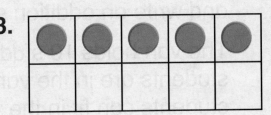

$5 + 0 = \underline{\phantom{0}}$

$\underline{\phantom{0}} + \underline{\phantom{0}} = 10$

Write an addition fact with 5. Then write an addition fact for 10.

4. 5 + ___ = ___
   6 + ___ = 10

5. 5 + ___ = ___
   9 + ___ = 10

6. 5 + ___ = ___
   8 + ___ = 10

7. Matt's mom made 10 pancakes in all. First, she made 6 pancakes. Then she made some more.
   Which addition fact shows how many more pancakes Matt's mom made?

   6 + 1 = 7
   ○

   6 + 4 = 10
   ○

   10 + 4 = 14
   ○

   6 + 6 = 12
   ○

8. **Extend Your Thinking** Draw counters and write an addition sentence to solve.

   Sara's camp has 7 tents in all. First, the campers set up 5 tents. How many more tents do the campers set up?

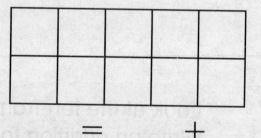

   ___ = ___ + ___

9. **Extend Your Thinking** Draw counters and write an addition sentence to solve.

   The van holds 10 students. Some students are in the van. How many more students can fit in the van?

   ___ + ___ = ___

Name _____

**Solve & Share**

Nia puts her teddy bears on shelves. Each shelf holds 10 bears. If she has 8 teddy bears on one shelf and collects 4 more, how many bears will she have in all?

Use counters and the ten-frames to find out. Then write a number sentence.

⭐ **TEKS 1.3D** Apply basic fact strategies to add and subtract within 20, including making 10 and decomposing a number leading to a 10. Also, 1.3, 1.3C. **Mathematical Process Standards 1.1B, 1.1C, 1.1E.**

Digital Resources at PearsonTexas.com

Solve    Learn    Glossary    Check    Tools    Games

____ + ____ = ____

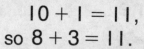

You can make 10 to add.

$$8$$
$$+\ 3$$

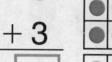

I can use ten-frames.

Use a ten-frame for each number.

$$8$$
$$+\ 3$$

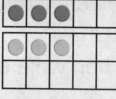

How can I make 10?

Move 2 from the bottom. Add it to 8. This makes 10.

$$10$$
$$+\ 1$$

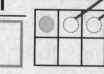

1 counter is left in the bottom ten-frame.

$10 + 1 = 11,$
so $8 + 3 = 11.$

8 + 3 is the same as 10 + 1.

## Do You Understand?

**Show Me!** How is $9 + 3$ like $10 + 2$?

## ☆ Guided Practice ☆ Write the missing numbers.

1.
$$9$$
$$+\ 3$$
$$\boxed{12}$$
→
$$10$$
$$+\ \boxed{2}$$
$$\boxed{12}$$

2.
$$7$$
$$+\ 4$$
$$\boxed{\phantom{0}}$$
→
$$10$$
$$+\ \boxed{\phantom{0}}$$
$$\boxed{\phantom{0}}$$

3.
$$6$$
$$+\ 5$$
$$\boxed{\phantom{0}}$$
→
$$10$$
$$+\ \boxed{\phantom{0}}$$
$$\boxed{\phantom{0}}$$

4.
$$9$$
$$+\ 5$$
$$\boxed{\phantom{0}}$$
→
$$10$$
$$+\ \boxed{\phantom{0}}$$
$$\boxed{\phantom{0}}$$

Name _____

Write the missing numbers.

5.   8          10
    +4      +  ☐
    ___        ___
    ☐          ☐

6.   7          10
    +5      +  ☐
    ___        ___
    ☐          ☐

7.   9          10
    +2      +  ☐
    ___        ___
    ☐          ☐

8.   9          10
    +6      +  ☐
    ___        ___
    ☐          ☐

9.   8          10
    +3      +  ☐
    ___        ___
    ☐          ☐

10.  6          10
    +4      +  ☐
    ___        ___
    ☐          ☐

Use the ten-frames.
Make 10 to add.

11. **Extend Your Thinking** Write 2 addition
sentences showing what you did.

____ + ____ = ____

____ + ____ = ____

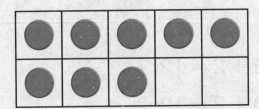

**12.** Billy has 8 green marbles and 4 blue marbles. How many marbles does Billy have in all?

Make 10 to solve.
Write 2 addition sentences.

$10 + \underline{\hspace{1cm}} = \underline{\hspace{1cm}}$

$\underline{\hspace{1cm}} + \underline{\hspace{1cm}} = \underline{\hspace{1cm}}$

**13.** Molly has 7 marbles inside a bag. She has 4 marbles outside the bag. How many marbles does she have in all?

Make 10 to solve.
Write 2 addition sentences.

$10 + \underline{\hspace{1cm}} = \underline{\hspace{1cm}}$

$\underline{\hspace{1cm}} + \underline{\hspace{1cm}} = \underline{\hspace{1cm}}$

**14.** ☆ Which addition sentence shows how to make 10 with these ten-frames?

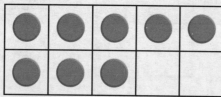
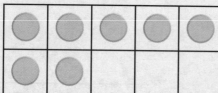

○ $10 + 2 = 12$

○ $10 + 3 = 13$

○ $10 + 4 = 14$

○ $10 + 5 = 15$

**15. Extend Your Thinking** Brad has 9 small rocks and 3 big rocks.

Draw counters and write 2 addition sentences to show how many rocks Brad has in all.

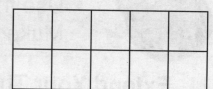

$\underline{\hspace{1cm}} + \underline{\hspace{1cm}} = \underline{\hspace{1cm}}$

$\underline{\hspace{1cm}} + \underline{\hspace{1cm}} = \underline{\hspace{1cm}}$

Name _____

**Another Look** You can make 10 to add.

7        4

8        3

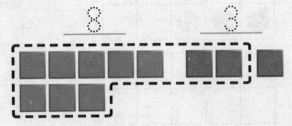

Circle a group of 10 squares.
Count the squares left over.
Write 2 addition sentences.

$10 + 1 = 11$

$7 + 4 = 11$

Circle a group of 10 squares.
Count the squares left over.
Write 2 addition sentences.

$10 + 1 = 11$

$8 + 3 = 11$

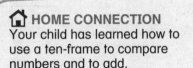

🏠 **HOME CONNECTION**
Your child has learned how to use a ten-frame to compare numbers and to add.

**HOME ACTIVITY** Sketch 2 ten-frames. Say 2 numbers between 4 and 10. Have your child place pennies that equal the first number in the top ten-frame and pennies that equal the second number in the bottom ten-frame. Then have your child make 10 to add.

Circle a group of 10.
Write 2 addition sentences.

1.     9          3

🧦🧦🧦🧦🧦🧦🧦
🧦🧦🧦🧦

$10 + \_\_\_ = 12$

$9 + 3 = \_\_\_$

2.     8          7

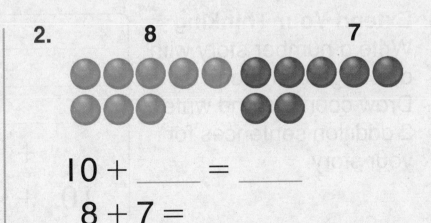

$10 + \_\_\_ = \_\_\_$

$8 + 7 = \_\_\_$

Write the missing numbers. Draw counters to help you.

3.
$$8 \rightarrow 10$$
$$+3 \quad + \boxed{\phantom{0}}$$
$$\boxed{\phantom{0}} \quad \boxed{\phantom{0}}$$
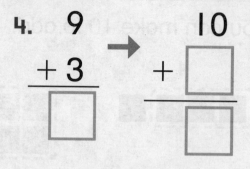

4.
$$9 \rightarrow 10$$
$$+3 \quad + \boxed{\phantom{0}}$$
$$\boxed{\phantom{0}} \quad \boxed{\phantom{0}}$$
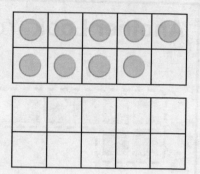

Choose the number sentence that shows a way to make 10 to solve.

5. Emma has 9 red apples.
⭐ She has 2 green apples.
How many apples does she have in all?

○ $10 + 1 = 11$

○ $10 + 2 = 12$

○ $10 + 3 = 13$

○ $10 + 4 = 14$

6. **Extend Your Thinking**
Write a number story with a sum greater than 10. Draw counters and write 2 addition sentences for your story.

_____

_____

_____

____ + ____ = ____

10 + ____ = ____

© Pearson Education, Inc. 1

Name _____

**Solve & Share**

There are 5 people on a bus. It stops and 2 people get off. Use counters to show how many people are still on the bus. Write the number.

⚙ TEKS 1.3D Apply basic fact strategies to add and subtract within 20, including making 10 and decomposing a number leading to a 10. Also, 1.5G. Mathematical Process Standards 1.1C, 1.1D, 1.1E.

STOP

Digital Resources at PearsonTexas.com

Solve   Learn   Glossary   Check   Tools   Games

_____ people are left on the bus.

Digital Resources at PearsonTexas.com

When you subtract 2, think 2 less than.

2 less than 7 is 5.

$$7 - 2 = 5$$

When you subtract 1, think 1 less than.

1 less than 7 is 6.

$$\begin{array}{r} 7 \\ -1 \\ \hline 6 \end{array}$$

When you subtract 0, think 0 less than.

0 less than 7 is 7. The number stays the same.

$$\begin{array}{r} 7 \\ -0 \\ \hline 7 \end{array}$$

## Do You Understand?

**Show Me!** Write subtraction sentences to show *0 less*, *1 less*, and *2 less*.

☆ **Guided Practice** ☆   Complete each subtraction fact and sentence.

1.
$$\begin{array}{r} 4 \\ -1 \\ \hline \boxed{3} \end{array} \qquad \begin{array}{r} 4 \\ -0 \\ \hline \boxed{4} \end{array}$$

2.
$$\begin{array}{r} 6 \\ -0 \\ \hline \boxed{\phantom{0}} \end{array} \qquad \begin{array}{r} 6 \\ -2 \\ \hline \boxed{\phantom{0}} \end{array}$$

1 less than 4 is _3_.

0 less than 4 is _4_.

0 less than 6 is ___.

2 less than 6 is ___.

© Pearson Education, Inc. 1

Name _____

Write each subtraction fact and sentence.

**3.**

□ − □ = □

I less than 6 is ____ .

**4.**

□ − □ = □

0 less than 8 is ____ .

**5.**

□ − □ = □

2 less than 10 is ____ .

Draw a picture to solve. Write a subtraction sentence.

**6. Extend Your Thinking** Amy and Ryan buy pencils at the store. Amy buys
11 pencils. Ryan buys 2 less. How many pencils did Ryan buy?

____ − ____ = ____

Solve each problem below.

7. Manuel picks a number. His number is 1 less than 8. What is Manuel's number?

Write a subtraction sentence to solve.

_____ − _____ = _____

Manuel's number is _____.

8. Beth is thinking of a number. It is 0 less than 10. What is Beth's number?

Write a subtraction sentence to solve.

_____ − _____ = _____

Beth's number is _____.

9. Jan has some tickets. She gave 2 tickets to her friends. Now she has 6 tickets. How many tickets did Jan have before giving away 2 tickets?

○ 8

○ 6

○ 4

○ 2

You can write a number sentence to help you solve the problem.

10. **Extend Your Thinking** Complete the subtraction sentence. Then write a story to match the sentence.

$5 - \underline{\quad} = 4$

_____

_____

_____

_____

© Pearson Education, Inc. 1

Name _____

**Another Look**

$4 - 2 = ?$

Start at 4.

Count back 2.   3, 2

Solve the problem.

$4 - 2 = 2$

$6 - 1 = ?$

Start at 6.

Count back 1.   _5_

Solve the problem.

$6 - 1 = \underline{5}$

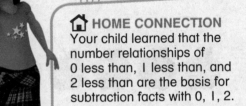

Count back to subtract 0, 1, or 2.

🏠 **HOME CONNECTION**
Your child learned that the number relationships of 0 less than, 1 less than, and 2 less than are the basis for subtraction facts with 0, 1, 2.

**HOME ACTIVITY** Using a collection of objects such as counters, count out 6. Then have your child tell what 2 less than 6 equals. Ask, "What subtraction sentence did you make?" Continue with other subtraction facts, having your child subtract 0, 1, or 2.

Count back to subtract 0, 1, or 2.

**1.**

Count back 1.   Solve the problem.

$9 - 1 =$ _____

**2.**

Count back 0.   Solve the problem.

$10 - 0 =$ _____

Write a subtraction sentence for each story.

**3.** There are 9 apples in Maya's basket.
She eats 1 apple.
How many apples are left?

_____ − _____ = _____

**4.** There are 12 cups on a tray. 2 cups are blue. The rest are red. How many cups are red?

_____ − _____ = _____

**5.** ⭐ Nicole has 12 pages left to read in her book. She reads some on the bus. Now she has 10 pages to read. Which subtraction sentence shows how many pages Nicole read on the bus?

○ $12 − 1 = 11$

○ $12 − 2 = 10$

○ $12 − 0 = 12$

○ $10 − 2 = 8$

**6. Extend Your Thinking** Write a subtraction sentence for 0 less, 1 less, or 2 less. Write a story to match your sentence.

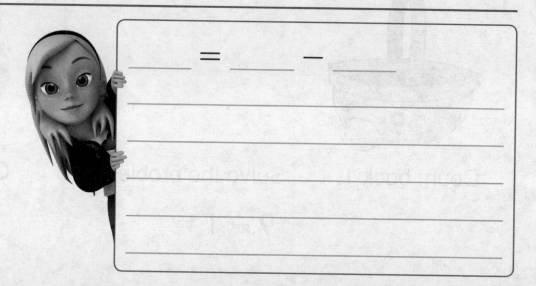

_____ = _____ − _____

Name _____

Solve & Share

Jenna has 6 beachballs. 4 of them blow to the other side of the pool. How many does she have left?

How can you use an addition fact to find the answer to 6 − 4 = _____? Use counters to help you solve the problem.

TEKS 1.3E Explain strategies to solve ... subtraction problems up to 20 using spoken words, objects, pictorial models, and number sentences. Also, 1.3, 1.3F. Mathematical Process Standards 1.1E, 1.1F.

Digital Resources at PearsonTexas.com

Solve    Learn    Glossary    Check    Tools    Games

_____ + _____ = _____    So, _____ − _____ = _____ .

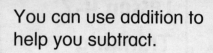

You can use addition to help you subtract.

$7 - 3 = \boxed{?}$

$3 + \boxed{?} = 7$

What can I add to 3 to make 7?

$3 + \boxed{4} = 7$

The missing part is 4.

Think of the addition fact to solve the subtraction fact.

$7 - 3 = \boxed{4}$

$3 + 4 = 7$

## Do You Understand?

**Show Me!** How can an addition fact help you solve $7 - 6$?

☆ **Guided Practice** ☆ Think addition to help you subtract. Draw the missing part. Then write the numbers.

1.
5

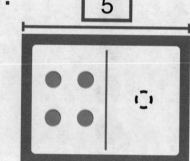

$5 - 4 = ?$
$4 + \underline{\phantom{00}} = 5$
So, $5 - 4 = \underline{\phantom{00}}$.

2.
6

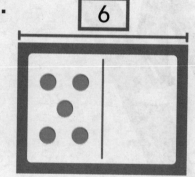

$6 - 5 = ?$
$5 + \underline{\phantom{00}} = 6$
So, $6 - 5 = \underline{\phantom{00}}$.

Name _____

**Independent Practice**    Think addition to help you subtract. Draw the missing part.
Then write the numbers.

3.

8

$6 + \underline{\quad} = 8$

So, $8 - 6 = \underline{\quad}$.

4.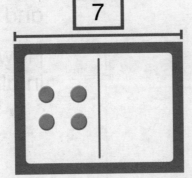

7

$4 + \underline{\quad} = 7$

So, $7 - 4 = \underline{\quad}$.

5.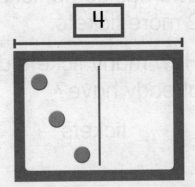

4

$3 + \underline{\quad} = 4$

So, $4 - 3 = \underline{\quad}$.

Draw the shape to complete the sentence.

6. **Extend Your Thinking**

If ⬤ + ▲ = ■ , then ■ − ⬤ = _____.

## Problem Solving
Solve. Then write an addition sentence and a subtraction sentence for each problem.

**7.** Pam needs 8 tickets to get on a ride. She has some tickets. She needs 2 more tickets.

How many tickets does Pam already have?

_____ tickets

_____ + _____ = _____

_____ − _____ = _____

**8.** Rosi buys some beads to make a bracelet. She buys 2 blue beads and 5 white beads.

How many beads does Rosi buy in all?

_____ beads

_____ + _____ = _____

_____ − _____ = _____

**9.** Which addition fact can help you solve the problem?

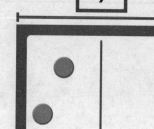

9 − 2 = ?

○ 3 + 6 = 9

○ 5 + 4 = 9

○ 2 + 7 = 9

○ 8 + 1 = 9

**10. Extend Your Thinking** Kathy has a box that holds 6 crayons. 4 crayons are inside the box. She uses addition to find how many are missing. Is Kathy correct? Explain.

6 + 4 = 10

10 crayons are missing.

© Pearson Education, Inc. 1

Name _____

**Another Look** Use an addition fact to solve a subtraction fact.

I know that
2 + 6 = 8
So, 8 – 6 = 2.

___3___ + ___6___ = ___9___

So, ___9___ – ___6___ = ___3___.

🏠 **HOME CONNECTION**
Your child learned how to use addition facts to solve subtraction facts.

**HOME ACTIVITY** Fold a sheet of paper in half so you have 2 equal boxes. Put 1–8 pennies in the box on the left. Say a number greater than the number of pennies in the box, but not greater than 9. Ask: "What subtraction sentence can you write? What addition sentence is related?" Continue with different number combinations.

Write an addition fact. Think of the addition fact to help you write and solve the subtraction fact.

1.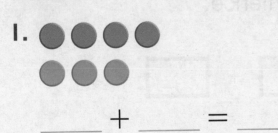

____ + ____ = ____

____ – ____ = ____

2.

____ + ____ = ____

____ – ____ = ____

3.

____ + ____ = ____

____ – ____ = ____

Draw counters. Write a subtraction and an addition sentence for each problem.

**4.**

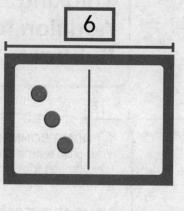

6

_____ − _____ = _____

_____ + _____ = _____

**5.**

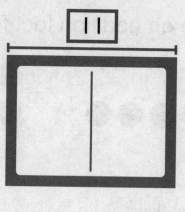

11

_____ − _____ = _____

_____ + _____ = _____

**6.** Tia and Sue make 8 baskets. If Sue makes 2 baskets, how many baskets does Tia make?

Which addition fact can help you subtract?

○  8 + 6 = 14

○  6 + 6 = 12

○  2 + 8 = 10

○  2 + 6 = 8

**Extend Your Thinking** Draw the shapes to complete each sentence.

**7.** If △ + ○ = ☐ ,

then _____ − _____ = _____ .

**8.** If ☐ = ☐ + ☐ ,

then _____ = _____ − _____ .

Name ______________________________

# Lesson 4-8
## Thinking Addition to 12 to Subtract

**Solve & Share** How can you use an addition fact to find the answer to $11 - 5 =$ ____? Use counters to help you solve the problem.

**TEKS 1.3E** Explain strategies used to solve … subtraction problems up to 20 using spoken words, objects, pictorial models, and number sentences. Also, 1.3, 1.3F. **Mathematical Process Standards** 1.1D, 1.1F.

Digital Resources at PearsonTexas.com

Solve | Learn | Glossary | Check | Tools | Games

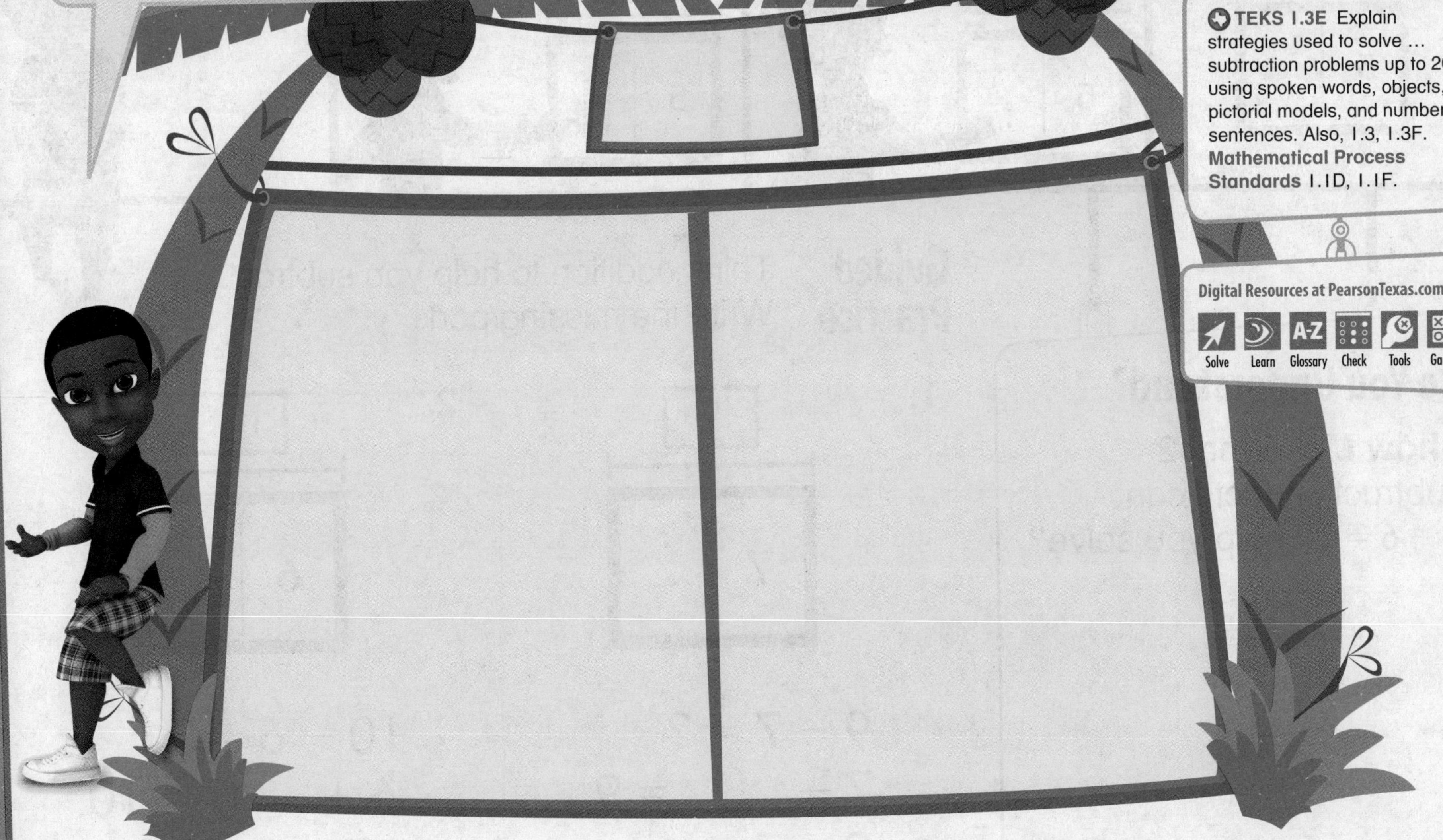

____ + ____ = ____   So, ____ − ____ = ____ .

Think addition to help you subtract.

$9 - 5 = \boxed{?}$

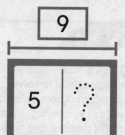

$5 + \boxed{?} = 9$

What can I add to 5 to make 9?

$5 + \boxed{4} = 9$

4 is the missing part.

Think of the addition fact to solve the subtraction fact.

$5 + 4 = 9,$
so $9 - 5 = 4.$

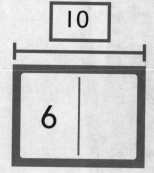

## Do You Understand?

**Show Me!** What 2 subtraction facts can $4 + 6 = 10$ help you solve?

☆ **Guided Practice** ☆ Think addition to help you subtract. Write the missing part.

1.

$9 - 7 = ?$
$7 + \underline{2} = 9$
So, $9 - 7 = \underline{2}.$

2.

$10 - 6 = ?$
$6 + \underline{\phantom{0}} = 10$
So, $10 - 6 = \underline{\phantom{0}}.$

© Pearson Education, Inc. 1

Name _____

☆ **Independent** ☆ **Practice**

Think addition to help you subtract. Write the missing part.

3.

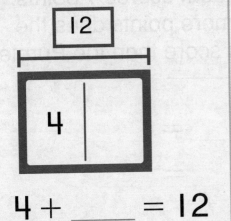

12

4 |

$4 + \underline{\quad} = 12$

So, $12 - 4 = \underline{\quad}$.

4.

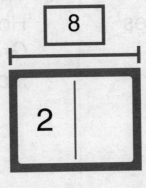

8

2 |

$2 + \underline{\quad} = 8$

So, $8 - 2 = \underline{\quad}$.

5.

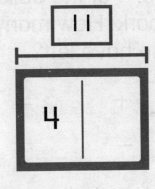

11

4 |

$4 + \underline{\quad} = 11$

So, $11 - 4 = \underline{\quad}$.

6. **Extend Your Thinking** Write an addition sentence and a subtraction sentence.

The Red team scored some goals.
The Blue team scored 7 goals.
Together the teams scored 10 goals.
How many goals did the Red team score?

You can think addition to help you subtract!

$\underline{\quad} + \underline{\quad} = \underline{\quad}$

$\underline{\quad} - \underline{\quad} = \underline{\quad}$       $\underline{\quad}$ goals

7. Jamie brings 10 baseballs to the game. 4 of the balls are hit out of the park. How many baseballs does Jamie have left?

_____ + _____ = _____

_____ − _____ = _____

_____ baseballs

8. The Purple team scores 5 points. The Green team scores 9 points. How many more points does the Green team score than the Purple team?

_____ + _____ = _____

_____ − _____ = _____

_____ points

9. Mrs. Kane has 12 students. Some are drawing pictures. 7 are reading books. How many students are drawing pictures?

Which addition fact can you use to find the answer?

○ $6 + 5 = 11$

○ $5 + 7 = 12$

○ $6 + 6 = 12$

○ $5 + 8 = 13$

10. **Extend Your Thinking** Write a subtraction story about the fish.

_____

_____

_____

_____ ◯ _____ = _____

_____ ◯ _____ = _____

Name _____

**Another Look** You can use addition facts to help you subtract. Look at the subtraction fact. Then look at the addition fact that can help.

$$9 - 1 = 8$$

$$8 + 1 = 9$$

$$8 - 2 = 6$$

$$6 + 2 = 8$$

🏠 **HOME CONNECTION** Your child used addition facts to 12 to solve related subtraction facts.

**HOME ACTIVITY** Give your child a subtraction fact to solve. Have him or her use pennies or other objects, such as counters, to solve the problem. Then have your child tell you the addition problem that is related. Continue with several subtraction facts.

Subtract. Then write the addition fact that helped you subtract.

1.

$$10 - \text{\_\_\_} = 8$$

$$8 + \text{\_\_\_} = 10$$

2.

$$11 - \text{\_\_\_} = 7$$

$$7 + \text{\_\_\_} = 11$$

3.

$$12 - \text{\_\_\_} = 3$$

$$3 + \text{\_\_\_} = 12$$

Think addition to help you subtract. Write the missing part.

4.

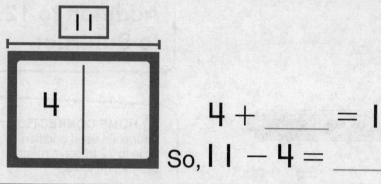

$4 + \underline{\hspace{1cm}} = 11$

So, $11 - 4 = \underline{\hspace{1cm}}$.

5.

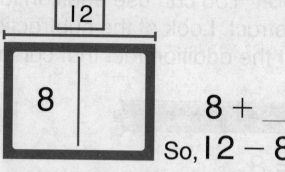

$8 + \underline{\hspace{1cm}} = 12$

So, $12 - 8 = \underline{\hspace{1cm}}$.

6. Solve the subtraction story. Write a related addition fact.

Paula has 11 kittens. She gives some away. She has 6 kittens left. How many kittens did she give away?

_____ kittens

$\underline{\hspace{0.8cm}} - \underline{\hspace{0.8cm}} = \underline{\hspace{0.8cm}}$

$\underline{\hspace{0.8cm}} + \underline{\hspace{0.8cm}} = \underline{\hspace{0.8cm}}$

7. Which addition fact can help you solve this number story?

Miguel and Andy pick apples. Miguel picks 9 apples. Andy picks 4 less. How many apples did Andy pick?

○ $9 + 4 = 13$

○ $6 + 3 = 9$

○ $4 + 8 = 12$

○ $4 + 5 = 9$

8. **Extend Your Thinking** Write a number story for $11 - 3$. Then write the addition fact that helped you solve the subtraction sentence.

© Pearson Education, Inc. 1

Name ______________________________

**Solve & Share**

6 fish swim by. Some more fish join them. Now there are 11 fish. How many fish joined the fish swimming by?
Draw a picture to solve the problem. Then write a number sentence.

___ + ___ = ___

## Problem Solving

# Lesson 4-9
# Draw a Picture and Write a Number Sentence

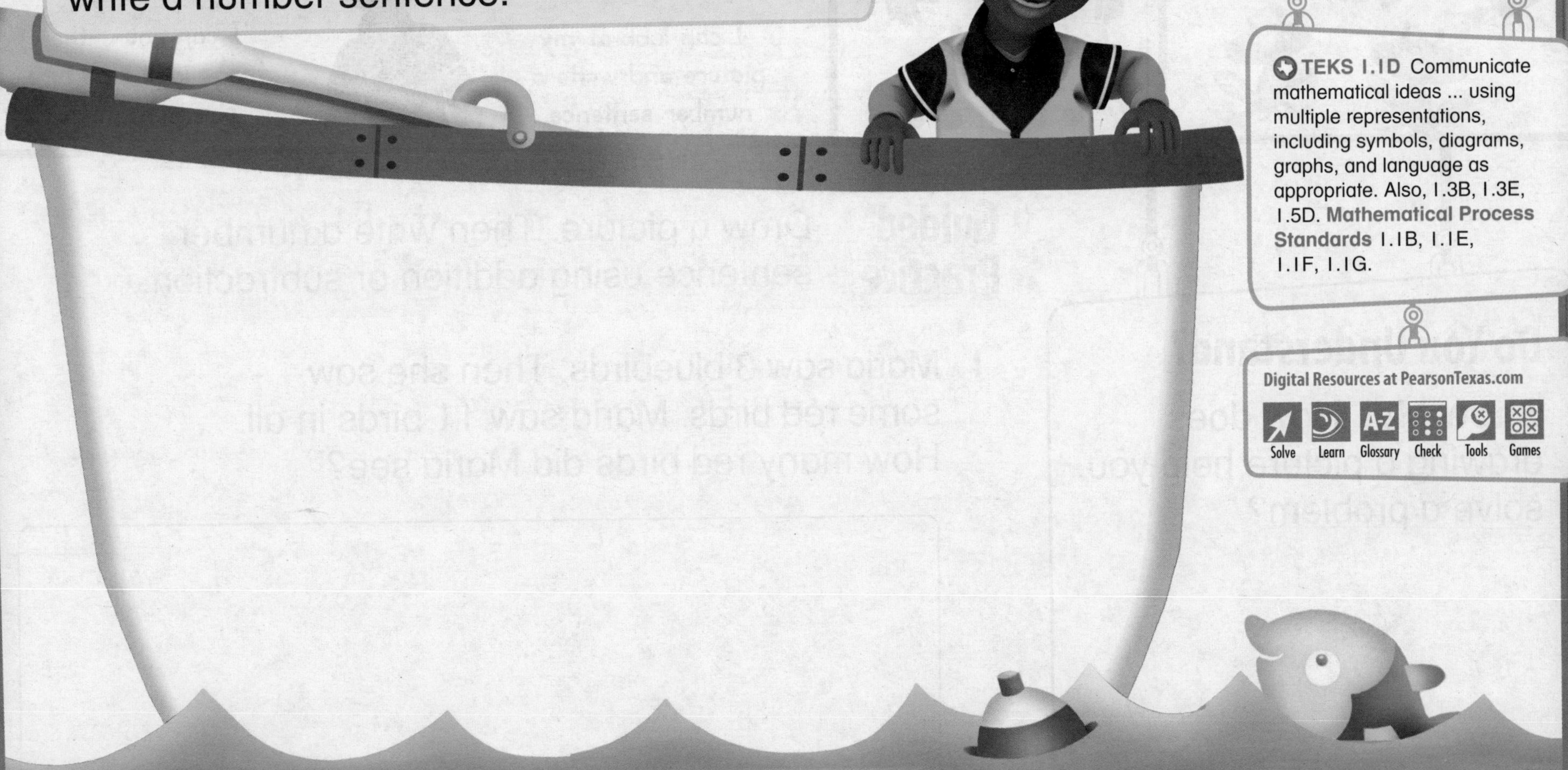

**TEKS 1.1D** Communicate mathematical ideas ... using multiple representations, including symbols, diagrams, graphs, and language as appropriate. Also, 1.3B, 1.3E, 1.5D. **Mathematical Process Standards** 1.1B, 1.1E, 1.1F, 1.1G.

**Digital Resources at PearsonTexas.com**

Solve | Learn | Glossary | Check | Tools | Games

## Analyze

There are 5 frogs in the pond. 4 more jump in.

How many frogs are in the pond now?

## Plan

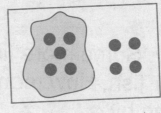
I can draw a picture to show the story.

## Solve and Justify

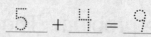

$$\underline{5} + \underline{4} = \underline{9}$$

I can look at my picture and write a number sentence.

## Evaluate

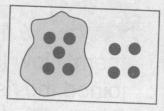

I can count the frogs in the picture to check my answer.

---

☆ **Guided Practice** ☆ Draw a picture. Then write a number sentence using addition or subtraction.

## Do You Understand?

**Show Me!** How does drawing a picture help you solve a problem?

1. Maria saw 3 bluebirds. Then she saw some red birds. Maria saw 11 birds in all. How many red birds did Maria see?

_____ ◯ _____ = _____

© Pearson Education, Inc. 1

Name _____

2. Jamal picks some berries. Then Ed picks 3 more. Jamal and Ed pick 12 berries in all. How many berries does Jamal pick?

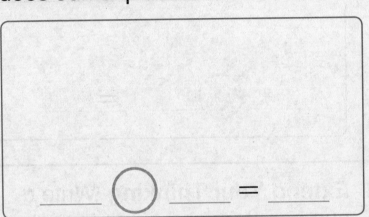

_____ ◯ _____ = _____

3. There are 8 flowers in Vicky's garden. Vicky picks 4 flowers. How many flowers are still in the garden?

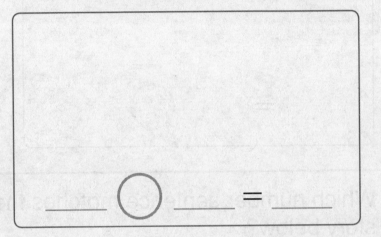

_____ ◯ _____ = _____

4. **Extend Your Thinking** Write a number story to match the picture. Then write a number sentence.

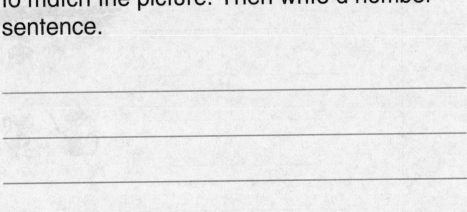

_____

_____

_____

_____ ◯ _____ = _____

Draw a picture. Then write a number sentence using addition or subtraction.

**5.** Charlie and Joey draw stars. Charlie draws 7 stars. Joey draws 4 less. How many stars did Joey draw?

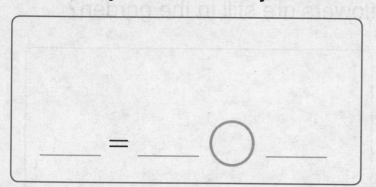

___ = ___ ◯ ___

**6.** Brian found 3 rocks on Monday. He found more rocks on Friday. In all, he found 8 rocks. How many rocks did Brian find on Friday?

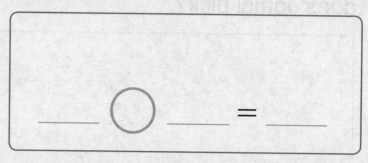

___ ◯ ___ = ___

**7.** Which number sentence matches the story below?

There are 8 ducks.
5 ducks are in a row.
Some more ducks join them.
How many ducks join them?

○ $5 - 3 = 2$ ducks

○ $6 + 5 = 11$ ducks

○ $6 - 3 = 3$ ducks

○ $5 + 3 = 8$ ducks

**8. Extend Your Thinking** Write a number story and number sentence for the picture.

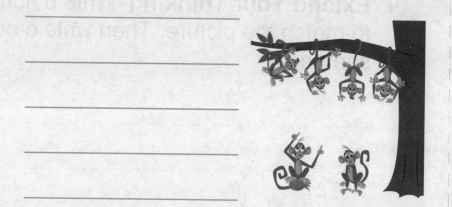

_____

_____

_____

_____

© Pearson Education, Inc. 1

Name _____

**Another Look** You can use pictures to solve a number story.

Linda has 4 buttons.
She buys some more.
Linda has 7 buttons in all.

How many buttons did Linda buy?

_3_ buttons

_4_ (+) _3_ = _7_

🏠 **HOME CONNECTION**
Your child drew pictures and wrote number sentences to solve story problems.

**HOME ACTIVITY** Tell your child a story that involves adding or subtracting. Say, "Draw a picture and write a number sentence for this story." Check to make sure the drawing and number sentence match the story. Repeat with 1 or 2 different stories.

 Write a number sentence to solve. Draw a picture to check.

1. Abby has 8 apples. Judy gives her some more apples.
Now Abby has 11 apples. How many apples did Judy give her?

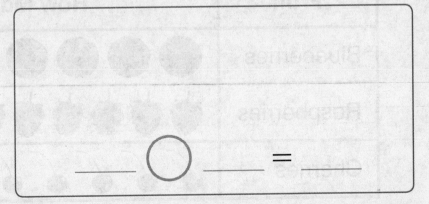

___ ◯ ___ = ___

Solve each problem below.

**2.** Tim has 9 pears.
3 pears are yellow.
The rest are green.
How many pears are green?

_____ ◯ _____ = _____

**3.** Ian has 5 red balloons.
Max has 6 blue balloons.
How many balloons do the
boys have in all?

_____ ◯ _____ = _____

**4.** Some birds are on a branch. 3 birds fly away. 4 birds stay.
⭐ How many birds were there to start?

Which subtraction sentence shows the story?

◯ $7 - 2 = 5$        ◯ $9 - 7 = 2$

◯ $7 - 3 = 4$        ◯ $4 - 3 = 1$

**5. Extend Your Thinking** Use the chart. Write a number story. Then write an addition or subtraction sentence to match your story.

| Fruit | How Many? |
|---|---|
| Blueberries | 🫐🫐🫐🫐 |
| Raspberries | 🫐🫐🫐🫐🫐🫐 |
| Cherries | 🍒🍒🍒🍒🍒🍒🍒🍒 |

_____

_____

_____

_____

Name _____

**Think about numbers** in the toy problems to make sense of addition and subtraction sentences.

**1.** Cross out the set of number sentences that does **not** match the problem.

Lauren has 12 toy cars.
She gives 5 toy cars to Jen.

How many toy cars does Lauren have left?

$12 - 5 = 7$          $7 - 5 = 2$

$5 + 7 = 12$          $5 + 2 = 7$

---

**2.** Tell how you can use addition or subtraction to solve the toy car problem.

_____

_____

_____

**3.** Jen has 5 toy cars. Write a subtraction sentence and an addition sentence to show how many toy cars Jen has left if she gives 3 cars to Ellie.

____ − ____ = ____

____ + ____ = ____

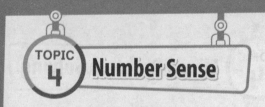

## Make a List

1. Mario makes a list to show the ways to make 12 with red and yellow counters. Use the pattern to find the missing numbers.

| ● | ● |
|---|---|
| 12 | 0 |
| | 1 |
| | |
| | |
| | 5 |
| | 6 |
| 5 | |
| | |
| | |
| 2 | 10 |
| | |
| | 12 |

## What's Wrong?

2. Cross out the model that can't be right. Complete the model that can be right.

Oliver and I have the same number of pencils.

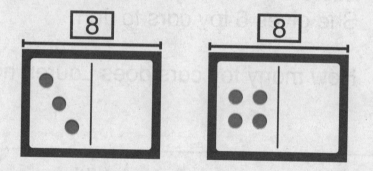

## Complete It!

3. Fill in the missing numbers.

$$\begin{array}{r} 9 \\ + \ \boxed{\phantom{0}} \\ \hline 12 \end{array} \qquad \begin{array}{r} \boxed{\phantom{0}} \\ - \ 3 \\ \hline 9 \end{array} \qquad \begin{array}{r} 3 \\ + \ \boxed{\phantom{0}} \\ \hline 11 \end{array}$$

Name _____

**Set A**

There are 8 peppers in the pot.
You can add 1 more by counting
1 more.

1 more than 8 is 9.

$8 + 1 = 9$

Add 1, 2, or 0 to find the sum.
Write the addition fact.

1.

___ + ___ = ___

2.

___ + ___ = ___

**Set B**

You can make 10 to add.

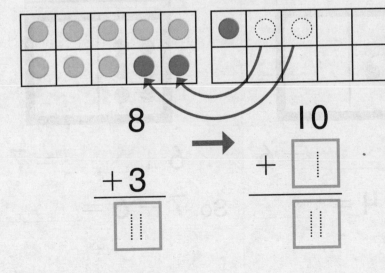

$8$
$+3$
□□□

→

$10$
$+□$
□□

Make 10 to add.

3.

$7$
$+4$
□

→

$10$
$+□$
□

4.

$9$
$+3$
□

→

$10$
$+□$
□

You can subtract by thinking 0 less than, 1 less than, or 2 less than.

2 less than 9 is ___7___.

Write the subtraction fact.

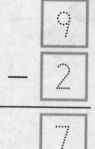

$$\begin{array}{r} 9 \\ -\ 2 \\ \hline 7 \end{array}$$

Subtract 0, 1, or 2 to find the difference. Write the subtraction fact.

5.

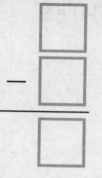

1 less than 4 is _____.

6.

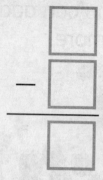

0 less than 6 is _____.

You can think addition to help you subtract.

8

?

The missing part is 3.

$5 + \underline{3} = 8$

So, $8 - 5 = \underline{3}$.

Think addition to help you subtract.

7.

6

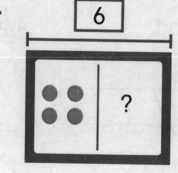

?

$4 + \underline{\phantom{0}} = 6$

So, $6 - 4 = \underline{\phantom{0}}$.

8.

7

?

$6 + \underline{\phantom{0}} = 7$

So, $7 - 6 = \underline{\phantom{0}}$.

Name _____

Set E

You can use a double to add.

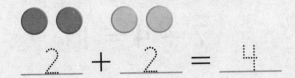

$2 + 2 = 4$

$3 + 3 = 6$

Both addends are the same.
They are doubles.

Set F

You can use doubles to add other numbers.

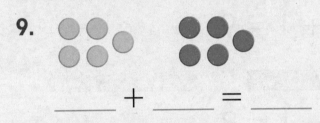

$2 + 2$     2 + 2 and
           1 more

$2 + 2 = 4$     $2 + 3 = 5$

Write an addition sentence
for each double.

9.

___ + ___ = ___

10.

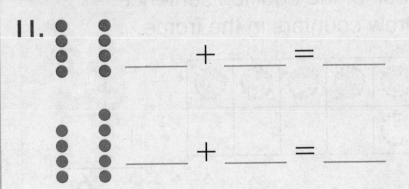

How many coins are there in all?

___ + ___ = ___

Find each sum.

11.

___ + ___ = ___

___ + ___ = ___

You can use addition facts to help you subtract.

$$8 + 1 = 9$$

$$9 - 1 = 8$$

$8 + 1 = 9$ and $9 - 1 = 8$ are related facts.

Use the addition fact to help you subtract.

12.

$$11 - 4 = \underline{\quad} \qquad 7 + 4 = 11$$

13.

$$12 - 9 = \underline{\quad} \qquad 3 + 9 = 12$$

You can use a ten-frame to learn facts with 5.

Look at the addition sentence. Draw counters in the frame.

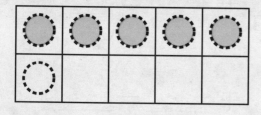

$$
\begin{array}{r}
5 \\
+\ 1 \\
\hline
6
\end{array}
$$

$$5 + 1 = 6$$

Draw counters and complete the addition sentences.

14.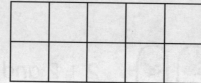

$$4 + 5 = \underline{\quad}$$

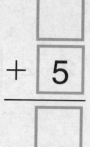

$$
\begin{array}{r}
\square \\
+\ 5 \\
\hline
\square
\end{array}
$$

© Pearson Education, Inc. 1

Name _____

**Test**

**1.** Molly has 9 toy cars. She got 2 more as a gift.
How many toy cars does Molly have now?

9        10        11        12

○        ○        ○        ○

**2.** Brad has 5 books.
His mother gives him 4 more.
How many books does Brad have
in all?

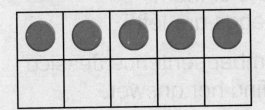

1        4        5        9

○        ○        ○        ○

**3.** Sammy earns 3 stars in gym class.
He earns 4 more stars in music class.
How many stars did Sammy earn?

6        7        8        9

○        ○        ○        ○

**4.** Which addition sentence helps you add 8 + 4?

$10 + 4 = 14$        $10 + 3 = 13$        $10 + 2 = 12$        $10 + 1 = 11$

○        ○        ○        ○

**5.** Add the near doubles.
Find the missing number.

$$3 + 4 = \underline{\phantom{?}}$$

| 4 | 5 | 6 | 7 |
|---|---|---|---|
| ○ | ○ | ○ | ○ |

**6.** Yuri is thinking of a number.
His number is 0 less than 9.
Use the subtraction sentence
to find his number.

$$9 - 0 = \underline{\phantom{?}}$$

| 6 | 7 | 8 | 9 |
|---|---|---|---|
| ○ | ○ | ○ | ○ |

**7.** Find the missing part.

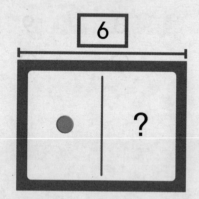

$$1 + \underline{\phantom{?}} = 6$$

$$6 - 1 = \underline{\phantom{?}}$$

| 4 | 5 | 6 | 7 |
|---|---|---|---|
| ○ | ○ | ○ | ○ |

**8.** Jessica had 12 eggs.
She cooked 8 of them.
How many eggs are left?

Find the number sentence Jessica
can use to find her answer.

○  $12 - 6 = 6$

○  $12 - 8 = 4$

○  $12 - 3 = 9$

○  $12 - 5 = 7$

© Pearson Education, Inc. 1

**9.** Which addition sentence helps you add $9 + 3$?

$10 + 2 = 12$
○

$10 + 4 = 14$
○

$10 + 3 = 13$
○

$10 + 5 = 15$
○

---

**10.** Lucy sees 12 turtles and 3 turtle eggs.
How many more turtles does she see than turtle eggs?

6
○

7
○

8
○

9
○

---

**11.** Paul has 5 grapes.
His friend gives him 3 more.
How many grapes does Paul
have in all?

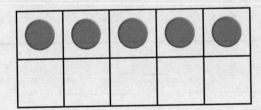

8
○

9
○

10
○

11
○

**12.** Nathan sees bugs in his yard.
He counts 3 bees and 5 ants.
How many bugs did Nathan see in all?

6
○

7
○

8
○

9
○

**13.** Add the doubles.
Find the missing number.

$$4 + 4 = \underline{\phantom{?}}$$

6      7      8      9
○      ○      ○      ○

**14.** Erin is thinking of a number.
Her number is 4 less than 8.
Use the subtraction sentence to
find her number.

$$8 - 4 = \underline{\phantom{?}}$$

3      4      5      6
○      ○      ○      ○

---

**15.** Find the missing part. Write the numbers.

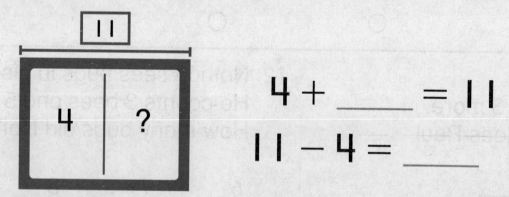

$$4 + \underline{\phantom{xxx}} = 11$$

$$11 - 4 = \underline{\phantom{xxx}}$$

---

**16.** Larry has 12 marbles.
He gives 7 to his sister.
How many marbles does
Larry have left?
Write a number sentence to solve.

$$\underline{\phantom{xx}} \bigcirc \underline{\phantom{xx}} = \underline{\phantom{xx}}$$

$$\underline{\phantom{xx}} \text{ marbles}$$

# Addition and Subtraction Facts to 20

**Essential Question:** What strategies can you use for adding and subtracting to 20?

Some animals have special teeth to eat plants.

Some animals have special teeth to eat meat.

Wow! Let's do this project and learn more.

## Math and Science Project: What Do They Eat?

**Find Out** Talk to friends and relatives about the things different animals eat. Ask why teeth are different depending on what animals eat.

**Journal: Make a Book** Show what you found out. In your book, also:

- Draw pictures of animals and what they eat.
- Make up and solve addition and subtraction problems about animals and what they eat.

# Review What You Know

## Vocabulary

**1.** Circle the problem that shows a **double**.

$$5 + 5 = 10$$

$$5 + 6 = 11$$

$$5 + 7 = 12$$

**2.** Circle the number sentences that are **related facts**.

$$5 + 7 = 12$$

$$12 - 7 = 5$$

$$4 + 5 = 9$$

$$9 - 3 = 6$$

**3.** Circle the **sum** in the number sentence below.

$$7 + 4 = 11$$

---

## Addition and Subtraction

**4.** Robin has 9 stamps. She gets 4 more stamps as a gift. How many stamps does Robin have now?

____ stamps

**5.** Jen has 18 treats for her cat. She feeds some treats to her cat. Jen has 9 treats left. How many treats did Jen give her cat?

____ treats

## Doubles Facts

**6.** Solve this doubles fact.

$$7 + 7 = \underline{\quad}$$

© Pearson Education, Inc. 1

# My Word Cards

Study the words on the front of the card. Complete the activity on the back.

## doubles-plus-1 fact

the addends are 1 apart

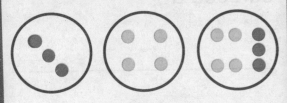

$3 + 4 = 7$

addends

## doubles-plus-2 fact

the addends are 2 apart

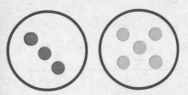

$3 + 5 = 8$

addends

## make 10

$7 + 4 = ?$

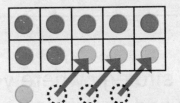

10          7
$+ 1$   so   $+ 4$
11          11

## fact family

$3 + 5 = 8$
$5 + 3 = 8$
$8 - 3 = 5$
$8 - 5 = 3$

## related facts

$2 + 3 = 5$

$5 - 2 = 3$

Use what you know to complete the sentences.
Extend learning by writing your own sentence using each word.

----------------------------------------

_____

_____

is a strategy where you first add or subtract until you reach 10.

----------------------------------------

When adding numbers that are 2 apart, you can use a

_____

_____.

----------------------------------------

When adding numbers that are 1 apart, you can use a

_____

_____.

----------------------------------------

If a subtraction fact and an addition fact have the same numbers, they are called

_____.

----------------------------------------

A group of related addition and subtraction facts is called a

_____

_____.

Name _____

Solve & Share

Carlos and I each picked 5 strawberries. What doubles fact shows how many strawberries we have in all?

If I pick 1 more strawberry, how could you find how many strawberries there are in all?

TEKS 1.3D Apply basic fact strategies to add and subtract within 20, including making 10 and decomposing a number leading to a 10. Also, 1.3. **Mathematical Process Standards** 1.1C, 1.1D, 1.1F.

Digital Resources at PearsonTexas.com

Solve    Learn    Glossary    Check    Tools    Games

___ + ___ = ___          ___ + ___ = ___

**Double**

You can use doubles to find **doubles-plus-1 facts**.

6
+ 7
---
?

Doubles–plus–1 facts are also called near doubles.

Double the 6.

6
+ 6
---
12

6 + 7 is 6 + 6 and 1 more.

6
+ 6
---
12

and 1 more

12 and 1 more is 13.

6
+ 7
---
13

---

## Do You Understand?

**Show Me!** How does knowing 7 + 7 help you find 7 + 8?

☆ **Guided Practice** ☆ Add the doubles. Then use the doubles to help you solve the doubles-plus-1 facts.

1.

$\underline{5} + \underline{5} = \underline{10}$

So, $5 + 6 = \underline{11}$.

2.

$\underline{\phantom{0}} + \underline{\phantom{0}} = \underline{\phantom{0}}$

So, $8 + 9 = \underline{\phantom{0}}$.

© Pearson Education, Inc. 1

Add the doubles. Then use the doubles to help you solve the doubles-plus-1 facts.

3.
$$\begin{array}{r} 7 \\ + 7 \\ \hline \square \end{array}$$
$$\begin{array}{r} 8 \\ + 7 \\ \hline \square \end{array}$$

4.
$$\begin{array}{r} 4 \\ + 4 \\ \hline \square \end{array}$$
$$\begin{array}{r} 4 \\ + 5 \\ \hline \square \end{array}$$

5.
$$\begin{array}{r} 5 \\ + 5 \\ \hline \square \end{array}$$
$$\begin{array}{r} 5 \\ + 6 \\ \hline \square \end{array}$$

6.
$$\begin{array}{r} 9 \\ + 9 \\ \hline \square \end{array}$$
$$\begin{array}{r} 9 \\ + 10 \\ \hline \square \end{array}$$

7.
$$\begin{array}{r} 6 \\ + 6 \\ \hline \square \end{array}$$
$$\begin{array}{r} 6 \\ + 7 \\ \hline \square \end{array}$$

8.
$$\begin{array}{r} 3 \\ + 3 \\ \hline \square \end{array}$$
$$\begin{array}{r} 3 \\ + 4 \\ \hline \square \end{array}$$

Use doubles and near doubles to help you solve the problem. Then draw a picture and write a number sentence to match.

9. **Extend Your Thinking** Max has some blue marbles. Tom has some purple marbles. Tom has 1 more marble than Max. How many marbles do they have in all?

_____ + _____ = _____

# Problem Solving   Solve each problem below.

**10.** Carrie and Pete each picked 7 cherries. Then Pete picked 1 more. How many cherries do they have in all?

Write an addition sentence.

_____ + _____ = _____

_____ cherries

**11.** Manny and Pam each bought 5 apples. Then Pam bought 1 more. How many apples do they have in all?

Write an addition sentence.

_____ + _____ = _____

_____ apples

---

**12.** Juan ate 8 grapes after lunch. Then he ate some more grapes after dinner. He ate 17 grapes in all. How many grapes did Juan eat after dinner?

○ 8

○ 9

○ 7

○ 1

You can use a double and near double to help you solve the problem.

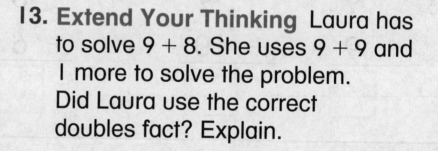

**13. Extend Your Thinking** Laura has to solve $9 + 8$. She uses $9 + 9$ and 1 more to solve the problem. Did Laura use the correct doubles fact? Explain.

_____

_____

_____

© Pearson Education, Inc. 1

Name _____

**Another Look** You can use doubles facts to add doubles-plus-1 facts.

$4 + 5 = ?$

$5 = 4 + 1$, so you can write

$4 + 5$ as $4 + 4 + 1$.

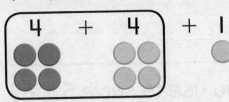

$4 + 4 = 8$

8 and 1 more is 9. So, $4 + 5 = 9$.

$2 + 3 = ?$

$3 = \underline{2} + \underline{1}$

$\underline{2} + \underline{2} = \underline{4}$

So, $\underline{2} + \underline{3} = \underline{5}$.

 Add the doubles. Then use the doubles to help you solve the doubles-plus-1 facts.

1.

$3 + 3 = \boxed{6}$

$3 + 4 = \boxed{7}$

2.
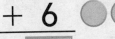
$6 + 6 = \boxed{\phantom{0}}$

$6 + 7 = \boxed{\phantom{0}}$

Draw 1 more cube. Then use the doubles to help you add 1 more.

3.

Think: _____ + _____ = _____.

So, 7 + 8 = _____.

4.

Think: _____ + _____ = _____.

So, 9 + 10 = _____.

5. Which should you use to solve 9 + 8?

○ 7 + 7 and 1 more

○ 8 + 8 and 1 more

○ 8 + 8 and 2 more

○ 9 + 9 and 1 more

6. Which should you use to solve 5 + 6?

○ 5 + 5 and 2 more

○ 4 + 5 and 1 more

○ 5 + 5 and 1 more

○ 4 + 4 and 1 more

7. **Extend Your Thinking** Use a doubles-plus-1 fact to solve the problem. Then draw a picture and write a number sentence to match.

Dan saw some cats and dogs. He saw 1 more dog than cat. How many dogs and cats did Dan see?

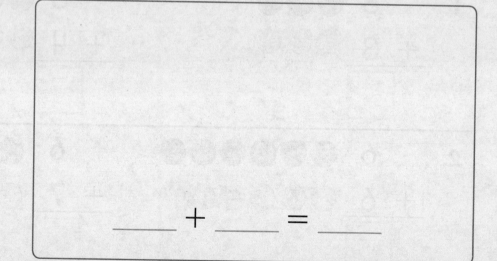

_____ + _____ = _____

Name _____

**Solve & Share**

Carlos and I each find 5 seashells. What doubles fact shows how many seashells we have in all?

If Carlos finds 2 more seashells, how could you find how many seashells there are in all?

⊙ TEKS 1.3D Apply basic fact strategies to add and subtract within 20, including making 10 and decomposing a number leading to a 10. Also, 1.3. Mathematical Process Standards 1.1B, 1.1E, 1.1F, 1.1G.

Digital Resources at PearsonTexas.com

Solve  Learn  Glossary  Check  Tools  Games

___ + ___ = ___        ___ + ___ = ___
**Double**

These are called **doubles-plus-2 facts**.

$$6 \qquad 9$$
$$\underline{+\,8} \quad \underline{+\,7}$$
$$? \qquad ?$$

There are different ways to solve a doubles-plus-2 fact.

$$6$$
$$\underline{+\,8}$$
$$?$$

Double the lesser number. Then add 2.

Think $6 + 6 = 12$ and 2 more.

Double 6 is 12. 2 more than 12 is 14.

$6 + 8 = 14$

Or, double the number between.

7 is between 6 and 8. Double 7 is 14.

## Do You Understand?

**Show Me!** Which doubles facts can help you solve $7 + 9$? Explain.

## ☆ Guided Practice ☆ Use a doubles fact to help you add.

1.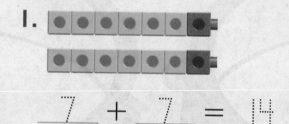

$7 + 7 = 14$

So, $6 + 8 = \underline{14}$.

2.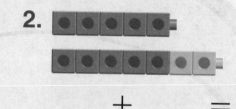

$\underline{\phantom{0}} + \underline{\phantom{0}} = \underline{\phantom{0}}$

So, $5 + 7 = \underline{\phantom{0}}$.

3.

$\underline{\phantom{0}} + \underline{\phantom{0}} = \underline{\phantom{0}}$

So, $10 + 8 = \underline{\phantom{0}}$.

4.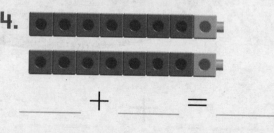

$\underline{\phantom{0}} + \underline{\phantom{0}} = \underline{\phantom{0}}$

So, $7 + 9 = \underline{\phantom{0}}$.

Name _____

# Independent ☆ Practice

Draw 2 more cubes. Use a doubles fact to help you add.

5. ___ + ___ = ___

So, 10 + 8 = ___.

6. ___ + ___ = ___

So, 9 + 11 = ___.

7. ___ + ___ = ___

So, 8 + 6 = ___.

8. ___ + ___ = ___

So, 7 + 5 = ___.

9. ___ + ___ = ___

So, 4 + 6 = ___.

10. ___ + ___ = ___

So, 3 + 5 = ___.

Use a doubles and a doubles-plus-2 fact to solve the problem. Draw cubes to help you.

11. **Extend Your Thinking** Dan made a red cube train. Kay made a yellow cube train. Kay's train has 2 more cubes than Dan's train. How many cubes do they have in all?

___ = ___ + ___

**12.** Kelly and Eric each made 6 sand castles. Then Kelly made 2 more. How many sand castles did they make in all?

Write an addition sentence.

____ + ____ = ____

_____ sand castles

**13.** Mark found 7 shells. Sue found 2 more than Mark. Together, they found 16 shells. How many shells did Sue collect?

Write an addition sentence.

____ + ____ = ____

_____ shells

**14.** Ben saw 7 starfish. Jamie saw 9 starfish. How many starfish did they see in all?

Which should you use to find how many starfish Ben and Jamie saw in all?

○   7 + 7 and 1 more

○   7 + 9 and 1 more

○   7 + 7 and 2 more

○   9 + 9 and 2 more

**15. Extend Your Thinking** Use a doubles-plus-2 fact to solve the problem. Write a number sentence to match.

There are some fish in a pond. Some fish are silver. Some fish are gold. There are 2 more gold fish than silver fish. How many fish are there in all?

____ + ____ = ____

silver     gold     fish
fish       fish

Name _____

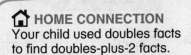

**Another Look** You can use doubles facts to add doubles-plus-2 facts.

6 + 8 = ?

8 = 6 + 2, so you can write

6 + 8 as 6 + 6 + 2.

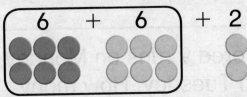

6 + 6 = 12

12 and 2 more is 14. So, 6 + 8 = 14.

2 + 4 = ?

4 = __2__ + __2__

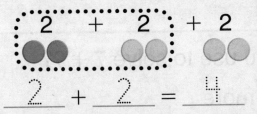

__2__ + __2__ = __4__

So, __2__ + __4__ = __6__.

🏠 **HOME CONNECTION**
Your child used doubles facts to find doubles-plus-2 facts.

**HOME ACTIVITY** Give your child a doubles fact, such as 4 + 4. Have your child use objects to show the doubles fact, such as two groups of 4 paper clips. Ask, "How many in all?" Then add 2 more paper clips to one of the groups. Ask, "What is the doubles-plus-2 fact? How many in all now?" Repeat with other doubles facts.

Add the doubles. Then use the doubles to help you solve the doubles-plus-2 facts.

1.

3

+ 3

[6]

3

+ 5

[8]

2.

4

+ 4

[ ]

6

+ 4

[ ]

Draw 2 more cubes. Then use the doubles to help you add 2 more.

3.

Think: _____ + _____ = _____.

So, $5 + 7 =$ _____.

4.

Think: _____ + _____ = _____.

So, $3 + 5 =$ _____.

5. Which should you use to solve $7 + 9$?

○  $7 + 7$ and 1 more

○  $7 + 7$ and 2 more

○  $8 + 8$ and 1 more

○  $8 + 8$ and 2 more

6. Max's team scored 9 runs on Monday and 11 runs on Tuesday. How many runs did the team score in all?

Which doubles fact will help you solve the problem?

○  $7 + 7$         ○  $9 + 9$

○  $8 + 8$         ○  $11 + 11$

7. **Extend Your Thinking** Use a doubles-plus-2 fact to solve the problem. Then draw a picture and write a number sentence to match.

Tanya and Kyle feed the same number of goats at the zoo. Then Kyle feeds 2 more goats. How many goats did they feed in all?

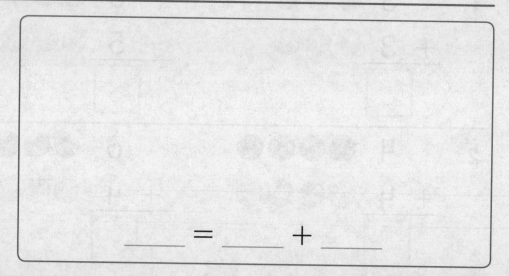

_____ = _____ + _____

Name _____

**Solve & Share**

Josh has 6 grapes. Tia gave him 5 more. On the top workmat, use cubes and a number sentence to show how many grapes Josh has in all.

Then Josh ate 3 grapes. On the bottom workmat, show how many grapes he has now.

TEKS 1.1B Use a problem-solving model that incorporates analyzing given information, formulating a plan or strategy, determining a solution, justifying the solution, and evaluating the problem-solving process and the reasonableness of the solution. Also, 1.3D, 1.5D. Mathematical Process Standard 1.1C, 1.1E.

Digital Resources at PearsonTexas.com

Solve   Learn   Glossary   Check   Tools   Games

1. _____ $\bigoplus$ _____ = _____

2. _____ $\bigcirc$ _____ = _____

 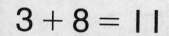

## Analyze

Emilio had 6 toys to sell. His brother had 5 toys to sell. How many toys did they have to sell in all?

Then they sold 8 toys. How many toys are left?

## Plan

$$6 + 5 = ?$$

There are two steps in this problem.

**Step 1:** Add to find how many toys in all.

**Step 2:** Use the answer from Step 1 to answer the last question.

## Solve and Justify

$$6 + 5 = \underline{11}$$

They have 11 toys to sell.

$$11 - 8 = \underline{3}$$

3 toys are left.

They sold 8 toys. So, 3 toys are left.

## Evaluate

$$3 + 8 = 11$$

They have 3 toys left. They sold 8 toys. So, they had 11 toys to sell.

---

☆ **Guided Practice** ☆  Write number sentences to solve each step of the problems below.

## Do You Understand?

**Show Me!** When you solve a two-step problem, why do you need to solve the problem in Step 1 before the problem in Step 2?

1. 8 friends sit at a table. 2 more friends join them. How many friends are at the table now?

$$\underline{8} \; \bigoplus \; \underline{2} = \underline{10}$$

3 friends leave the table. How many friends are still at the table?

$$\underline{10} \; \bigominus \; \underline{3} = \underline{7}$$

2. Rachel blows up 12 balloons. 2 balloons pop. How many balloons are left?

$$\underline{\phantom{0}} \; \bigcirc \; \underline{\phantom{0}} = \underline{\phantom{0}}$$

She blows up 9 more balloons. How many balloons are there now?

$$\underline{\phantom{0}} \; \bigcirc \; \underline{\phantom{0}} = \underline{\phantom{0}}$$

**Topic 5** | Lesson 3

Name _____

☆
**Independent**
☆ **Practice** Write number sentences to solve each step of the problems below.

**3.** 6 students are hiking on a trail.
2 adults go with them.
How many people are hiking in all?

_____ ◯ _____ = _____

4 more adults join the hikers.
How many hikers are there now?

_____ ◯ _____ = _____

**4.** 12 birds sit on a roof.
5 of the birds fly away.
How many birds are still on the roof?

_____ ◯ _____ = _____

5 more birds fly away.
Now how many birds are on the roof?

_____ ◯ _____ = _____

Choose numbers to use in the problem below.
Then write number sentences to solve each step.

**5. Extend Your Thinking** There are
10 pennies in Jake's bank. He spends
some of the pennies on a toy car. How
many pennies are left in Jake's bank?

_____ ◯ _____ = _____

Jake's dad gives him some pennies.
How many pennies does Jake have in
his bank now?

_____ ◯ _____ = _____

**Topic 5 | Lesson 3**

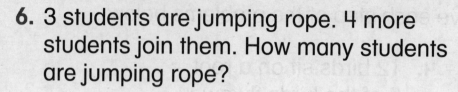

**Problem Solving** Solve each problem below.

6. 3 students are jumping rope. 4 more students join them. How many students are jumping rope?

_____ ◯ _____ = _____ students

2 students leave and go home. How many students are jumping rope now?

_____ ◯ _____ = _____ students

7. Beth has 5 crayons. She gives 2 crayons to Leo. How many crayons does Beth have left?

_____ ◯ _____ = _____ crayons

Beth buys 8 more crayons. How many crayons does she have now?

_____ ◯ _____ = _____ crayons

8. Mary found 8 shells. She gives 3 away. How many shells does Mary have now?

Mary finds 5 more shells. How many shells does she have now?

Choose the number sentences that match the story.

○  8 + 3 = 11 and 11 + 5 = 16

○  8 + 3 = 11 and 11 − 5 = 6

○  8 − 3 = 5 and 5 + 5 = 10

○  8 − 3 = 5 and 5 − 5 = 0

9. **Extend Your Thinking** Draw pictures that show a two-step problem for 4 + 2 = 6 and then 6 − 3 = 3. Tell your friend a story about the picture.

© Pearson Education, Inc. 1

Name _____

**Another Look** Use number sentences to solve each step.

Jill has 6 marbles. She gets 5 more. How many marbles does she have in all?

I can use the answer from the first step to answer the question in the second step.

$6 + 5 =$ ___11___ marbles

Jill gives 8 marbles to Sal. How many marbles does Jill have now?

___11___ $-$ ___8___ $=$ ___3___   Jill has ___3___ marbles left.

🏠 **HOME CONNECTION** Your child solved two-step problems by using the answer from the first step to solve the second step.

**HOME ACTIVITY** Give your child 3 pennies. Then give your child 2 more pennies. Have your child tell a number sentence for the number of pennies in all. Then take 1 penny from your child. Have your child tell a number sentence for the number of pennies left. Repeat using a different number of pennies.

Write number sentences to solve each step of the problems below.

1. Jack has 4 model cars. He buys 3 more. How many model cars does Jack have in all?

   ____ $+$ ____ $=$ ____ model cars

   For his birthday, Jack gets 5 model cars. How many model cars does he have now?

   ____ $+$ ____ $=$ ____ model cars

2. Nikki uses 6 red beads to make a bracelet. She adds 8 blue beads. How many beads does Nikki use to make her bracelet?

   ____ $+$ ____ $=$ ____ beads

   On the way home, Nikki loses 4 beads. How many beads does Nikki have left on her bracelet?

   ____ $-$ ____ $=$ ____ beads

Write number sentences to solve each problem below.

**3.** 8 monkeys are in a tree. 5 monkeys climb down. Then 2 more monkeys climb up. How many monkeys are in the tree?

_____ ◯ _____ = _____

_____ ◯ _____ = _____

**4.** There are 9 apples on the table. Mary puts 2 more apples on the table. Then she gives 4 apples to a friend. How many apples are on the table now?

_____ ◯ _____ = _____

_____ ◯ _____ = _____

**5.** Alan has 7 marbles. He buys 6 more marbles. Then he gives 5 marbles to Deb. How many marbles does Alan have now? Which number sentence solves the first step?

○ $7 - 6 = 1$         ○ $13 - 5 = 8$

○ $7 + 6 = 13$        ○ $13 + 5 = 18$

**6.** 10 students are in Mr. Park's class. 3 students join his class. 1 student moves away. How many students are in Mr. Park's class now? Which number sentence solves the second step?

○ $13 - 1 = 12$       ○ $10 - 3 = 7$

○ $10 - 1 = 9$        ○ $10 - 4 = 6$

**7. Extend Your Thinking** Write numbers to solve the problem.

10 butterflies are in a garden. _____ more join them. How many butterflies are there in all?

Then _____ butterflies fly away. How many butterflies are left in the garden?

_____

_____

© Pearson Education, Inc. I

Name ____________________

**Solve & Share**

Put 9 counters on the ten-frame. Put 5 counters outside of the ten-frame. How can you find how many counters there are in all without counting each counter?

____ + ____ = ____

# Lesson 5-4
## Making 10 to Add

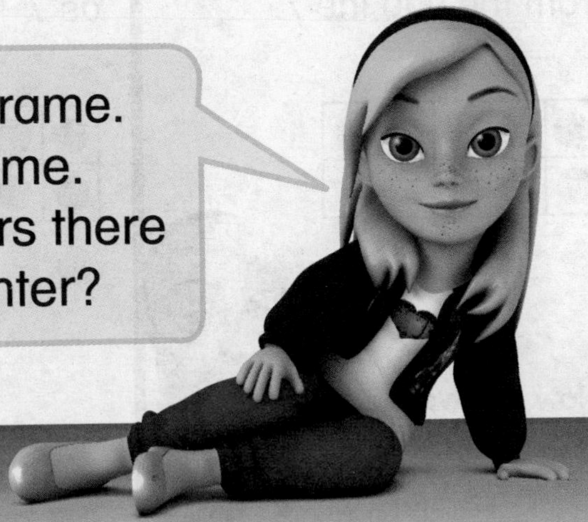

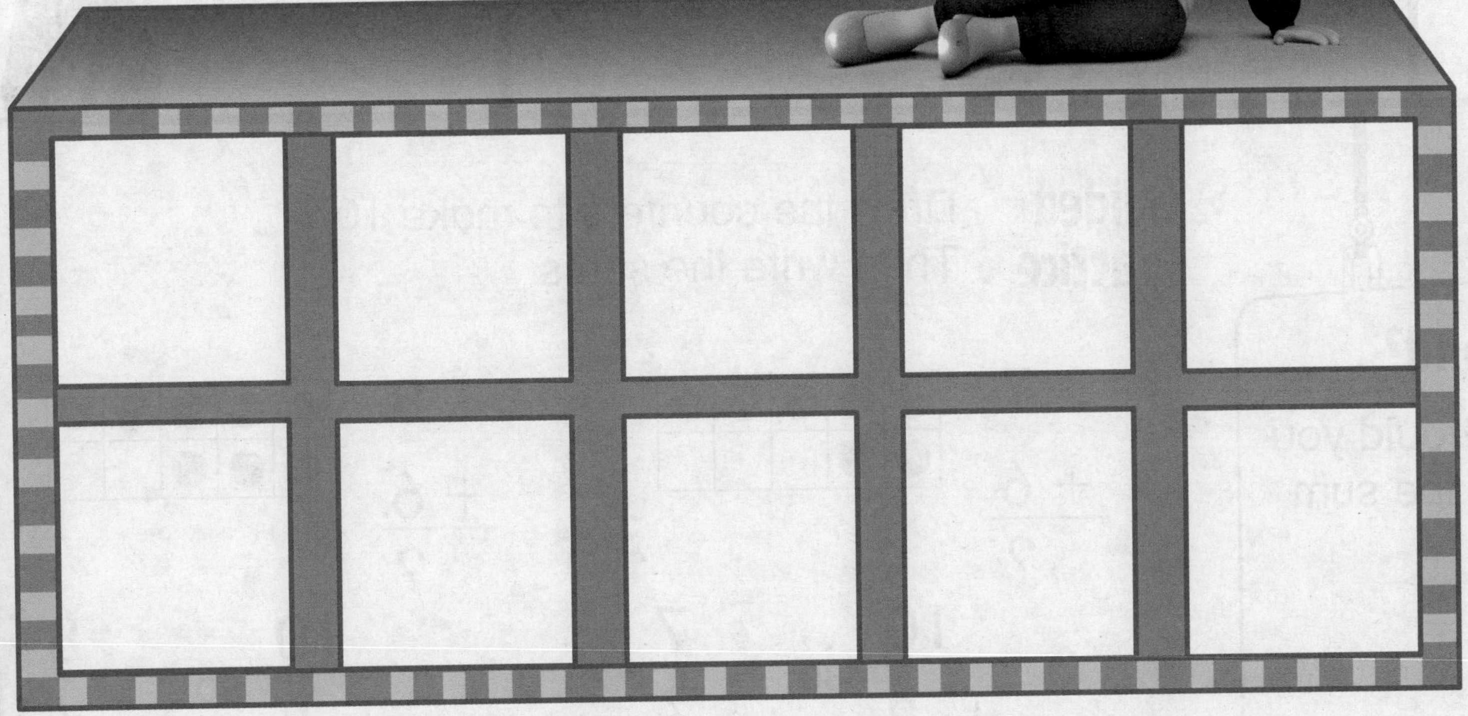

**TEKS 1.3D** Apply basic fact strategies to add and subtract within 20, including making 10 and decomposing a number leading to a 10. Also, 1.3, 1.3C. **Mathematical Process Standards** 1.1E, 1.1F, 1.1G.

**Digital Resources at PearsonTexas.com**

Solve Learn Glossary Check Tools Games

**Make 10** to help you add.

$$\begin{array}{r} 7 \\ + 4 \\ \hline \end{array}$$

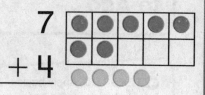

Move 3 counters from the 4 to the 7.

Now I have 10 and 1.

10 + 1 is the same as 7 + 4.

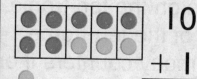

$$\begin{array}{r} 10 \\ + 1 \\ \hline \end{array}$$

$$\begin{array}{r} 10 \\ + 1 \\ \hline 11 \end{array} \quad so \quad \begin{array}{r} 7 \\ + 4 \\ \hline 11 \end{array}$$

The sums are the same!

## Do You Understand?

**Show Me!** How would you make a 10 to find the sum of 4 + 9?

☆ **Guided Practice** ☆   Draw the counters to make 10. Then write the sums.

1.
$$\begin{array}{r} 7 \\ + 6 \\ \hline ? \end{array}$$

$$\begin{array}{r} 10 \\ + 3 \\ \hline \boxed{13} \end{array} \quad so \quad \begin{array}{r} 7 \\ + 6 \\ \hline \Box \end{array}$$

2.
$$\begin{array}{r} 8 \\ + 6 \\ \hline ? \end{array}$$

$$\begin{array}{r} 10 \\ + 4 \\ \hline \Box \end{array} \quad so \quad \begin{array}{r} 8 \\ + 6 \\ \hline \Box \end{array}$$

© Pearson Education, Inc. 1

Name _____

**Independent Practice**

Draw the counters to make 10. Then write the sums.

3.
$$\begin{array}{r} 7 \\ + 8 \\ \hline ? \end{array}$$
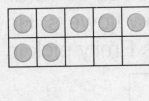

$$\begin{array}{r} 10 \\ + 5 \\ \hline \square \end{array}$$
so
$$\begin{array}{r} 7 \\ + 8 \\ \hline \square \end{array}$$

4.
$$\begin{array}{r} 9 \\ + 6 \\ \hline ? \end{array}$$
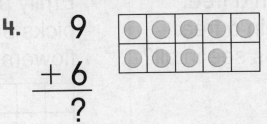

$$\begin{array}{r} 10 \\ + 5 \\ \hline \square \end{array}$$
so
$$\begin{array}{r} 9 \\ + 6 \\ \hline \square \end{array}$$

5.
$$\begin{array}{r} 7 \\ + 7 \\ \hline ? \end{array}$$

$$\begin{array}{r} 10 \\ + 4 \\ \hline \square \end{array}$$
so
$$\begin{array}{r} 7 \\ + 7 \\ \hline \square \end{array}$$

Draw counters to help you solve each problem.
Use 2 different colors.

6. **Extend Your Thinking** There are 11 cats on a fence. There are 5 black cats. The rest of the cats are white.

How many white cats are on the fence?

_____

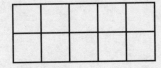

7. **Extend Your Thinking** Ann buys 15 ribbons for her hair. Some of the ribbons are blue. 6 of the ribbons are pink.

How many ribbons are blue?

_____

# Problem Solving
Draw counters to help you solve each problem below.
Use 2 different colors.

**8.** Carlos sees 7 yellow birds in a tree. Then he sees 6 white birds in a tree. How many birds does Carlos see in all?

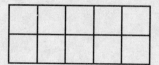

_____ birds

**9.** Emily picks 8 red flowers. Then she picks 8 yellow flowers. How many flowers does Emily pick in all?

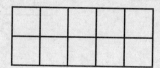

_____ flowers

**10.** 8 people are on a bus. Then 7 more people get on. Which shows how to make a 10 to find the number of people on the bus?

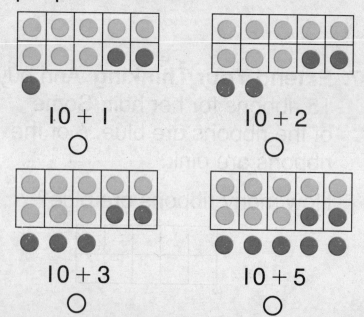

10 + 1
○

10 + 2
○

10 + 3
○

10 + 5
○

**11. Extend Your Thinking** Look at the model. Complete the number sentences to match what the model shows.

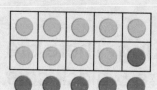

10 + _____ = _____

So, _____ + _____ = _____.

Name _____

**Another Look** Making 10 can help you add.

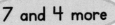
7 and 4 more

$7 + 4 = ?$

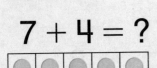

Make a 10.

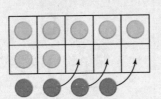

10 and 1 more
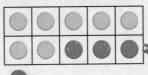

So, 7 + 4 and 10 + 1 have the same sum.

$10 + 1 = \underline{\quad}$ so $7 + 4 = \underline{\quad}$.

🏠 **HOME CONNECTION**
Your child made 10 to help make addition easier.

**HOME ACTIVITY** Have your child use small objects to show 7 + 6. Tell your child to move some objects to make a 10. Then have your child give the 2 number sentences: 10 + 3 = 13, so 7 + 6 = 13.

Draw the counters to make 10. Then write the sums.

1.
$$\begin{array}{r} 9 \\ + 6 \\ \hline ? \end{array}$$

$$\begin{array}{r} 10 \\ + 5 \\ \hline \square \end{array}$$

so

$$\begin{array}{r} 9 \\ + 6 \\ \hline \square \end{array}$$

2.
$$\begin{array}{r} 7 \\ + 6 \\ \hline ? \end{array}$$

$$\begin{array}{r} 10 \\ + 3 \\ \hline \square \end{array}$$

so

$$\begin{array}{r} 7 \\ + 6 \\ \hline \square \end{array}$$

Draw the counters to make 10. Then write the sums.

3. 9
   + 5
   ───
   ?

   10        9
   + 4   so  + 5
   ───       ───
   ☐         ☐

4. 8
   + 3
   ───
   ?

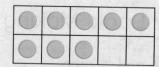

   10        8
   + 1   so  + 3
   ───       ───
   ☐         ☐

5. **Algebra** Which number belongs
   ⭐ in the ☐ ?

   $9 + 6 =$ ___?___

   So, $10 +$ ☐ $=$ ___?___ .

   9    5    8    6
   ○    ○    ○    ○

6. **Algebra** Which number belongs
   ⭐ in the ☐ ?

   $8 + 5 =$ ___?___

   So, ☐ $+ 3 =$ ___?___ .

   7    8    9    10
   ○    ○    ○    ○

7. **Extend Your Thinking** Circle 2 numbers.

Draw counters to make 10. Use 2 different colors.
Then write 2 addition sentences to match.

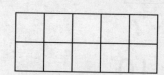

$10 +$ _____ $=$ _____

So, _____ $+$ _____ $=$ _____ .

© Pearson Education, Inc. 1

Name _____

**Solve & Share**

9 + 6 = ?

Choose a strategy to solve the problem. Use words, objects, or pictures to explain your work.

⊙ TEKS 1.3E Explain strategies used to solve addition ... problems up to 20 using spoken words, objects, pictorial models, and number sentences. Also, 1.3, 1.3D. Mathematical Process Standards 1.1B, 1.1C, 1.1E.

Digital Resources at PearsonTexas.com

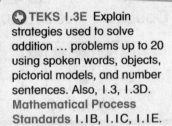

Solve   Learn   Glossary   Check   Tools   Games

**Doubles**

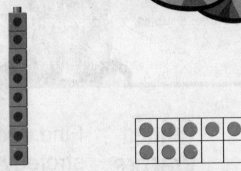

**Near Doubles**

**Make 10**

____ + ____ = ____

You can use different ways to remember addition facts.

Doubles    Near Doubles

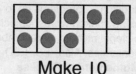

Make 10

$$4$$
$$+4$$

Doubles

Both numbers are the same. These are doubles.

$$6 + 7$$

Near Doubles

The numbers are 1 apart. These are near doubles.

$$8 + 5$$

Make 10

One number is close to 10. You can make 10.

$$10$$
$$+3$$

---

## Do You Understand?

**Show Me!** What strategy could you use to solve 7 + 8? Why is it a good strategy?

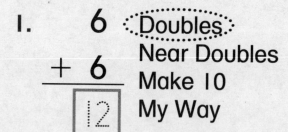

☆ **Guided Practice** ☆   Find each sum. Circle the strategy that you used.

1.
$$6$$
$$+6$$
$$\boxed{12}$$
Doubles
Near Doubles
Make 10
My Way

2.
$$9$$
$$+7$$
$$\boxed{\phantom{0}}$$
Doubles
Near Doubles
Make 10
My Way

3.
$$6$$
$$+7$$
$$\boxed{\phantom{0}}$$
Doubles
Near Doubles
Make 10
My Way

4.
$$8$$
$$+9$$
$$\boxed{\phantom{0}}$$
Doubles
Near Doubles
Make 10
My Way

© Pearson Education, Inc. 1

Name _____

**Independent Practice**    Find each sum.

5.  6
   + 8
    ☐

6.  8
   + 8
    ☐

7.  4
   + 9
    ☐

8.  9
   + 9
    ☐

9.  7
   + 6
    ☐

10.  8
    + 3
     ☐

11.  9
    + 8
     ☐

12.  6
    + 5
     ☐

13.  8
    + 5
     ☐

14.  6
    + 9
     ☐

15.  7
    + 4
     ☐

16.  7
    + 7
     ☐

Solve the problem. Explain the strategy you used.

**17. Extend Your Thinking** Jan has
9 green marbles and some red marbles.
She has 11 marbles in all.

_____

_____

How many red marbles does Jan have?

_____

_____ red marbles

**18.** Brett has 8 shirts in his closet. He puts more shirts in the dresser. Now he has 16 shirts. How many shirts did Brett put in the dresser?

Brett put _____ shirts in the dresser.

Circle the strategy you used to find the sum.

Doubles            Make 10
Near Doubles       My Way

**19.** Sara has 7 big books. She has 8 small books. Which strategy could **not** help you find how many books Sara has in all?

○  Doubles

○  Near Doubles

○  Make 10

○  My Way

**20. Extend Your Thinking** Manuel and Jake have 13 pencils in all. How many pencils could each boy have?

Circle the strategy you used.

Draw a picture to help you solve the problem.

$13 = \underline{\phantom{00}} + \underline{\phantom{00}}$

Doubles            Make 10
Near Doubles       My Way

Name _____

**Another Look** You can use different strategies to solve problems.

5 and 6 are 1 apart.
They are near doubles.

    5          5  ●●●●●
  + 6        + 5  ●●●●●
  ___        ___
    ?         [10]

          5  ●●●●●
        + 6  ●●●●●●
        ___
         [11]

9 is close to 10.
Make a 10.

    9
  + 5
  ___
    ?

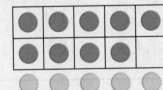

   10         9
  + 4   so  + 5
  ___        ___
  [14]       [14]

🏠 **HOME CONNECTION**
Your child chose a strategy to add. Then your child explained why he or she chose that strategy.

**HOME ACTIVITY** Have your child use small objects to show 8 + 9. Tell him or her to use one of the following strategies to find the sum: Doubles, Doubles Plus 1, Make 10, or My Way. Ask your child to explain how he or she used that strategy to find the answer.

 Find each sum. Circle the strategy that you used.

1.      5      Think: 5 and 4 are 1 apart.
      + 4
      ___      Doubles
      [ ]      Near Doubles
               Make 10

2.      8      Think: 8 is close to 10.
      + 3
      ___      Doubles
      [ ]      Near Doubles
               Make 10

Find each sum. Circle the strategy that you used.

3.
$$\begin{array}{r} 9 \\ +\ 3 \\ \hline \end{array}$$
□

Doubles
Near Doubles
Make 10

4.
$$\begin{array}{r} 7 \\ +\ 7 \\ \hline \end{array}$$
□

Doubles
Near Doubles
Make 10

5.
$$\begin{array}{r} 5 \\ +\ 6 \\ \hline \end{array}$$
□

Doubles
Near Doubles
Make 10

Find the missing number for each problem.

6. Algebra ✪

$6 + \underline{\ ?\ } = 12$

6    8    10    18
○    ○    ○    ○

7. Algebra ✪

$\underline{\ ?\ } + 4 = 11$

5    6    7    15
○    ○    ○    ○

8. Algebra ✪

$7 + 8 = \underline{\ ?\ }$

2    10    15    20
○    ○    ○    ○

9. **Extend Your Thinking** Write a story problem that can be solved by making 10. Then explain how to solve the problem.

Name ______________________

**Solve & Share**

How can thinking about 10 help you find the answer to the subtraction fact $13 - 7$?

# Lesson 5-6
## Making 10 to Subtract

**TEKS 1.3D** Apply basic fact strategies to add and subtract within 20, including making 10 and decomposing a number leading to a 10. Also, 1.3, 1.5F. **Mathematical Process Standards** 1.1B, 1.1E, 1.1F, 1.1G.

**Digital Resources at PearsonTexas.com**

Solve Learn Glossary Check Tools Games

_____ − _____ = _____

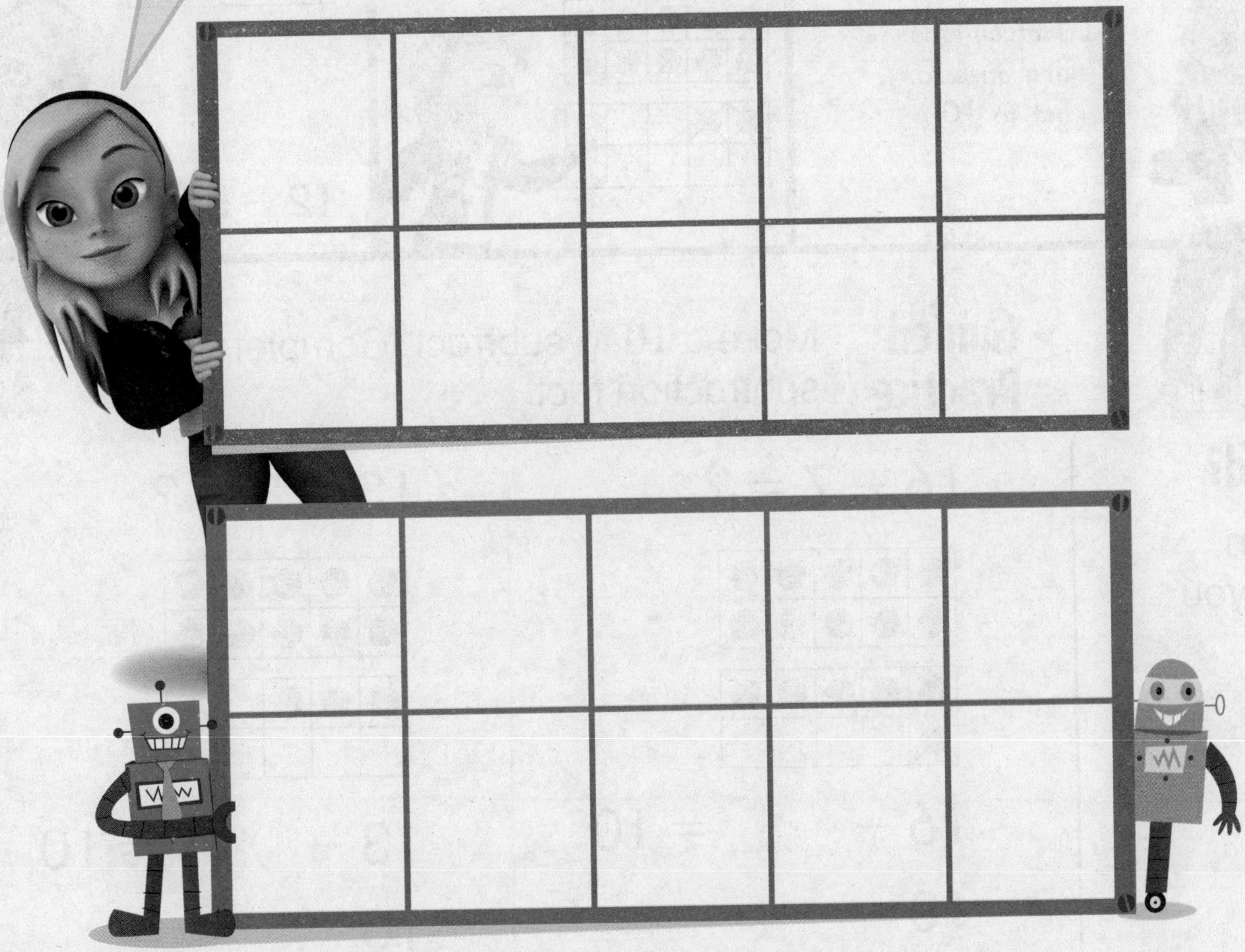

$12 - 5 = ?$

You can make a 10 to help you subtract.

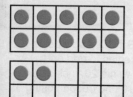

Start with 12.

Subtract 2 to get to 10.

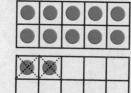

I subtract the extra ones to get to 10.

Subtract 3 more because $2 + 3 = 5$.

I subtracted 5 in all.

There are 7 left.

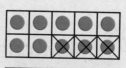

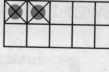

The answer is 7!

$12 - 5 = \underline{7}$

## Do You Understand?

**Show Me!** How can finding $14 - 4$ help you find $14 - 6$?

⭐ **Guided Practice** ⭐ Make a 10 to subtract. Complete each subtraction fact.

1. $16 - 7 = ?$

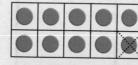

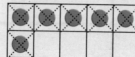

$16 - \underline{6} = 10$

$10 - \underline{1} = \underline{9}$

So, $16 - 7 = \underline{9}$.

2. $13 - 8 = ?$

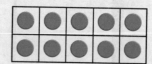

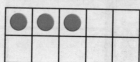

$13 - \underline{\phantom{0}} = 10$

$10 - \underline{\phantom{0}} = \underline{\phantom{0}}$

So, $13 - 8 = \underline{\phantom{0}}$.

**280** two hundred eighty

© Pearson Education, Inc. 1

**Topic 5** | Lesson 6

Name _____

Make a 10 to subtract. Complete each subtraction fact.

3.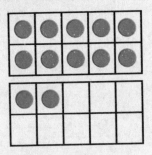

$12 - 4 =$ _____

4.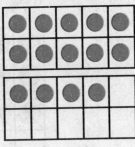

$14 - 6 =$ _____

5.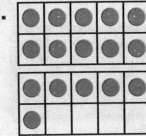

$16 - 9 =$ _____

6.

$17 - 8 =$ _____

7.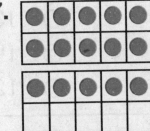

$15 - 7 =$ _____

8.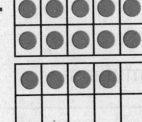

$14 - 9 =$ _____

Draw counters in the ten-frames to show your work.

9. **Extend Your Thinking** Show how you can make 10 to find $13 - 7$.

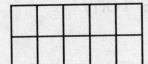

**10.** Kyle baked 12 muffins. His friends ate 6 muffins. How many muffins are left?

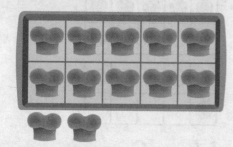

$12 - \underline{\hspace{2cm}} = 10$

$10 - \underline{\hspace{2cm}} = \underline{\hspace{2cm}}$

$\underline{\hspace{2cm}}$ muffins

**11.** Which number sentence matches the ten-frames?

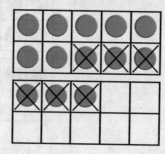

○  $13 - 5 = 8$

○  $13 - 6 = 7$

○  $14 - 6 = 8$

○  $12 - 4 = 8$

**12. Extend Your Thinking** Choose a number less than 15 to use in the problem below. Then draw a picture and write a number sentence to solve the problem.

Tony picks 15 flowers.
He gives some flowers to his mother.
How many flowers does Tony have left?

$\underline{\hspace{2cm}}$ flowers

$\underline{\hspace{1.5cm}} - \underline{\hspace{1.5cm}} = \underline{\hspace{1.5cm}}$

Name _____

**Another Look** Making a 10 can help you subtract.
Another way to make 10 is to add on.

14 − 6 = ?

Start with 6.

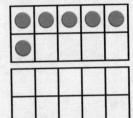

Add 4 to
make 10.

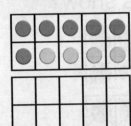

Add 4 more
to make 14.

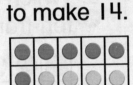

6 + __4__ = 10     10 + __4__ = __14__

I added 8 to
6 to make 14.
So, 14 − 6 = 8.

🏠 **HOME CONNECTION**
Your child used the making
10 strategy to subtract.

**HOME ACTIVITY** Write
12 − 6 = ? on a piece of paper.
Have your child use small
objects to find the difference.
Tell your child to make a 10 to
subtract: by adding on to get
10 or by subtracting to get 10.
Have your child explain each
step of the process as he or
she solves the problem.

Make a 10 to subtract.
Complete each subtraction fact.

1.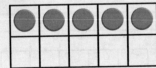

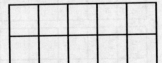

14 − 5 = _____

2.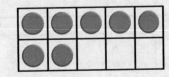

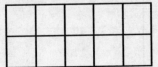

16 − 7 = _____

3.

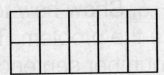

15 − 9 = _____

Make a 10 to help you find the missing number in each problem.

**4. Algebra**

$5 = 12 -$ _____

**5. Algebra**

_____ $- 6 = 8$

**6. Algebra**

$15 - 8 =$ _____

**7.** Which subtraction fact do the ten-frames show?

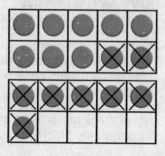

○ $17 - 8 = 9$

○ $16 - 9 = 7$

○ $16 - 10 = 6$

○ $16 - 8 = 8$

**8.** Which subtraction fact do the ten-frames show?

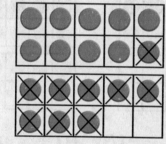

○ $9 = 18 - 9$

○ $8 = 17 - 9$

○ $10 = 18 - 8$

○ $9 = 17 - 8$

**9. Extend Your Thinking** Write a subtraction story problem for $15 - 6$. Show how to make 10 to solve the problem. Then complete the number sentence.

$15 - 6 =$ _____

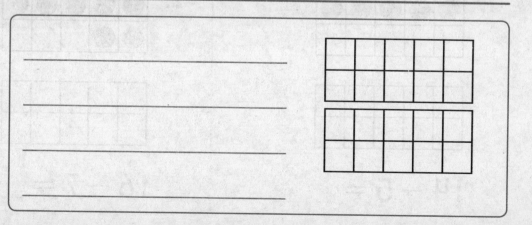

Name ____________________

# Lesson 5-7
## Fact Families

**Solve & Share**

Can you write 2 addition and 2 subtraction facts that use the numbers 8, 9, and 17? Use cubes to help you.

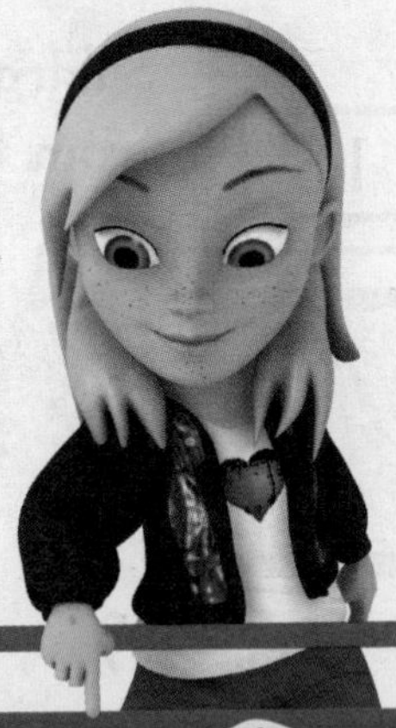

TEKS 1.5F Determine the unknown whole number in an addition or subtraction equation when the unknown may be any one of the three or four terms in the equation. Also, 1.5E, 1.5G. **Mathematical Process Standards** 1.1C, 1.1E, 1.1F.

Digital Resources at PearsonTexas.com

Solve Learn Glossary Check Tools Games

___ + ___ = ___      ___ − ___ = ___

___ + ___ = ___      ___ − ___ = ___

You can write 2 addition facts for this model.

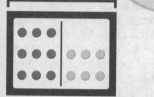

15

Add the parts in any order.

$9 + 6 = 15$
$6 + 9 = 15$

You can also write 2 subtraction facts.

15

Subtract 1 part from the whole.

$15 - 6 = 9$

Subtract the other part from the whole.

15

$15 - 9 = 6$

These are **related facts**. They are a **fact family**.

$9 + 6 = 15$
$6 + 9 = 15$

$15 - 6 = 9$
$15 - 9 = 6$

## Do You Understand?

**Show Me!** Can $9 = 15 - 6$ be written as $15 - 6 = 9$?

## ☆ Guided Practice ☆

Write the fact family for each model.

1.

14

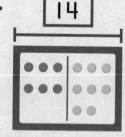

$14 = 6 + 8$

$14 = 8 + 6$

$8 = 14 - 6$

$6 = 14 - 8$

2.

16

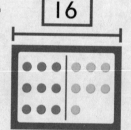

___ + ___ = ___

___ + ___ = ___

___ − ___ = ___

___ − ___ = ___

© Pearson Education, Inc. 1

**Topic 5** | Lesson 7

Name _____

**Independent ☆ Practice**   Write the fact family for each model.

3.

[17]

| 9 | 8 |

___ + ___ = ___

___ + ___ = ___

___ − ___ = ___

___ − ___ = ___

4.

[13]

| 7 | 6 |

___ = ___ + ___

___ = ___ + ___

___ = ___ − ___

___ = ___ − ___

5.

[12]

| 4 | 8 |

___ + ___ = ___

___ + ___ = ___

___ − ___ = ___

___ − ___ = ___

6. **Extend Your Thinking**  Are the following number sentences a fact family? Explain your answer.

$9 + 5 = 14$

$15 - 5 = 10$

$4 + 4 = 8$

$15 = 6 + 9$

*What is the whole? What are the parts?*

_____

_____

_____

_____

_____

**Problem Solving** Write a fact family for each set of counters below.

**7.**

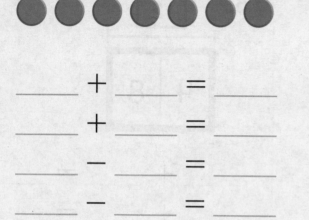

_____ + _____ = _____

_____ + _____ = _____

_____ − _____ = _____

_____ − _____ = _____

**8.**

_____ = _____ + _____

_____ = _____ + _____

_____ = _____ − _____

_____ = _____ − _____

**9.** Which related facts match the picture?

$9 = 9 + 0$
$0 = 9 - 9$
○

$11 = 9 + 2$
$2 = 11 - 9$
○

$18 = 9 + 9$
$9 = 18 - 9$
○

$17 = 9 + 8$
$8 = 17 - 9$
○

**10. Extend Your Thinking** Write a number sentence to solve the problem below. Then write 3 related facts to complete a fact family.

Tanya has 8 stickers. Miguel gave her 5 more. How many stickers does Tanya have in all? _____ stickers

_____ ○ _____ = _____

_____ ○ _____ = _____

_____ ○ _____ = _____

_____ ○ _____ = _____

## Another Look

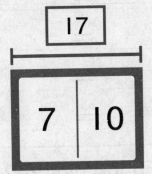

| 17 |
|---|
| 7 | 10 |

$7 + 10 = 17$

$10 + 7 = 17$

$17 - 10 = 7$

$17 - 7 = 10$

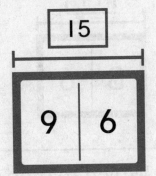

| 15 |
|---|
| 9 | 6 |

$9 + 6 = 15$

$6 + 9 = 15$

$15 - 6 = 9$

$15 - 9 = 6$

Fact families use the same numbers.

🏠 HOME CONNECTION
Your child used a part-part-whole model to find the subtraction facts and addition facts in a fact family.

HOME ACTIVITY Write an addition problem, such as $9 + 4 = ?$ Have your child find the sum and write the related addition fact. $(4 + 9 = 13)$ Then ask your child to write the 2 related subtraction sentences to complete the fact family. $(13 - 9 = 4$ and $13 - 4 = 9)$ Continue with several other fact families.

Write the fact family for each model.

1.

| 18 |
|---|
| 10 | 8 |

___ + ___ = ___

___ + ___ = ___

___ − ___ = ___

___ − ___ = ___

2.

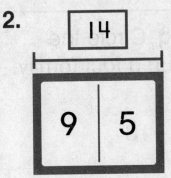

| 14 |
|---|
| 9 | 5 |

___ + ___ = ___

___ + ___ = ___

___ − ___ = ___

___ − ___ = ___

Digital Resources at PearsonTexas.com

Write the fact family for each model.

**3.**

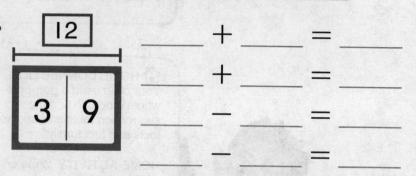

| 12 |
|----|

| 3 | 9 |

_____ + _____ = _____

_____ + _____ = _____

_____ − _____ = _____

_____ − _____ = _____

**4.**

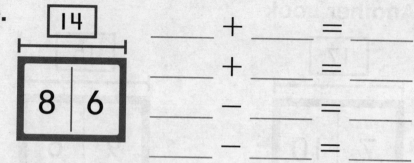

| 14 |
|----|

| 8 | 6 |

_____ + _____ = _____

_____ + _____ = _____

_____ − _____ = _____

_____ − _____ = _____

**5.** Which related facts match the picture?

○  4 + 11 = 15 and 15 − 4 = 11

○  11 − 4 = 7 and 7 + 4 = 11

○  3 + 7 = 10 and 10 − 3 = 7

○  7 − 4 = 3 and 7 − 3 = 4

**6.** Which related facts match the picture?

○  9 − 7 = 2 and 7 + 2 = 9

○  2 + 7 = 9 and 7 − 5 = 2

○  7 + 9 = 16 and 16 − 7 = 9

○  9 − 2 = 7 and 16 − 16 = 0

**7. Extend Your Thinking** Circle the
3 numbers that make up a fact family.
Write the fact family.

5     7     8     4     13

_____ + _____ = _____

_____ + _____ = _____

_____ − _____ = _____

_____ − _____ = _____

Name _____

**Solve & Share**

$14 - 5 = ?$

How can you use a related fact to help you find the difference? Write the related addition and subtraction facts. Use counters to help you.

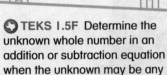

⭐ **TEKS 1.5F** Determine the unknown whole number in an addition or subtraction equation when the unknown may be any one of the three or four terms in the equation. Also, 1.3, 1.3D. **Mathematical Process Standards 1.1C, 1.1E, 1.1F.**

Digital Resources at PearsonTexas.com

Solve  Learn  Glossary  Check  Tools  Games

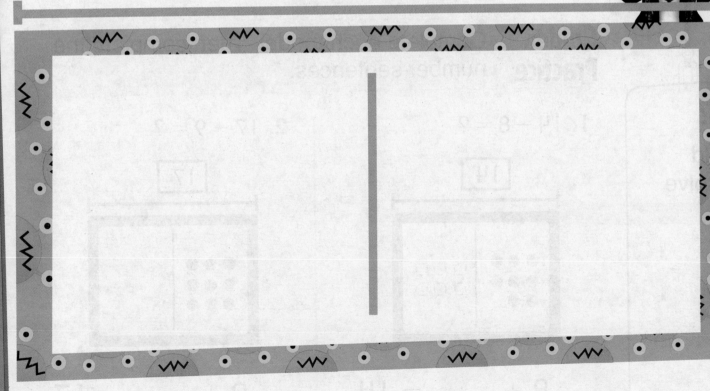

____ + ____ = ____        ____ − ____ = ____

$13 - 8 = ?$

Use addition to help you subtract.

13

?

$8 + ? = 13$

What can I add to 8 to make 13?

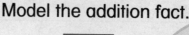

Model the addition fact.

13

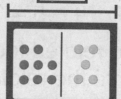

The missing part is 5.
$8 + 5 = 13$,
so $13 - 8 = 5$.

## Do You Understand?

**Show Me!** How could you use addition to solve $16 - 9$?

☆ **Guided Practice** ☆ Complete each model. Then complete the number sentences.

1. $14 - 8 = ?$

14

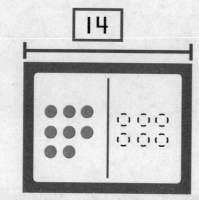

$8 + \underline{6} = 14$

$14 - 8 = \underline{6}$

2. $17 - 9 = ?$

17

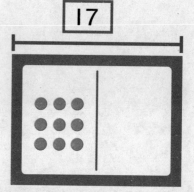

$9 + \underline{\phantom{0}} = 17$

$17 - 9 = \underline{\phantom{0}}$

© Pearson Education, Inc. 1

Name _____

**Independent Practice** Complete each model. Then complete the number sentences.

**3.** $17 - 9 = ?$

17

9

$9 + \underline{\phantom{00}} = 17$

$17 - 9 = \underline{\phantom{00}}$

**4.** $20 - 10 = ?$

20

10

$10 + \underline{\phantom{00}} = 20$

$20 - 10 = \underline{\phantom{00}}$

**5.** $15 - 7 = ?$

15

7

$7 + \underline{\phantom{00}} = 15$

$15 - 7 = \underline{\phantom{00}}$

 Draw the missing shape for each problem.

**6. Extend Your Thinking**

If ● + ■ = ▲ ,

then ▲ − ■ = _____ .

**7. Extend Your Thinking**

If ▬ − ▮ = ▮ ,

then _____ + ▮ = ▬ .

## Problem Solving
Write a related addition and subtraction fact to help you solve each problem.

8. There are 17 robot parts in a box. Fred uses some of the parts. Now there are 8 left. How many parts did Fred use?

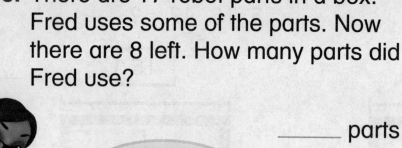

Related facts have the same whole and the same parts.

_____ parts

_____ + _____ = _____

_____ − _____ = _____

9. Maria invites 10 friends to her party. 3 cannot come. How many friends will be at Maria's party?

_____ friends

_____ + _____ = _____

_____ − _____ = _____

10. Which addition fact will help you subtract?

$$13 - 7 = ?$$

○ $5 + 7 = 12$

○ $7 + 6 = 13$

○ $7 + 7 = 14$

○ $12 - 7 = 5$

11. **Extend Your Thinking** Write a subtraction sentence about Fred and a box of 16 robot parts. Then write a related addition fact you could use to solve it.

_____

_____

_____

_____ + _____ = _____

_____ − _____ = _____

© Pearson Education, Inc. 1

Name _____

**Another Look** You can use an addition fact to help you solve a related subtraction fact.

$18 - 8 = ?$

18

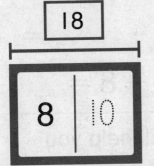

8 | 10

$8 + 10 = 18$
$18 - 8 = 10$

$15 - 6 = ?$

15

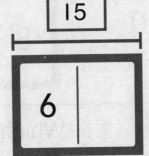

6 |

$6 + \underline{9} = 15$
$15 - 6 = \underline{9}$

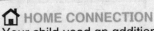

🏠 **HOME CONNECTION**
Your child used an addition fact to solve a related subtraction fact.

**HOME ACTIVITY** Write a subtraction problem for your child to solve. Have him or her say a related addition fact to help solve the subtraction problem. Provide pennies or other small objects to be used as counters, if necessary. Repeat using different subtraction problems.

Complete each model.
Then complete the number sentences.

1. $11 - 6 = ?$

11

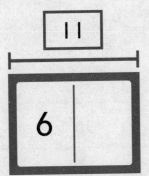

6 |

$6 + \underline{\phantom{0}} = 11$
$11 - 6 = \underline{\phantom{0}}$

2. $12 - 9 = ?$

12

9 |

$9 + \underline{\phantom{0}} = 12$
$12 - 9 = \underline{\phantom{0}}$

Complete each model. Then complete the number sentences.

**3.** $10 - 6 = ?$

$6 + \underline{\hspace{2em}} = 10$

$10 - 6 = \underline{\hspace{2em}}$

**4.** $16 - 8 = ?$

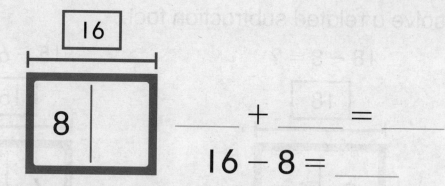

$\underline{\hspace{2em}} + \underline{\hspace{2em}} = \underline{\hspace{2em}}$

$16 - 8 = \underline{\hspace{2em}}$

**5.** Which addition fact will help you solve $14 - 9$?

○ $5 + 14 = 19$

○ $5 + 9 = 14$

○ $4 + 9 = 13$

○ $5 + 7 = 12$

**6.** Which addition fact will help you solve $18 - 6$?

○ $6 + 13 = 19$

○ $10 + 8 = 18$

○ $8 + 11 = 19$

○ $12 + 6 = 18$

**7. Extend Your Thinking** Draw the missing shape. Then explain how you know your answer is correct.

If ⬭ + ⬯ = △ ,

then △ − ⬭ = __.

© Pearson Education, Inc. 1

Name _____

⭐ TEKS 1.5F Determine the unknown whole number in an addition or subtraction equation when the unknown may be any one of the three or four terms in the equation. Also, 1.3D. Mathematical Process Standards 1.1B, 1.1C, 1.1E, 1.1F.

**Solve & Share**

Complete the subtraction facts. Use the addition facts on the right to help you.

How are the subtraction facts and the completed addition facts the same? What parts are alike?

Digital Resources at PearsonTexas.com

Solve  Learn  Glossary  Check  Tools  Games

$18 - 9 = $ _____

$17 - 9 = $ _____

$16 - 9 = $ _____

$9 + 9 = 18$

$9 + 8 = 17$

$9 + 7 = 16$

For every subtraction fact there is a related addition fact.

$$15$$
$$- 7$$
$$\boxed{?}$$

You can think addition to help you subtract.

$$15$$
$$- 7$$
$$\boxed{?}$$

$$7$$
$$+ \boxed{?}$$
$$15$$

I add 8 to 7 to make 15.

$$7$$
$$+ \boxed{8}$$
$$15$$

If $7 + 8 = 15$, then $15 - 7 = 8$.

$$15$$
$$- 7$$
$$\boxed{8}$$

## Do You Understand?

**Show Me!** How does the fact $6 + 9 = 15$ help you solve $15 - 6$?

**Guided Practice** Complete the addition fact. Then solve the subtraction fact.

1.
$$9$$
$$+ \boxed{5}$$
$$14$$

$$14$$
$$- 9$$
$$\boxed{5}$$

2.
$$10$$
$$+ \boxed{\phantom{0}}$$
$$20$$

$$20$$
$$- 10$$
$$\boxed{\phantom{0}}$$

3.
$$7$$
$$+ \boxed{\phantom{0}}$$
$$11$$

$$11$$
$$- 7$$
$$\boxed{\phantom{0}}$$

4.
$$8$$
$$+ \boxed{\phantom{0}}$$
$$13$$

$$13$$
$$- 8$$
$$\boxed{\phantom{0}}$$

© Pearson Education, Inc. 1

Name _____

**Independent Practice**    Solve each subtraction fact.

5.   15
    −  8
    ☐

6.   18
    −  9
    ☐

7.   13
    −  9
    ☐

8.   11
    −  2
    ☐

9.   16
    −  7
    ☐

10.   14
    −  8
    ☐

11.   17
    −  7
    ☐

12.   12
    −  4
    ☐

**Extend Your Thinking**  Look at the related facts below. Circle **True** or **False** to show whether or not the facts are correct.

13. If $8 + 8 = 16$,

    then $16 − 8 = 8$.

    True      False

14. If $7 + 6 = 15$,

    then $15 − 7 = 6$.

    True      False

## Problem Solving

Write a related subtraction and addition fact to help you solve each problem.

**15.** Sam had some crayons. He found 6 more. Now Sam has 13 crayons. How many crayons did Sam have before he found more?

_____ + _____ = _____

_____ − _____ = _____

_____ crayons

**16.** Ted has 15 problems to solve. So far, he has solved 7. How many problems does Ted have left to solve?

_____ + _____ = _____

_____ − _____ = _____

_____ problems

**17.** Susan solved a subtraction problem. She used $8 + 6 = 14$ to help her solve it.

Which related subtraction problem did she solve?

○  $16 - 8 = 8$

○  $14 - 6 = 8$

○  $13 - 8 = 5$

○  $8 - 6 = 2$

**18. Extend Your Thinking** Solve $13 - 4$. Use pictures, numbers, or words to show how you solved it.

© Pearson Education, Inc. 1

Name _____

**Another Look** You can use a related addition fact to help you subtract.

8 − 5 = ?

Think: What plus 5 equals 8?
You can use the cubes to add.

If 3 + 5 = 8, then 8 − 5 = 3.

9 − 7 = ?

If __7__ + __2__ = __9__,

then __9__ − __7__ = __2__.

🏠 **HOME CONNECTION**
Your child used addition facts to solve related subtraction problems.

**HOME ACTIVITY** Collect 15 pennies to use as counters. Make a subtraction problem for your child to solve by removing some of the pennies. Have him or her tell you the subtraction sentence. Then have your child say the related addition sentence that helped him or her subtract.

Complete each addition fact.
Then solve each subtraction fact.

1. 16 − 7 = ?

   If 7 + ____ = 16,

   then 16 − 7 = ____ .

2. 14 − 6 = ?

   If 6 + ____ = 14,

   then 14 − 6 = ____ .

3. 17 − 8 = ?

   If 8 + ____ = 17,

   then 17 − 8 = ____ .

4. 13 − 7 = ?

   If 7 + ____ = 13,

   then 13 − 7 = ____ .

Digital Resources at PearsonTexas.com

Write a related subtraction and addition fact to solve each problem.

**5.** Josh has 12 pencils. He gives some of them to his friends. Now he has 7 pencils left. How many pencils did Josh give to his friends?

____ + ____ = ____

____ − ____ = ____

**6.** Amy found some shells at the beach. She gave 6 to her brother. Now she has 10 shells. How many shells did Amy find on the beach?

____ + ____ = ____

____ − ____ = ____

**7.** Which addition fact helps you solve
$12 - 3 = ?$

- ○ $10 + 3 = 13$
- ○ $3 + 6 = 9$
- ○ $2 + 10 = 12$
- ○ $3 + 9 = 12$

**8.** Which addition fact helps you solve
$17 - 7 = ?$

- ○ $6 + 7 = 13$
- ○ $7 + 8 = 15$
- ○ $10 + 7 = 17$
- ○ $10 + 4 = 14$

**9. Extend Your Thinking** Your friend says $4 + 7 = 11$ helps him solve $11 - 3 = ?$. Is your friend correct?

Explain your answer.

© Pearson Education, Inc. 1

**Solve & Share**

Jeff has 12 apples. He gives away 6 apples. How many apples are left? Use words, counters, pictures, or number sentences to explain how many are left.

⭐ TEKS 1.3E Explain strategies used to solve ... subtraction problems up to 20 using spoken words, objects, pictorial models, and number sentences. Also, 1.3B, 1.3D, 1.5D. Mathematical Process Standard 1.1B, 1.1C, 1.1F.

Digital Resources at PearsonTexas.com

| | | | | | |
|---|---|---|---|---|---|
| Solve | Learn | Glossary | Check | Tools | Games |

_____ apples are left.

You can use different ways to solve subtraction facts.

$14 - 6 = ?$

You can think addition to subtract $14 - 6$.

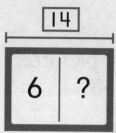

| 14 |
|---|

| 6 | ? |
|---|---|

$6 + \underline{8} = 14$

$14 - 6 = \underline{8}$

You can make a 10 to subtract $12 - 8$.

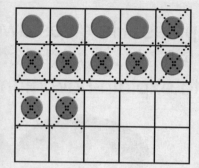

$12 - 8 = \underline{4}$

For other subtraction facts, you can think of a number that is the same, 1 less, or 2 less to subtract 0, 1, or 2.

$10 - 0 = \underline{10}$

$10 - 1 = \underline{9}$

$10 - 2 = \underline{8}$

## Do You Understand?

**Show Me!** What is one strategy you can use to solve $13 - 4 = ?$

☆ **Guided Practice** ☆  Make a 10 to subtract. Draw counters to help you subtract.

1. $15 - 9 = \underline{6}$

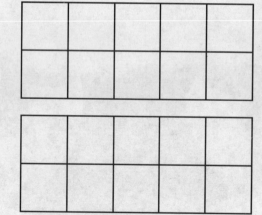

2. $17 - 8 = \underline{\phantom{0}}$

© Pearson Education, Inc. 1

**Independent Practice**  Think addition to subtract. Complete the number sentences.

3. 12 − 5 = ?

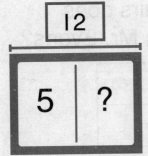

12

| 5 | ? |

5 + ___ = 12

12 − 5 = ___

4. 16 − ? = 6

16

| 6 | ? |

6 + ___ = 16

16 − ___ = 6

5. 5 = 11 − ?

11

| 5 | ? |

11 = 5 + ___

5 = 11 − ___

Write a subtraction sentence to solve the problem. Explain which strategy you used.

6. **Extend Your Thinking**  Maya has a box of 16 crayons. 7 crayons are broken. The rest are **not** broken. How many crayons are **not** broken?

___ − ___ = ___ crayons

_____

_____

_____

_____

Draw counters to help you subtract. Then complete the
subtraction sentence.

**7.** Holly has 11 books. She has 4 more
books than Jack. How many books
does Jack have?

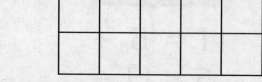

_____ − _____ = _____ books

**8.** Mrs. Potts has 19 chairs in her room.
Mr. Evans has 10 chairs in his room.
How many more chairs does
Mrs. Potts have than Mr. Evans?

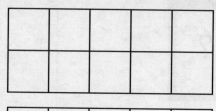

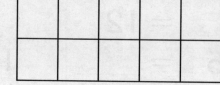

_____ − _____ = _____ chairs

**9.** Which addition fact will help you solve
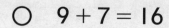 16 − 9 = ?

- ○ 9 + 7 = 16
- ○ 7 + 11 = 18
- ○ 8 + 4 = 12
- ○ 10 + 7 = 17

**10. Extend Your Thinking** What strategy
would you use to solve 14 − 1 = ?

_____

_____

_____

_____

© Pearson Education, Inc. 1

Name _____

**Another Look** There are different ways to solve subtraction sentences. You can use an addition fact to help you solve a related subtraction problem.

$18 - ? = 9$

| 18 |
|---|

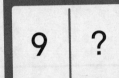

| 9 | ? |
|---|---|

$9 + 9 = 18$

$18 - 9 = 9$

$14 - 6 = ?$

| 14 |
|---|

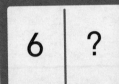

| 6 | ? |
|---|---|

$6 + \underline{8} = 14$

$14 - 6 = \underline{8}$

🏠 **HOME CONNECTION**
Your child explained different strategies to solve subtraction problems.

**HOME ACTIVITY** Write a subtraction sentence. Ask your child to solve the problem. Ask what strategy he or she used to solve the problem, for example, making 10, using a related addition fact, drawing pictures, or another strategy.

 Think addition. Complete the number sentences.

1. $11 - 5 = ?$

| 11 |
|---|

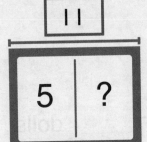

| 5 | ? |
|---|---|

$5 + \underline{\hspace{1cm}} = 11$

$11 - 5 = \underline{\hspace{1cm}}$

2. $15 - ? = 6$

| 15 |
|---|

| 6 | ? |
|---|---|

$6 + \underline{\hspace{1cm}} = 15$

$15 - \underline{\hspace{1cm}} = 6$

Make a 10 to solve each problem. Draw counters in each ten-frame to help you.

3.

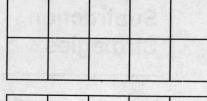

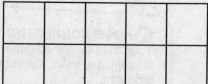

$15 - 7 =$ _____

4.

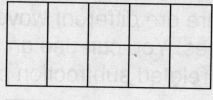

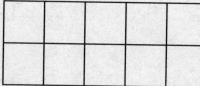

$14 - 9 =$ _____

5. Ben has 10 baseballs. Andy has 2 less than Ben. How many baseballs does Andy have?

Which subtraction fact would you use to solve the problem?

○ $10 - 0 = 10$

○ $10 - 2 = 8$

○ $10 - 1 = 9$

○ $10 - 3 = 7$

6. **Extend Your Thinking** Use pictures, numbers, or words to solve the problem.

Beth found 13 dolls in her room. 2 of the dolls have curly hair. How many dolls do **not** have curly hair?

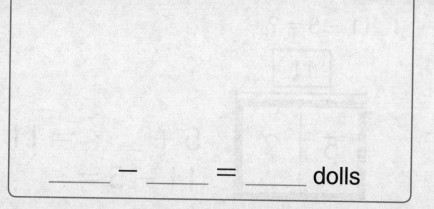

_____ − _____ = _____ dolls

Name _____

**Solve & Share**

Write a related subtraction fact for $6 + 8 = 14$. Create a story problem for the fact. Then draw a picture or use counters to solve the problem.

**TEKS 1.1G** Display, explain, and justify mathematical ideas and arguments ... .
**TEKS 1.3F** Generate and solve problem situations ... involving addition or subtraction of numbers within 20. Also, 1.3B, 1.3D, 1.5D. **Mathematical Process Standards** 1.1A, 1.1B, 1.1C, 1.1D.

_____

_____

_____

Digital Resources at PearsonTexas.com

Solve   Learn   Glossary   Check   Tools   Games

_____ − _____ = _____

## Analyze

Create a story for the number sentence below.

$5 + 7 = 12$

The + tells me to write an addition story.

## Plan

I can use objects to model the addition. Then I will write a story.

My story will be about adding bugs.

## Solve and Justify

Lee sees 5 bugs.
Then 7 more bugs
fly into her garden.
How many bugs
does Lee see in all?
12 bugs in all.

I created a story about joining objects.

## Evaluate

I will ask a friend to write a number sentence for my story.

$5 + 7 = 12$

---

## Do You Understand?

**Show Me!** How would you act out $5 + 9 = ?$

---

☆ **Guided Practice** ☆   Use counters or draw a picture to model each number sentence. Then fill in the blanks.

1. $18 - 9 = 9$

Carlos has ___18___ dog treats.

Tom has ___9___ dog treats.

How many more treats than Tom does Carlos have? ___9___

---

2. $7 + 8 = 15$

Rosi has ____ paintings. She paints ____ more.
How many paintings does she have in all? ____

© Pearson Education, Inc. 1

Name _____

Use counters to model each number sentence.
Then write a story or draw a picture to match.

3. $8 - 4 = 4$

4. $12 - 4 = 8$

**Extend Your Thinking** Complete the number sentence.
Then write a story problem to match.

5. $7 +$ _____ $=$ _____

Draw a picture to
show your work.

6. Ann buys ____ apples. Her family eats ____ apples. How many apples does Ann have left?

____ ◯ ____ = ____

____ apples

7. Judy has some hats. ____ of the hats are purple. 8 of the hats are yellow. How many hats does Judy have in all?

____ ◯ ____ = ____

____ hats

8. Mike bakes some muffins. His friends eat 9 muffins. There are 7 left over.

Which number sentence matches the story?

7 + 9 = 16          9 + 7 = 16
   ◯                    ◯

16 − 9 = 7          15 − 8 = 7
   ◯                    ◯

9. **Extend Your Thinking** There are 4 orange fish in a bowl. There are 7 blue fish in the same bowl. How many fish are in the bowl?

$$4 + 7 = 13$$

Does the number sentence match the story? Tell why or why not. If not, write the correct number sentence.

_____

_____

_____

© Pearson Education, Inc. 1

Name _____

**Another Look** You can use counters to solve a number sentence. Then you can write a number story to match.

$$12 - 5 = 7$$

Cindy picks 12 lemons from a tree. She gives 5 to her aunt. Now Cindy has 7 lemons.

$$9 + 5 = \underline{14}$$

Sarah picks ___9___ flowers.

Then she picks ___5___ more.

Sarah picks ___14___ flowers in all.

⌂ **HOME CONNECTION**
Your child used counters to solve number sentences. Then he or she wrote a number story for the number sentence.

**HOME ACTIVITY** Collect some small objects to use as counters. Write a number sentence for your child. Have him or her use the counters to solve the number sentence and then tell you a number story for the sentence. Repeat using several different number sentences.

Use counters to model each number sentence. Then write a story to match.

1. $14 - 8 = \underline{\phantom{000}}$

_____

_____

_____

2. $8 + 8 = \underline{\phantom{000}}$

_____

_____

_____

Write an addition or subtraction sentence to match each picture.

3.

_____ ◯ _____ = _____

4.

_____ ◯ _____ = _____

Find the missing number for each problem.

5. Algebra ⭐

$12 - 6 = \,?$

| 4 | 5 | 6 | 7 |
|---|---|---|---|
| ◯ | ◯ | ◯ | ◯ |

6. Algebra ⭐

$11 = 4 + \,?$

| 6 | 7 | 8 | 9 |
|---|---|---|---|
| ◯ | ◯ | ◯ | ◯ |

7. Algebra ⭐

$\,? - 9 = 9$

| 18 | 17 | 16 | 15 |
|----|----|----|----|
| ◯ | ◯ | ◯ | ◯ |

8. **Extend Your Thinking** Write a number sentence. Then write a story problem to match. Draw counters or pictures to check your work.

_____

_____

_____

_____ _____ = _____ ◯ _____

Name _____

You can **use a model** to solve addition and subtraction problems.

1. Cross out the model that does **not** match the problem.

   5 students are running.
   6 more students join them.
   How many students are there in all?

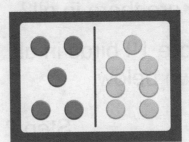 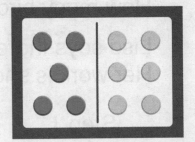

2. Write an addition or a subtraction sentence for the problem in Exercise 1.

   _____ ◯ _____ = _____

3. Explain how you knew to add or subtract using objects, pictures, or words.

4. Some adults are running in the park. Some adults leave and go home. Now there are 7 adults running in the park. Write a subtraction sentence to match the story.

   _____ − _____ = _____

   Tell which strategy you used to solve the problem using objects, pictures, or words.

## What's Wrong?

**1.** 7 birds are at the bird bath. 8 birds fly to join them.
How many birds are there in all?

Lisa says there are 14 birds in all.
Her work is shown below.

Step 1

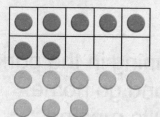

Step 2

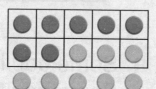

Step 3

$7 + 3 = 10$

$10 + 4 = 14$

So, $7 + 8 = 14$.

Circle the step that has an error. Then explain Lisa's error using objects,
pictures, or words.

**2.** Correct Lisa's work in Exercise 1.

**3.** How many birds are there in all?

_____ birds

Set A

**Reteaching**

A doubles-plus-1 fact is a
doubles fact and 1 more.

$$8 \atop {+7 \over ?}$$

$$8 \atop {+7 \over \boxed{15}}$$

7 + 7 = 14.
14 and 1 more is 15.

Add the doubles. Then use the
doubles to help you add 1 more.

1.
$$5 \atop {+5 \over \square}$$
$$6 \atop {+5 \over \square}$$

2.
$$8 \atop {+8 \over \square}$$
$$8 \atop {+9 \over \square}$$

Set B

A doubles-plus-2 fact is a
doubles fact and 2 more.

$$9 \atop {+7 \over ?}$$

$$9 \atop {+7 \over \boxed{16}}$$

7 + 7 = 14.
14 and 2 more is 16.

Add the doubles. Then use the
doubles to help you add 2 more.

3.
$$5 \atop {+5 \over \square}$$
$$7 \atop {+5 \over \square}$$

4.
$$6 \atop {+6 \over \square}$$
$$8 \atop {+6 \over \square}$$

You can make 10 to add.

$$8$$
$$+6$$
$$?$$

$$10 \quad so \quad 8$$
$$+4 \qquad +6$$
$$\boxed{14} \qquad \boxed{14}$$

Find the sum. Draw counters in the ten-frame to help you.

5.
$$7$$
$$+8$$
$$?$$

$$10 \quad so \quad 7$$
$$+5 \qquad +8$$
$$\boxed{\phantom{0}} \qquad \boxed{\phantom{0}}$$

You can choose different ways to add.

 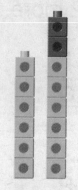 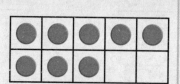

Doubles     Near Doubles     Make 10

Find each sum. Circle the strategy that you used.

6.
$$8$$
$$+4$$
$$\boxed{\phantom{0}}$$

Doubles

Near Doubles

Make 10

My Way

7.
$$7$$
$$+8$$
$$\boxed{\phantom{0}}$$

Doubles

Near Doubles

Make 10

My Way

Name _____

## Set E

You can make a 10 to subtract.

$15 - 6 = ?$

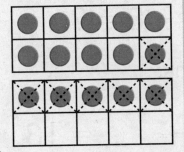

First subtract 5 from 15 to get to 10.

$15 - 5 = 10$

Then take away 1 more to get to 6.

$15 - 6 = \underline{9}$

Make a 10 to subtract. Then complete the subtraction fact.

8. $16 - 7 = \underline{\hspace{1cm}}$

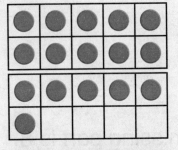

9. $13 - 6 = \underline{\hspace{1cm}}$

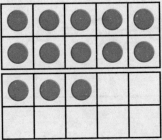

## Set F

You can write a fact family to match the model.

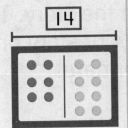

$14 = 6 + 8$

$\underline{14} = \underline{8} + \underline{6}$

$6 = 14 - 8$

$\underline{8} = \underline{14} - \underline{6}$

Write a fact family to match the model.

10. $\underline{\hspace{1cm}} + \underline{\hspace{1cm}} = \underline{\hspace{1cm}}$

$\underline{\hspace{1cm}} + \underline{\hspace{1cm}} = \underline{\hspace{1cm}}$

$\underline{\hspace{1cm}} - \underline{\hspace{1cm}} = \underline{\hspace{1cm}}$

$\underline{\hspace{1cm}} - \underline{\hspace{1cm}} = \underline{\hspace{1cm}}$

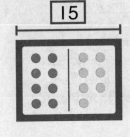

You can use addition to help you subtract.

$15 - 7 = ?$

Think:

$7 + \underline{8} = 15$

The missing part is 8.

So, $15 - 7 = 8.$

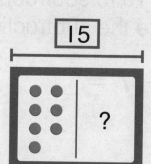
15

Think addition to subtract.
Then complete the number sentences.

11. $13 - 8 = ?$

Think:

$8 + \underline{\phantom{0}} = 13$

So, $13 - 8 = \underline{\phantom{0}}.$

13

You can write and solve your own addition and subtraction stories.

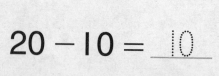
Tom washes 20 dogs. Mary washes 10 dogs. How many more dogs does Tom wash than Mary?

You can act out my story with counters and draw a picture to solve it.

Write a math story for each problem on another piece of paper. Use objects to act out the story. Then draw a picture to show your story on your paper. Write your answer here.

12. $9 + 4 = \underline{\phantom{0}}$

13. $18 - 9 = \underline{\phantom{0}}$

$20 - 10 = \underline{10}$

© Pearson Education, Inc. 1

1. Frank has 7 paper airplanes.
He makes 9 more.
How many paper airplanes does
Frank make in all?

- ○ 18
- ○ 17
- ○ 16
- ○ 15

2. Mark has 7 red marbles.
He has 8 blue marbles.
How many marbles does
Mark have in all?

- ○ 14
- ○ 15
- ○ 16
- ○ 17

3. Which fact family matches the picture?

$8 + 0 = 8$
$0 + 8 = 8$
$8 - 0 = 8$
$8 - 8 = 0$
○

$5 + 9 = 14$
$9 + 5 = 14$
$14 - 5 = 9$
$14 - 9 = 5$
○

$5 + 8 = 13$
$8 + 5 = 13$
$13 - 5 = 8$
$13 - 8 = 5$
○

$8 + 9 = 17$
$9 + 8 = 17$
$17 - 9 = 8$
$17 - 8 = 9$
○

**4.** Which related subtraction fact can be solved using $7 + 8 = 15$?

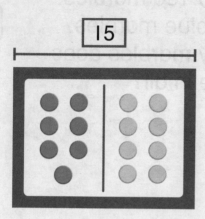

15

- ○ $15 - 8 = 7$
- ○ $14 - 7 = 7$
- ○ $8 - 7 = 1$
- ○ $8 - 8 = 0$

**5.** There are 13 birds in a tree.
Then 6 birds fly away.
How many birds are still in the tree?

Make a 10 to solve.

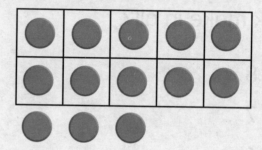

- ○ 4
- ○ 5
- ○ 6
- ○ 7

**6.** Gloria has 7 yellow pencils. She has 9 red pencils. Which strategy would **not** help you find how many pencils she has in all?

- ○ Doubles Plus 1
- ○ Make 10
- ○ Doubles Plus 2
- ○ My Way

7. Nina bakes 14 corn muffins.
She gives away 8 corn muffins.
There are 6 left over.

Which number sentence
matches the story?

○ $15 - 8 = 7$

○ $7 + 8 = 15$

○ $14 - 8 = 6$

○ $8 + 6 = 14$

8. Which related addition fact
can help you solve the
subtraction fact?

$$16 - 7 = ?$$

○ $7 + 7 = 14$

○ $7 + 8 = 15$

○ $6 + 7 = 13$

○ $9 + 7 = 16$

9. Sandy makes 9 bracelets and gives 3 of them away.
How many bracelets does Sandy have left?
Then Sandy made 4 more bracelets.
How many bracelets does she have now?

Which pair of number sentences match the story?

$9 + 3 = 12$
$12 + 4 = 16$
○

$9 - 3 = 6$
$6 + 4 = 10$
○

$9 - 3 = 6$
$10 - 4 = 6$
○

$9 + 3 = 12$
$12 - 4 = 8$
○

**10.** Ming has 5 books.
She buys 8 more books.
How many books does
she have in all?

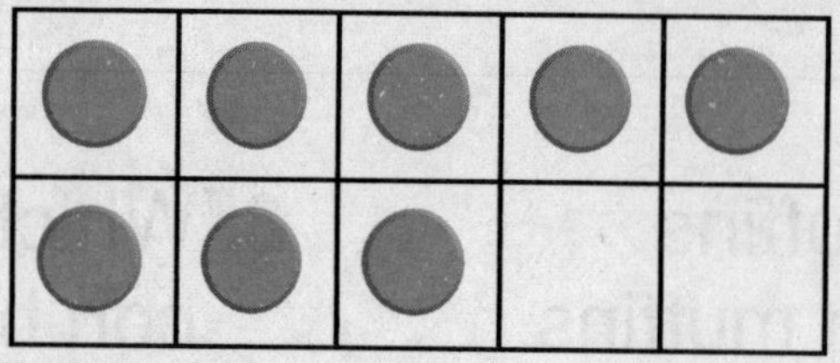

Make a 10 to solve.

11 books      13 books      15 books      17 books
○          ○          ○          ○

**11.** A box has 16 skateboard parts. Maria used some of the parts.
Now there are 8 parts left. Write a subtraction sentence to show
how many parts Maria used.

_____ − _____ = _____

**12.** Write an addition or subtraction story using the numbers 9, 10, and 19.

Then use objects, pictures, or words to solve your problem.

© Pearson Education, Inc. 1

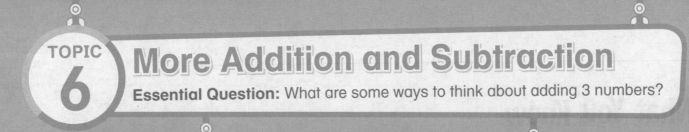

# TOPIC 6
# More Addition and Subtraction

**Essential Question:** What are some ways to think about adding 3 numbers?

Coal is a rock that is useful in many ways.

One way coal can be used is to make heat.

Wow! Let's do this project and learn more.

**Math and Science Project:** Many Uses of Rocks

**Find Out** Talk to friends and relatives about ways coal can be used. Ask how they use, or have used, coal.

**Journal: Make a Book** Show what you found out. In your book, also:

- Draw a picture to show one way to use coal.

- Make up and solve addition and subtraction problems about coal.

Name _____

# Review What You Know

## Vocabulary

**1.** Circle the number that is the **sum** in the number sentence.

$$17 = 9 + 8$$

**2.** Circle the word that tells which strategy can be used to add the numbers.

$$7 + 8 = ?$$

**doubles**

**near doubles**

**fact family**

**3.** Circle the word that tells what part is missing.

$$7 + \underline{?} = 17$$

**sum**

**equals**

**addend**

## Find the Sum

**4.** Margie found 7 rocks. Kara found 6 rocks. How many rocks did they find in all?

_____ rocks

**5.** Tom has 6 toy cars. Jane has some toy cars. They have 11 toy cars in all. How many toy cars does Jane have?

_____ toy cars

## Subtraction Facts

**6.** Find the missing number to solve this subtraction fact.

$$\underline{\hspace{1cm}} = 15 - 5$$

© Pearson Education, Inc. 1

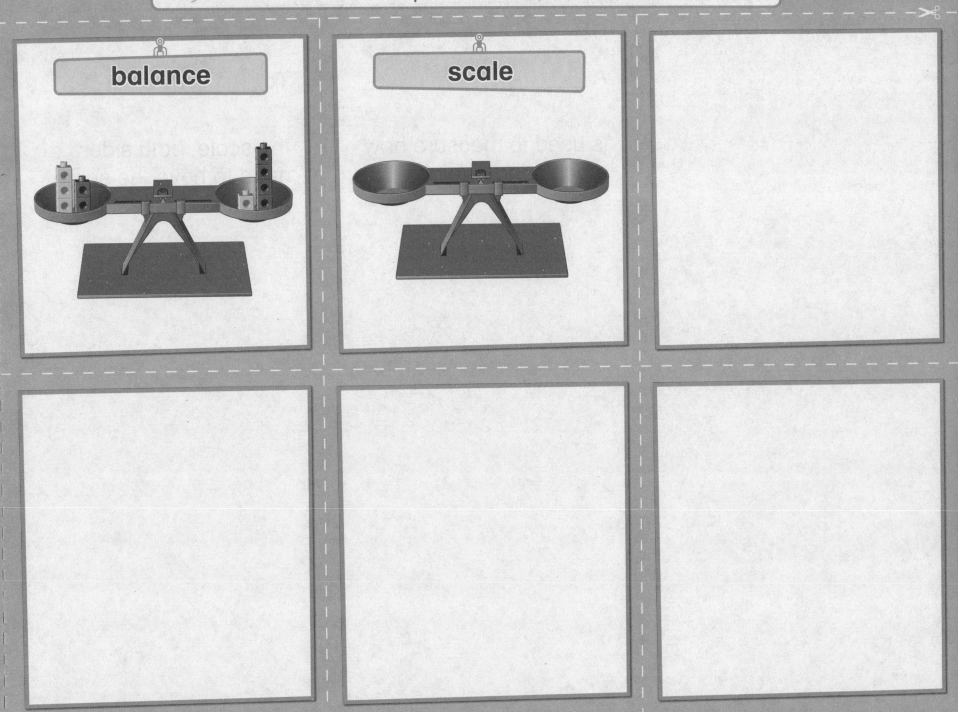

balance

scale

# My Word Cards

Use what you know to complete the sentences.
Extend learning by writing your own sentence using each word.

A _____

is used to measure how much things weigh.

To _____

the scale, both sides need to have the same number of cubes.

© Pearson Education, Inc. 1

Name ____________________

Solve & Share

How can you use addition to find the number of books in all 3 stacks?

Write 2 different number sentences to show how many books in all.

# Lesson 6-1
## Adding Three Numbers

TEKS 1.5G Apply properties of operations to add and subtract two or three numbers. Also, 1.3C, 1.3D. **Mathematical Process Standards** 1.1B, 1.1F.

Digital Resources at PearsonTexas.com

Solve Learn Glossary Check Tools Games

____ + ____ + ____ = ____

____ + ____ + ____ = ____

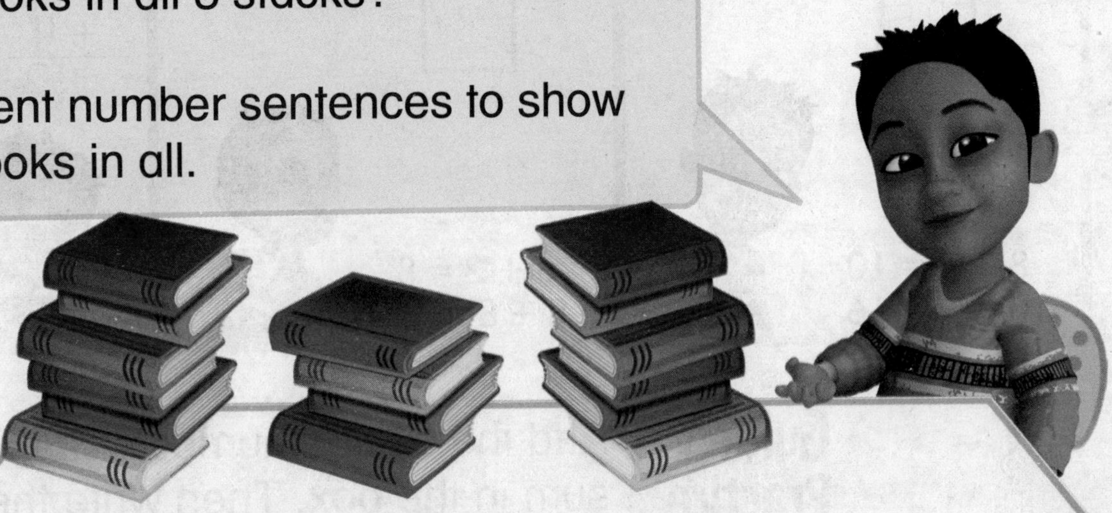

| You can add 3 numbers. | You can make 10. | You can make a double. | You can add any 2 numbers first. |
|---|---|---|---|

**You can add 3 numbers.**

$$8 + 6 + 2$$

Pick 2 numbers to add first.

**You can make 10.**

$$\text{⑧} + 6 + \text{②} = \underline{16}$$

10

$$8 + 2 = 10$$
$$10 + 6 = 16$$

**You can make a double.**

$$8 + \text{⑥} + \text{②} = \underline{16}$$

8

$$6 + 2 = 8$$
$$8 + 8 = 16$$

**You can add any 2 numbers first.**

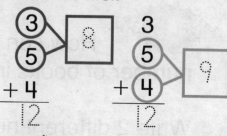

$$\begin{array}{r} ③ \\ ⑤ \\ + ④ \\ \hline 12 \end{array} \quad 8$$

$$\begin{array}{r} 3 \\ ⑤ \\ + ④ \\ \hline 12 \end{array} \quad 9$$

The sums are the same.

---

## Do You Understand?

**Show Me!** Why can you pick any 2 numbers to add first when you add 3 numbers?

☆ **Guided Practice** ☆ Add the circled numbers first. Write their sum in the box. Then write the sum of all 3 numbers.

**1.**

$$\text{②} + \text{⑨} + 1 = \underline{12}$$

11

$$2 + \text{⑨} + \text{①} = \underline{12}$$

10

**2.**

$$\text{⑥} + \text{③} + 2 = \underline{\quad}$$

$$6 + \text{③} + \text{②} = \underline{\quad}$$

---

Name _____

## ☆ Independent ☆
## ☆ Practice

Circle 2 numbers to add first. Write their sum in the box at the right. Then write the sum of all 3 numbers.

3.
```
    6
    6
  + 1
  ┌─┐
  └─┘
```
☐

4.
```
    3
    7
  + 8
  ┌─┐
  └─┘
```
☐

5.
```
    2
    8
  + 3
  ┌─┐
  └─┘
```
☐

6.
```
    7
    3
  + 3
  ┌─┐
  └─┘
```
☐

7.
```
    2
    2
  + 8
  ┌─┐
  └─┘
```
☐

8.
```
    5
    0
  + 9
  ┌─┐
  └─┘
```
☐

9. **Extend Your Thinking** Find the missing numbers.
The numbers on each branch add up to 15.

10. Maya put 5 books on a shelf and 3 books on another shelf. Then she put 4 books on the last shelf. How many books did Maya put on all the shelves?

____ + ____ + ____ = ____

____ books

11. Ellen saved 3 dimes on Monday. She saved 3 more dimes on Tuesday. She also saved some dimes on Friday. Ellen saved 12 dimes in all. How many dimes did she save on Friday?

____ + ____ + ____ = ____

____ dimes

12. Ken bought 4 pencils, 6 markers, and 7 pens. He wants to know how many items he bought in all. He added 4 + 6 first. What should Ken add next?

- ○ 4 + 6
- ○ 4 + 13
- ○ 6 + 7
- ○ 10 + 7

13. **Extend Your Thinking** Explain how to add 7 + 2 + 3. Use pictures, numbers, or words.

© Pearson Education, Inc. 1

**Topic 6** | Lesson 1

Name _____

**Another Look** When you add 3 numbers, look for facts you know. Then add the third number.

⑥
④
+ 3
[13]

$6 + 4 = 10$

$10 + 3 = 13$

I can add the numbers in a different order.

The sum is the same.

⑥
4
+ ③
[13]

$3 + 6 = \underline{9}$

$9 + 4 = \underline{13}$

🏠 HOME CONNECTION
Your child learned how to add 3 numbers in any order.

HOME ACTIVITY Tell your child 3 numbers that have a sum less than or equal to 20. Have him or her add the 3 numbers to find the sum. Ask your child to think aloud as he or she adds the first 2 numbers, and then the third number to that sum. Repeat with several sets of numbers.

Find each sum. Add the circled numbers first. Then add the third number.

1.
⑤
2
+ ⑤
[ ]

$5 + 5 = \underline{\phantom{..}}$

$\underline{\phantom{..}} + 2 = \underline{\phantom{..}}$

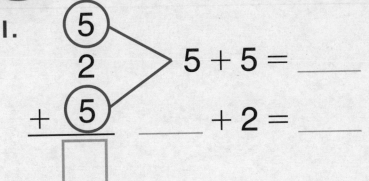

5
②
+ ⑤
[ ]

$2 + 5 = \underline{\phantom{..}}$

$\underline{\phantom{..}} + 5 = \underline{\phantom{..}}$

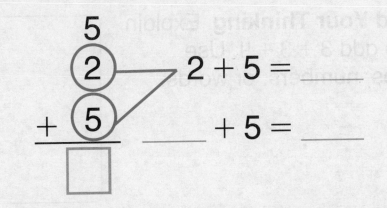

Add the numbers shown. Circle the numbers you add first.

2.

```
  □
  □
  □
+ □
─────
  □  turtles
```

3.

```
  □
  □
  □
+ □
─────
  □  fish
```

4. ⭐ Lucy brought 4 bats, 4 gloves, and 7 baseballs to the game. She wants to know how many items she brought in all. She added 4 + 4 first. What should Lucy add next?

- ○ 8 + 4
- ○ 8 + 6
- ○ 8 + 7
- ○ 8 + 8

5. ⭐ Matt bought pieces to make a model car. He bought 1 block of wood, 4 tires, and 2 cans of paint. If Matt added 1 + 2 first, what should Matt add next?

- ○ 3 + 4
- ○ 6 + 1
- ○ 5 + 2
- ○ 7 + 4

6. **Extend Your Thinking** Explain how to add 3 + 3 + 4. Use pictures, numbers, or words.

© Pearson Education, Inc. 1

Name ____________________________________________

**Solve & Share**

I have oranges, Alex has pears, and Jada has apples. How many pieces of fruit do we have in all?

Write 2 different addition sentences to solve the problem.

# Lesson 6-2
## Word Problems with Three Addends

**TEKS 1.5G** Apply properties of operations to add and subtract two or three numbers. Also, 1.3, 1.3D, 1.3F, 1.5D, 1.5F. **Mathematical Process Standards** 1.1A, 1.1B, 1.1C, 1.1F.

**Digital Resources at PearsonTexas.com**

Solve | Learn | Glossary | Check | Tools | Games

_____ + _____ + _____ = _____

_____ + _____ + _____ = _____

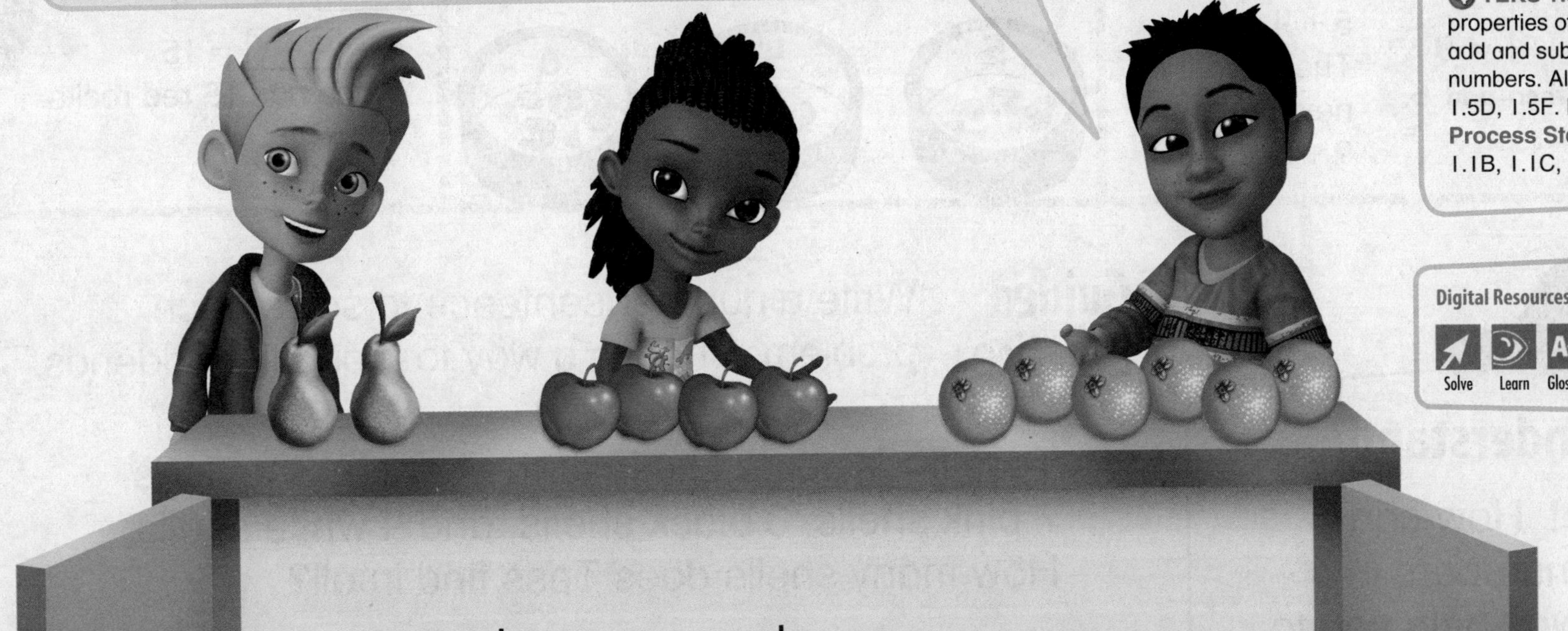

Vince collects red rocks.
He separates them into 3 baskets. How many red rocks does he have in all?

 5  4  6

5 + 4 = 9 and then add 6.

5 + 4 = 9
Then add the next number.
9 + 6 = 15

5 + 4 + 6 = ?
I can add 4 + 6 to make 10 and then add 5.

4 + 6 = 10
Then add the other number.
10 + 5 = 15

 5  4  6

I can group the numbers either way. The sum is the same.

5 + 4 + 6 = 15
5 + 4 + 6 = 15
Vince has 15 red rocks.

## Do You Understand?

**Show Me!** How can grouping numbers in a different way help you to solve a problem?

☆ **Guided Practice** ☆ Write a number sentence to solve each problem. Choose a way to group the addends.

1. Tess finds some shells at the beach. She finds 7 pink shells, 3 black shells, and 4 white shells. How many shells does Tess find in all?

   _7_ + _3_ + _4_ = _14_ shells

2. Tom sees some birds. He sees 4 red birds, 2 blue birds, and 6 black birds. How many birds does Tom see in all?

   ____ + ____ + ____ = ____ birds

☆ **Independent**
☆ **Practice**

Write a number sentence to solve each problem. Choose a way to group the addends.

**3.** Pat has cards of his favorite athletes. He has 8 baseball cards, 2 football cards, and 3 basketball cards. How many cards does Pat have in all?

____ + ____ + ____ = ____

____ cards

**4.** Bob plants seeds. He plants 2 brown seeds, 6 white seeds, and 8 black seeds. How many seeds does Bob plant in all?

____ + ____ + ____ = ____

____ seeds

Write the missing numbers for each problem.

**5. Algebra** $16 = 7 + \underline{\phantom{0}} + 6$

**6. Algebra** $11 = 2 + 2 + \underline{\phantom{0}}$

**7. Extend Your Thinking** Julio finds 3 ladybugs and some ants. Then he finds 5 beetles. Julio finds 14 bugs in all. How many ants did Julio find?

____ = ____ + ____ + ____

Julio finds ____ ants.

**8. Extend Your Thinking** Rosa picks 12 flowers from her garden. She picks some purple flowers. Then she picks 4 pink flowers and 3 yellow flowers. How many purple flowers did Rosa pick?

____ = ____ + ____ + ____

She picks ____ purple flowers.

# Problem Solving  Solve each problem below.

**9.** Dan threw 3 beanbags at the target. The numbers on the target show the score for each beanbag.

Write an addition sentence to find Dan's score.

____ + ____ + ____ = ____

**10.** Gail threw 3 beanbags at the target. The numbers on the target show the score for each beanbag.

Write an addition sentence to find Gail's score.

____ + ____ + ____ = ____

---

**11.** Joy threw 3 beanbags at the target. She scored 15 points. Which picture shows her target?

○

○

○

○

**12. Extend Your Thinking** Write a story problem about toys. The story should match the addition sentence below.

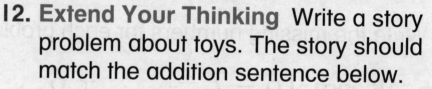

4 + 1 + 9 = 14

_____

_____

_____

_____

© Pearson Education, Inc. 1

Name _____

**Another Look** You can group addends in different ways.
Then you can write a number sentence.

 +  +

Sally has some fruit.
She has 3 apples,
5 bananas, and 5 pears.
How many pieces of fruit
does she have in all?

First, add the apples and bananas.

$$3 + 5 = \underline{8}$$

Then add the pears.

$$\underline{8} + \underline{5} = \underline{13}$$

Sally has __13__ pieces of fruit in all.

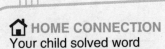 **HOME CONNECTION**
Your child solved word problems with 3 addends.

**HOME ACTIVITY** Gather several different kinds of small objects, such as buttons, paper clips, and pennies. Tell your child a word problem using the objects. Have your child add the objects together, telling you how many in all.

 Find each sum. Choose the best way to group the addends.

1.

____ + ____ + ____ = ____

2.

____ + ____ + ____ = ____

3. Todd is playing with some blocks. He has 3 red blocks, 3 yellow blocks, and 6 blue blocks. How many blocks is Todd playing with in all?

____ + ____ + ____ = ____

____ blocks

4. Emma has 7 green beads, some purple beads, and 6 yellow beads. She has 17 beads in all. How many purple beads does Emma have?

____ + ____ + ____ = ____

____ purple beads

5. Risa plants 3 different kinds of vegetable seeds. In all, she plants 16 seeds. Which group of addends could show the number of seeds for each kind of vegetable Risa planted?

○ 4 + 5 + 7        ○ 6 + 6 + 6

○ 4 + 6 + 7        ○ 5 + 9 + 5

6. Kami walks 3 dogs. She walks a total of 13 blocks. Which number sentence could show how far Kami walked each dog?

○ 4 + 4 + 7 = 15      ○ 6 + 6 + 6 = 18

○ 4 + 3 + 6 = 13      ○ 5 + 6 + 5 = 16

7. **Extend Your Thinking** Write a story problem about the lunchroom that matches the number sentence.

5 + 8 + 2 = 15

_____

_____

8. **Extend Your Thinking** The numbers in each row and column equal the sum in the gray box. Find the missing numbers.

|   | 6 | 8 | 16 |
|---|---|---|----|
| 7 | 4 |   | 12 |
| 3 | 5 | 9 |    |
| 12 |   | 18 | ✕ |

© Pearson Education, Inc. 1

Name ____________________

**Solve & Share** Pick 2 numbers to be the 2 parts in a fact family. Then write all of the facts in the family. You can use counters to help you.

___ + ___ = ___ | ___ − ___ = ___

___ + ___ = ___ | ___ − ___ = ___

# Lesson 6-3
## Make Your Own Fact Families

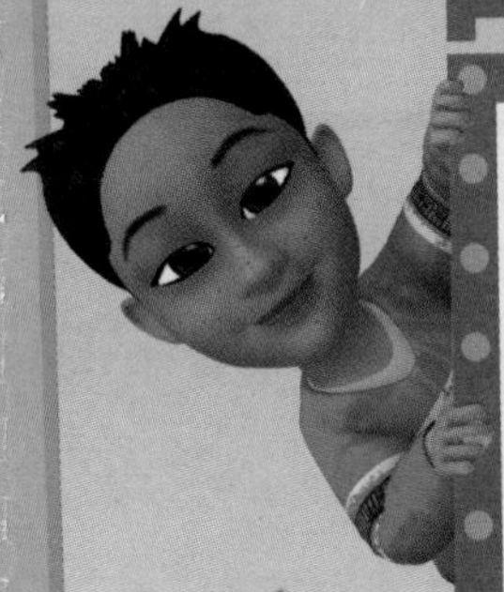

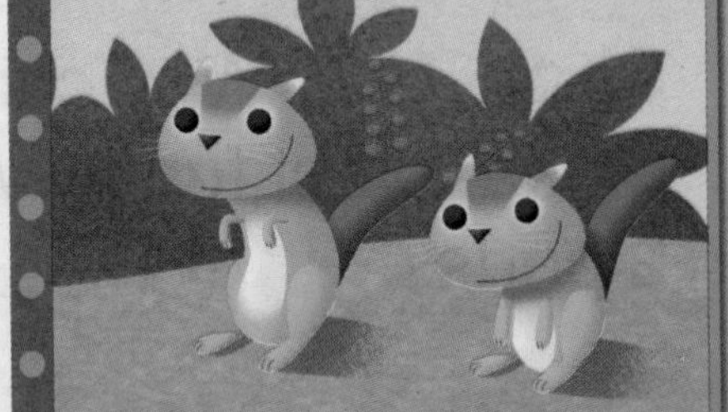

**TEKS 1.5F** Determine the unknown whole number in an addition or subtraction equation when the unknown may be any one of the three or four terms in the equation. Also, 1.5G. **Mathematical Process Standards** 1.1B, 1.1E, 1.1F.

**Digital Resources at PearsonTexas.com**

Solve Learn Glossary Check Tools Games

You can make your own fact family.

Add the parts.
Then write 2 addition facts.

These 2 number cards are like 2 parts.

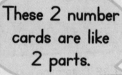

**3**   **9**

$3 + 9 = 12$
$9 + 3 = 12$

Use the addition facts to write 2 related subtraction facts.

$12 - 9 = 3$
$12 - 3 = 9$

If $3 + 9 = 12$, then $12 - 9 = 3$ and $12 - 3 = 9$!

You know a fact family for the numbers 3 and 9.

$3 + 9 = 12$
$9 + 3 = 12$

$12 - 9 = 3$
$12 - 3 = 9$

## Do You Understand?

**Show Me!** Why can you make a fact family with 2 parts?

☆ **Guided Practice** ☆  Choose 2 number cards. Write one number in each box. Then write the fact family for the 2 parts.

1.     6   7

$6 + 7 = 13$

___ + ___ = ___

$13 - 7 = 6$

___ − ___ = ___

2.

___ + ___ = ___

___ + ___ = ___

___ − ___ = ___

___ − ___ = ___

**Topic 6** | Lesson 3

Name _____

☆
**Independent**
☆ **Practice**

Write a fact family for the number in each box.

3.

**15**

_____ + _____ = 15

_____ + _____ = _____

15 − _____ = _____

_____ − _____ = _____

4.

**11**

_____ + _____ = 11

_____ + _____ = _____

11 − _____ = _____

_____ − _____ = _____

5.

**14**

_____ + _____ = 14

_____ + _____ = _____

14 − _____ = _____

_____ − _____ = _____

6.

**17**

_____ + _____ = 17

_____ + _____ = 17

17 − _____ = _____

17 − _____ = _____

7. **Extend Your Thinking** Dawn says that the facts on the paper belong to the same fact family. Is she correct? Explain.

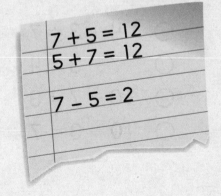

7 + 5 = 12
5 + 7 = 12

7 − 5 = 2

_____

_____

_____

## Problem Solving  Solve each problem below.

**8.** Maria and Ted pick 2 numbers.
Maria picks 9. Ted picks 5.
What fact family can Maria and
Ted make with the parts 9 and 5?

| **9** | **5** |

_____ + _____ = _____

_____ + _____ = _____

_____ − _____ = _____

_____ − _____ = _____

**9.** Mark and Andy pick 2 numbers.
Mark picks 6. Andy picks 7.
What fact family can Mark and
Andy make with the parts 6 and 7?

| **6** | **7** |

_____ + _____ = _____

_____ + _____ = _____

_____ − _____ = _____

_____ − _____ = _____

**10.** Which fact is missing
from the fact family?

○  $4 + 3 = 7$

○  $7 − 3 = 4$

○  $10 − 7 = 3$

○  $10 − 3 = 7$

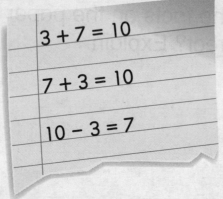

3 + 7 = 10

7 + 3 = 10

10 − 3 = 7

**11. Extend Your Thinking** Write a fact
family that has only 1 addition fact
and 1 subtraction fact.

_____ + _____ = _____

_____ − _____ = _____

Name _____

**Another Look** Use the parts 2 and 5.

Write the addition facts for these 2 parts.

$$2 + 5 = 7$$
$$5 + 2 = 7$$

Now write the subtraction facts for these 2 parts.

$$7 - 2 = 5$$
$$7 - 5 = 2$$

Now make your own fact family with the parts 6 and 4.

$$6 + 4 = 10$$
$$4 + 6 = 10$$

$$10 - 6 = 4$$
$$10 - 4 = 6$$

🏠 **HOME CONNECTION**
Your child learned how to make a fact family.

**HOME ACTIVITY** Play a game with number cards. Have your child choose 2 cards. Using the 2 numbers on those cards, have him or her write 2 addition facts and 2 subtraction facts.

Pick 2 numbers. Write a fact family for your 2 numbers.

1. My 2 numbers are ____ + ____ = ____        ____ – ____ = ____

____ and ____.        ____ + ____ = ____        ____ – ____ = ____

Solve each problem below.

**2.** Jessica and Karl pick 2 numbers. Jessica picks 3. Karl picks 4.

What fact family can Jessica and Karl make with 3 and 4?

_____ + _____ = _____

_____ + _____ = _____

_____ − _____ = _____

_____ − _____ = _____

**3.** Dennis and Janet pick 2 numbers. Dennis picks 2. Janet picks 6.

What fact family can Dennis and Janet make with their numbers?

_____ + _____ = _____

_____ + _____ = _____

_____ − _____ = _____

_____ − _____ = _____

**4.** ⭐ Which fact is missing from the fact family?

○ $11 + 5 = 16$

○ $6 + 11 = 17$

○ $11 - 6 = 5$

○ $6 - 5 = 1$

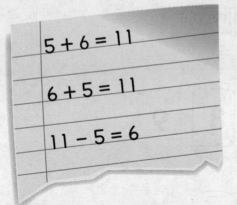

$5 + 6 = 11$

$6 + 5 = 11$

$11 - 5 = 6$

**5. Extend Your Thinking** Make a fact family for a doubles fact. How many facts did you make? Why?

Name _____

**Solve & Share**

How many cubes should you add to the right side of the scale so that both sides have the same amount? Draw that number of cubes.

Complete the number sentence to show how many cubes are on the right side.

★ **TEKS 1.5E** Understand that the equal sign represents a relationship where expressions on each side of the equal sign represent the same value(s). Also, 1.5F. **Mathematical Process Standards** 1.1B, 1.1C, 1.1D, 1.1F.

**Digital Resources at PearsonTexas.com**

Solve   Learn   Glossary   Check   Tools   Games

$$3 + 4 = \underline{\quad} + \underline{\quad}$$

How can you **balance** the **scale**?

Make the number of cubes the same on both sides.

The numbers of cubes on both sides of the scale should be equal.

I need to find the missing number of cubes to balance the scale.

$4 + 7 = 6 + ?$

Find how many more cubes to add to balance the scale.

$4 + 7 = 11$ and $6 + 5 = 11$ so, $4 + 7 = 6 + 5$. Both sides are the same!

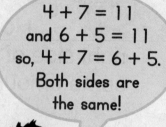

$4 + 7 = 6 + 5$

## Do You Understand?

**Show Me!** How are these 2 number sentences alike?

$$12 - 5 = 7$$
$$14 - 7 = 7$$

☆ **Guided Practice** ☆   Draw or cross out cubes to balance each scale. Then complete the number sentence.

**1.**

$11 - 3 = 10 - \underline{2}$

**2.**

$3 + 4 = 5 + \underline{\phantom{0}}$

Name _____

Draw or cross out cubes to balance each scale.
Then complete the number sentence.

3.

$12 - 5 = 8 - \underline{\quad}$

4.

$6 + 4 = 5 + \underline{\quad}$

Write the missing number for each problem.

5. Algebra  $8 + \underline{\quad} = 9 + 4$

6. Algebra  $12 - \underline{\quad} = 7 - 3$

7. Algebra  $15 - 9 = 12 - \underline{\quad}$

8. Algebra  $7 + 4 = 8 + \underline{\quad}$

Extend Your Thinking  What number is missing? How do you know?

9. $6 + 3 = 9 - \underline{\ ?\ }$

10. $16 - \underline{\ ?\ } = 3 + 4$

_____

_____

_____

The sum and
difference on
each side of the
equal sign should
be the same.

**11.** 1 green cube was removed. How many blue cubes do you need to remove to balance the scale? Complete the number sentence to show the two amounts are equal.

_____ blue cubes

$15 - \underline{\phantom{xx}} = 14 - 1$

**12.** How many cubes should you add to balance the scale? Complete the number sentence to show the two amounts are equal.

Add _____ cubes.

$4 + 5 = 6 + \underline{\phantom{xx}}$

**13.** Which weights will balance the weights on the scale?

○          ○          ○          ○

**14. Extend Your Thinking** Carlos said 11 is the missing number in the problem below. Is he correct? Explain.

$\underline{\phantom{?}} + 9 = 16 + 4$

_____

_____

_____

© Pearson Education, Inc. 1

Name _____

**Another Look** When the number of cubes on each side of the scale are the same, the scale is balanced. How can you balance the scale?

How many cubes are needed to balance the right side?

$8 + 4 = 6 + ?$

There are 12 cubes in all on the left side of the scale.

The scale is balanced by adding

_6_ cubes to the right side.

$8 + 4 = $ _12_

So, $6 + $ _6_ $ = 12.$

🏠 **HOME CONNECTION**
Your child found the missing number to make 2 number sentences equal.

**HOME ACTIVITY** Fold a piece of paper in half. Explain that each half of the paper is like one side of a scale. Gather pennies. Put piles of pennies on each half of the paper. Ask your child if the "scale" is balanced. If not, have him or her add pennies to balance the scale. Invite your child to write number sentences that are equal.

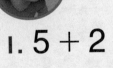 Find the missing number to balance each scale. Then complete each number sentence.

1. $5 + 2$ 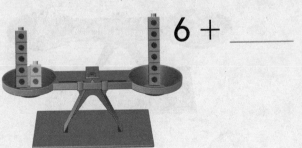 $6 + $ ___

$5 + 2 = 6 + $ ___

2. $11 - 5$ 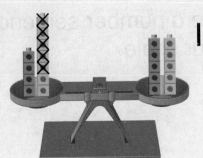 $10 - $ ___

$11 - 5 = 10 - $ ___

Balance each scale below. Circle **Add** or **Subtract**. Then write the number.

3.

**Add**

_____ cubes.

**Subtract**

4.
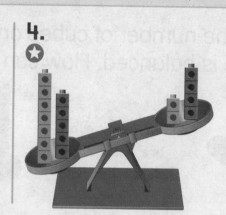
**Add**

_____ cubes.

**Subtract**

Find the missing number to complete each number sentence.

5. **Algebra**

$14 - 4 = 11 - \underline{?}$

4     3     2     1
○     ○     ○     ○

6. **Algebra**

$13 - 6 = 12 - \underline{?}$

4     5     6     7
○     ○     ○     ○

7. **Algebra**

$9 + \underline{?} = 7 + 7$

3     4     5     8
○     ○     ○     ○

8. **Extend Your Thinking** Draw cubes on each side to balance the scale.

Then write a number sentence to match your scale.

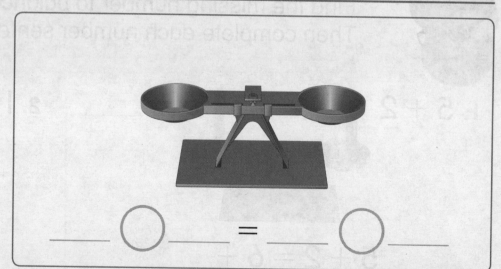

_____ ○ _____ = _____ ○ _____

© Pearson Education, Inc. 1

**Topic 6** | Lesson 4

Name _____

**Solve & Share**

The cubes on the scale show how many shells Rosi and James found. How many more shells does James need to find to have the same number as Rosi? Draw that number of cubes.

Then write a number sentence to show that Rosi's number of shells equals James's number of shells.

⭐ **TEKS 1.1D** Communicate mathematical ideas, reasoning, and their implications using multiple representations. Also, 1.3B, 1.5E, 1.5F. **Mathematical Process Standards 1.1B, 1.1C, 1.1G.**

**Digital Resources at PearsonTexas.com**

Solve   Learn   Glossary   Check   Tools   Games

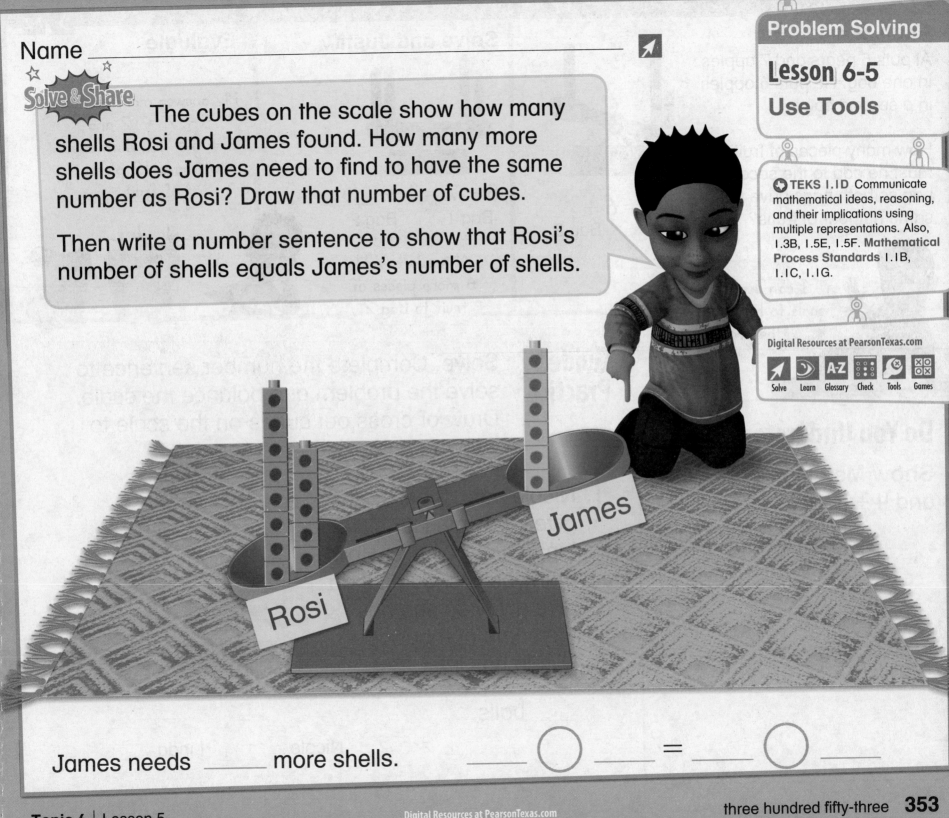

James

Rosi

James needs _____ more shells.       _____ ◯ _____ = _____ ◯ _____

## Analyze and Plan

Al puts 5 pears and 7 apples in one bag. He puts 6 apples in a second bag.

How many pieces of fruit must he add to the second bag so both bags have the same number of fruits?

$$5 + 7 = 6 + \underline{\phantom{0}}$$
Bag 1       Bag 2

*I can use a balance scale to help think about the problem.*

## Solve and Justify

$$5 + 7 = 6 + \underline{6}$$
Bag 1       Bag 2

*Al needs to add 6 more pieces of fruit to Bag 2.*

## Evaluate

*My answer makes sense. 5 + 7 = 12 and 6 + 6 = 12. Both bags will have 12 pieces of fruit.*

## Do You Understand?

**Show Me!** How are $3 + 5$ and $4 + 4$ equal?

## ☆ Guided Practice ☆

Solve. Complete the number sentence to solve the problem and balance the scale. Draw or cross out cubes on the scale to show that the sides are equal.

1. Nicole has 10 balls. She gives 3 away. Her sister Linda has 12 balls. How many balls should Linda give away so she has the same number as Nicole has left?

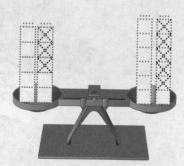

_____ balls

$\underline{\phantom{00}} - \underline{\phantom{00}} = \underline{\phantom{00}} - \underline{\phantom{00}}$
    Nicole       Linda

© Pearson Education, Inc. 1

Name _____

Complete the number sentences to solve each problem and balance the scale. Draw or cross out cubes on the scale to show that the sides are equal.

2. Ella saved 3 dimes on Monday and 8 dimes on Tuesday. Chris saved 9 dimes on Monday. How many dimes does he need to save on Tuesday to save the same number as Ella?

_____ dimes

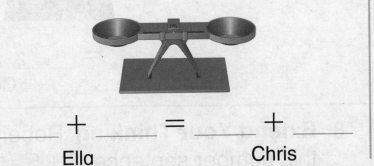

_____ + _____ = _____ + _____
Ella                 Chris

3. Kim has 15 flowers. She sells 6 of them. Felix has 13 flowers. How many does he need to sell to have the same number as Kim?

_____ flowers

_____ − _____ = _____ − _____
Kim                 Felix

4. **Extend Your Thinking** Look at the scale. Rick says that the scale is balanced. Is he correct? Explain.

_____

_____

_____

Write a number sentence to solve each problem and balance the scale. Draw or cross out cubes to show that the sides are equal.

**5.** Lori has 3 goldfish. She buys 9 more. Vic has 5 goldfish. How many goldfish must Vic buy to have the same number of fish as Lori?

_____ goldfish

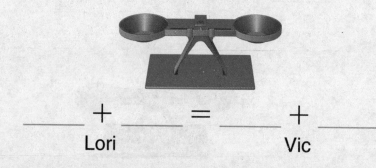

_____ + _____ = _____ + _____
   Lori                 Vic

**6.** Brad has 10 tomatoes. He gives 3 tomatoes away. Gary has 15 tomatoes. How many tomatoes does Gary need to give away to have the same number of tomatoes as Brad?

_____ tomatoes

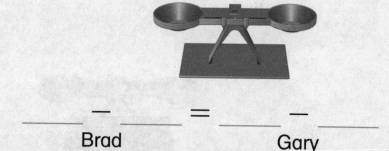

_____ − _____ = _____ − _____
   Brad                 Gary

**7.** Which number makes both sides equal?

$$7 + 9 = 8 + \underline{\ ?\ }$$

○ 7

○ 8

○ 9

○ 10

**8. Extend Your Thinking** Robert wrote this number sentence: $8 + 5 = 10 + 4$. Did Robert use the equal sign correctly? Why or why not?

_____
_____
_____

© Pearson Education, Inc. 1

Name _____

**Another Look** You can use a scale to show how both sides of a number sentence are equal.

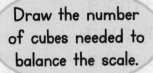

Draw the number of cubes needed to balance the scale.

🏠 **HOME CONNECTION** Your child solved story problems by completing number sentences. Your child visualized the equal sides of the number sentences using a scale.

**HOME ACTIVITY** Tell your child a story problem and ask him or her to write the number sentence that matches. Be sure your story problem involves writing equal sides of equations. Encourage him or her to draw cubes if necessary. Continue with more story problems.

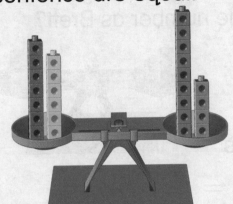

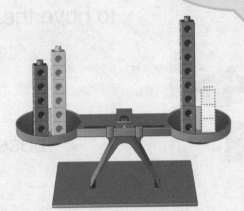

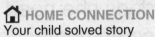

$$7 + 6 = 9 + 4$$

$$\underline{\phantom{0}} + 6 = 8 + \underline{\phantom{0}}$$

Complete the number sentence to solve the problem and balance the scale. Draw or cross out cubes on each side to show that the sides are equal.

1. Karen blows up 14 balloons. She popped 8 of them. Nadia blows up 12 balloons. How many should she pop so she has the same number as Karen?

_____ balloons

$$\underline{\phantom{0}} - \underline{\phantom{0}} = \underline{\phantom{0}} - \underline{\phantom{0}}$$

Solve each problem below. Draw or cross out cubes to help you.

**2.** David has 5 fish. He buys 4 more. Sarah has 2 fish. How many more does she need to buy to have the same number as David?

_____ fish

_____ + _____ = _____ + _____

**3.** Brett has 5 baseballs. He gives 3 of them away. Josie has 6 baseballs. How many does she need to give away to have the same number as Brett?

_____ baseballs

_____ − _____ = _____ − _____

**4.** Which number sentence matches the scale?

○ $3 + 8 = 5 + 6$

○ $11 + 3 = 8 + 6$

○ $11 - 3 = 8 - 0$

○ $5 + 8 = 6 + 7$

**5. Extend Your Thinking** Complete the number sentence. Draw cubes on the scale. Explain how you know it is correct.

$7 + 8 =$ _____ ○ _____

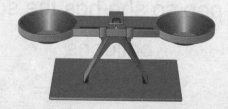

_____

_____

_____

Name _____

Think about how you can **use a model** when you solve these problems.

**1.** Cross out the model that does **not** match the problem.

3 friends score 13 points in a game.
Larry scores 6 points.
Yoshi scores some points.
Nia scores 3 points.

How many points did Yoshi score?

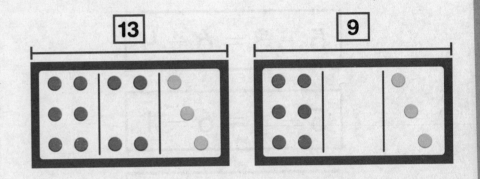

**2.** Write a number sentence to show the scores.

____ + ____ + ____ = ____

**3.** Write a different number sentence to show the scores.

____ + ____ + ____ = ____

**4.** Tell how you could use subtraction to solve the problem.

_____

_____

_____

_____

## Are They Equal?

1. Draw an X on any number sentences that are **not** correct. Try to find out by adding or subtracting in your head.

$$5 - 3 = 6 - 4$$

$$5 - 1 = 6 - 1$$

$$2 + 7 = 7 + 3$$

$$6 + 4 = 5 + 5$$

$$10 - 4 = 3 + 3$$

$$9 - 2 = 9 + 2$$

## What's Wrong?

2. Draw or cross out counters to make each model right.

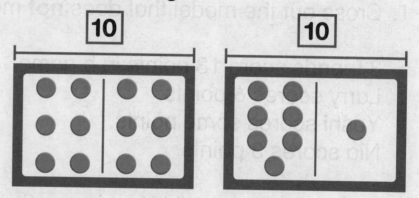

## Complete It!

3. Fill in the missing numbers.

$$9 \; + \; \boxed{\phantom{0}} \; + \; 3 \; = \; 15$$

$$4 \; + \; \boxed{\phantom{0}} \; + \; 4 \; = \; 12$$

$$\boxed{\phantom{0}} \; + \; 3 \; + \; 2 \; = \; 11$$

$$5 \; + \; 4 \; + \; 1 \; = \; \boxed{\phantom{0}}$$

TOPIC
6

Set A

You can add 3 numbers in any order.

Make a 10. Then add 2.

$(2) + (8) + 2 = \underline{12}$

Make a double. Then add 8.

$(2) + 8 + (2) = \underline{12}$

Find the sum.

1. $5 + 5 + 4 = \underline{\phantom{XX}}$

2. $9 + 5 + 1 = \underline{\phantom{XX}}$

3. $6 + 4 + 4 = \underline{\phantom{XX}}$

4. $3 + 3 + 5 = \underline{\phantom{XX}}$

Set B

Write the missing number.

$4 + 7 = 6 + ?$

Both sides should be equal.

$4 + 7 = 11$

So, $6 + ? = 11$.

The missing number is 5.

$4 + 7 = 6 + \underline{5}$

Find and write the missing number.

5. $10 + 5 = 6 + \underline{\phantom{XX}}$

6. $9 - \underline{\phantom{XX}} = 13 - 10$

7. $14 - \underline{\phantom{XX}} = 13 - 6$

8. $\underline{\phantom{XX}} + 8 = 7 + 5$

Use the parts and the whole to
write the fact family for the model.

$\underline{14} = \underline{6} + \underline{8}$

$\underline{14} = \underline{8} + \underline{6}$

$\underline{6} = \underline{14} - \underline{8}$

$\underline{8} = \underline{14} - \underline{6}$

| 14 |

Write the fact family for
the model.

9. $\underline{\hspace{1cm}} = \underline{\hspace{1cm}} + \underline{\hspace{1cm}}$

$\underline{\hspace{1cm}} = \underline{\hspace{1cm}} + \underline{\hspace{1cm}}$

$\underline{\hspace{1cm}} = \underline{\hspace{1cm}} - \underline{\hspace{1cm}}$

$\underline{\hspace{1cm}} = \underline{\hspace{1cm}} - \underline{\hspace{1cm}}$

| 15 |

There are some trees in the yard.
There are 7 maple trees, 3 oak
trees, and 7 elm trees. How many
trees are there in all?

You can add the 3 numbers in
any order.

$(7) + (3) + 7 = \underline{17}$

$(7) + 3 + (7) = \underline{17}$

Write a number sentence. Choose
the best way to group the addends.

10. There are 14 fish in a pond. There are
4 red fish, 5 orange fish, and some blue
fish. How many blue fish are there?

$\underline{\hspace{1cm}} + \underline{\hspace{1cm}} + \underline{\hspace{1cm}} = \underline{\hspace{1cm}}$

11. There are 6 blue birds, 3 red birds,
and 6 brown birds in a tree. How many
birds are in the tree in all?

$\underline{\hspace{1cm}} + \underline{\hspace{1cm}} + \underline{\hspace{1cm}} = \underline{\hspace{1cm}}$

1. Look at the model. Which fact is missing from this fact family?

$5 + 9 = 14$

$9 + 5 = 14$

$14 - 9 = 5$

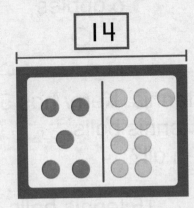

14

$9 - 4 = 5$
○

$9 - 5 = 4$
○

$14 - 5 = 9$
○

$14 - 7 = 7$
○

2. Which number is missing?

$$16 - \underline{\ \ ?\ \ } = 2 + 6$$

10
○

9
○

8
○

7
○

3. Tasha has 2 dogs and 3 cats. She also has 7 goldfish.
Which number sentence tells how many pets Tasha has in all?

$2 + 3 + 7 = 12$
○

$1 + 3 + 9 = 13$
○

$1 + 5 + 9 = 15$
○

$2 + 3 + 10 = 15$
○

**4.** Bill has 10 apples. He uses 8 of them to make muffins. Josh has 6 apples. How many should he use so he has the same number as Bill?

| 4 apples | 5 apples | 6 apples | 7 apples |
|:---:|:---:|:---:|:---:|
| ○ | ○ | ○ | ○ |

**5.** Kerry, Tom, and Nicole want to play tennis. Kerry has 5 tennis balls. Tom has 5 tennis balls. Nicole has 3 tennis balls. How many tennis balls do they have in all?

| 13 tennis balls | 14 tennis balls | 15 tennis balls | 16 tennis balls |
|:---:|:---:|:---:|:---:|
| ○ | ○ | ○ | ○ |

**6.** Which weights will balance the weights on the scale?

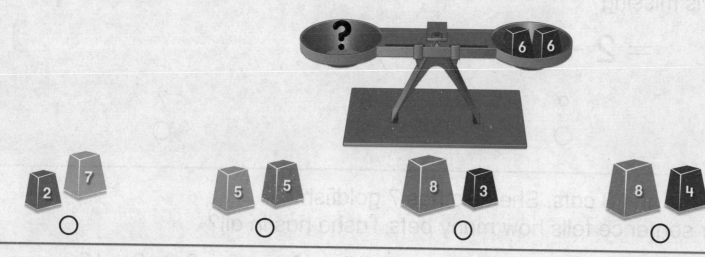

| ○ | ○ | ○ | ○ |
|:---:|:---:|:---:|:---:|

**7.** Write the missing number.

$$15 = 4 + \underline{\phantom{00}} + 8$$

# Counting and Number Patterns to 100

**Essential Question:** What are some patterns you can see on a hundred chart?

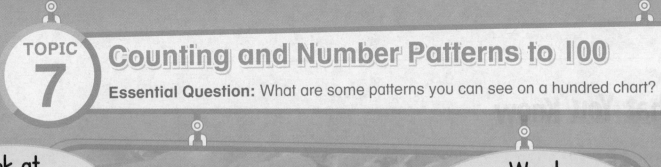

Look at all of the legs.

Animals that are alike usually have the same number of legs.

Wow! Let's do this project and learn more.

## Math and Science Project: How Many Legs?

**Find Out** Talk to friends and relatives about different animals. Ask them about animals with 2 legs and animals with 4 legs.

**Journal: Make a Book** Show what you found out. In your book, also:

- Draw some animals with 2 legs and some with 4 legs.
- Show counting patterns using animals with 2 legs or 4 legs.

Name _____

# Review What You Know

## Vocabulary

**1.** Circle the cubes that will **balance** the scale.

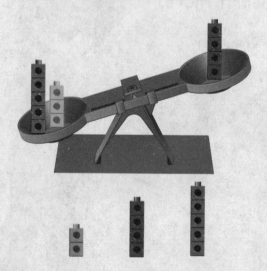

**2.** Circle the number sentence that is a **related fact** for $14 - 8 = 6$.

$$8 - 6 = 2$$

$$8 + 6 = 14$$

**3.** Circle the number that will complete the **fact family**.

$$3 + \underline{\phantom{?}} = 11$$

$$\underline{\phantom{?}} + 3 = 11$$

$$11 - 3 = \underline{\phantom{?}}$$

$$11 - \underline{\phantom{?}} = 3$$

| 8 | 14 | 7 | 5 |

---

## Find the Missing Part

**4.** Write the number that will balance the scale.

$$15 - 8 = \underline{\phantom{xx}} + 1$$

**5.** Write each missing number.

$$5 + 3 + 2 = \underline{\phantom{xx}}$$

$$9 + \underline{\phantom{xx}} + 7 = 17$$

## Related Facts

**6.** Write the related subtraction facts.

$$12 = 5 + 7$$

$$\underline{\phantom{xx}} = \underline{\phantom{xx}} - \underline{\phantom{xx}}$$

$$\underline{\phantom{xx}} = \underline{\phantom{xx}} - \underline{\phantom{xx}}$$

# My Word Cards

Study the words on the front of the card. Complete the activity on the back.

A-Z

## hundred chart

| 1 | 2 | 3 | 4 | 5 | 6 | 7 | 8 | 9 | 10 |
|---|---|---|---|---|---|---|---|---|---|
| 11 | 12 | 13 | 14 | 15 | 16 | 17 | 18 | 19 | 20 |
| 21 | 22 | 23 | 24 | 25 | 26 | 27 | 28 | 29 | 30 |
| 31 | 32 | 33 | 34 | 35 | 36 | 37 | 38 | 39 | 40 |
| 41 | 42 | 43 | 44 | 45 | 46 | 47 | 48 | 49 | 50 |
| 51 | 52 | 53 | 54 | 55 | 56 | 57 | 58 | 59 | 60 |
| 61 | 62 | 63 | 64 | 65 | 66 | 67 | 68 | 69 | 70 |
| 71 | 72 | 73 | 74 | 75 | 76 | 77 | 78 | 79 | 80 |
| 81 | 82 | 83 | 84 | 85 | 86 | 87 | 88 | 89 | 90 |
| 91 | 92 | 93 | 94 | 95 | 96 | 97 | 98 | 99 | 100 |

## ones digit

The **ones digit** in 43 is 3.

ones digit

## tens digit

The **tens digit** in 25 is 2.

tens digit

## column

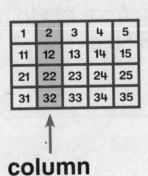

column

## row

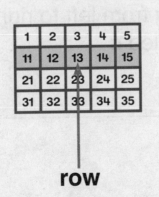

row

## skip count

5, 10, 15, 20, 25

# My Word Cards

Use what you know to complete the sentences.
Extend learning by writing your own sentence using each word.

A number that tells how many tens is called a

_____

_____.

A number that tells how many ones is called a

_____

_____.

A _____

_____

shows all of the numbers from 1 to 100.

When you _____

_____

_____,

you use a pattern to count.

A straight line of numbers or objects going from left to right is called a

_____.

A straight line of numbers or objects going from top to bottom is called a

_____.

© Pearson Education, Inc. 1

**Solve & Share**

Pick a number from the hundred chart. Write the number in the box. How can you find the number that is 1 more? Write that number. Then write the next 3 numbers.

⭐ TEKS 1.5A Recite numbers forward and backward from any given number between 1 and 120. Mathematical Process Standards 1.1B, 1.1C, 1.1F.

Digital Resources at PearsonTexas.com

Solve  Learn  Glossary  Check  Tools  Games

| 1 | 2 | 3 | 4 | 5 | 6 | 7 | 8 | 9 | 10 |
|---|---|---|---|---|---|---|---|---|----|
| 11 | 12 | 13 | 14 | 15 | 16 | 17 | 18 | 19 | 20 |
| 21 | 22 | 23 | 24 | 25 | 26 | 27 | 28 | 29 | 30 |
| 31 | 32 | 33 | 34 | 35 | 36 | 37 | 38 | 39 | 40 |
| 41 | 42 | 43 | 44 | 45 | 46 | 47 | 48 | 49 | 50 |
| 51 | 52 | 53 | 54 | 55 | 56 | 57 | 58 | 59 | 60 |
| 61 | 62 | 63 | 64 | 65 | 66 | 67 | 68 | 69 | 70 |
| 71 | 72 | 73 | 74 | 75 | 76 | 77 | 78 | 79 | 80 |
| 81 | 82 | 83 | 84 | 85 | 86 | 87 | 88 | 89 | 90 |
| 91 | 92 | 93 | 94 | 95 | 96 | 97 | 98 | 99 | 100 |

_____ , _____ , _____ , _____

You can find patterns when you count forward on a **hundred chart**.

| 1 | 2 | 3 | 4 | 5 | 6 | 7 | 8 | 9 | 10 |
|---|---|---|---|---|---|---|---|---|----|
| 11 | 12 | 13 | 14 | 15 | 16 | 17 | 18 | 19 | 20 |
| 21 | 22 | 23 | 24 | 25 | 26 | 27 | 28 | 29 | 30 |
| 31 | 32 | 33 | 34 | 35 | 36 | 37 | 38 | 39 | 40 |
| 41 | 42 | 43 | 44 | 45 | 46 | 47 | 48 | 49 | 50 |
| 51 | 52 | 53 | 54 | 55 | 56 | 57 | 58 | 59 | 60 |
| 61 | 62 | 63 | 64 | 65 | 66 | 67 | 68 | 69 | 70 |
| 71 | 72 | 73 | 74 | 75 | 76 | 77 | 78 | 79 | 80 |
| 81 | 82 | 83 | 84 | 85 | 86 | 87 | 88 | 89 | 90 |
| 91 | 92 | 93 | 94 | 95 | 96 | 97 | 98 | 99 | 100 |

The tens digit in each number in this row is 1.

| 1 | 2 | 3 | 4 |
|---|---|---|---|
| 11 | 12 | 13 | 14 |
| 21 | 22 | 23 | 24 |
| 31 | 32 | 33 | 34 |

The ones digit in each number in this column is 4.

| 1 | 2 | 3 | 4 |
|---|---|---|---|
| 11 | 12 | 13 | 14 |
| 21 | 22 | 23 | 24 |
| 31 | 32 | 33 | 34 |

The last number in each row ends in 0.

| 1 | 2 | 3 | 4 | 5 | 6 | 7 | 8 | 9 | 10 |
|---|---|---|---|---|---|---|---|---|----|
| 11 | 12 | 13 | 14 | 15 | 16 | 17 | 18 | 19 | 20 |
| 21 | 22 | 23 | 24 | 25 | 26 | 27 | 28 | 29 | 30 |

Look at 29 and 30. The tens digit changes from 2 to 3. The ones digit changes from 9 to 0.

# Do You Understand?

**Show Me!** How do the numbers in a hundred chart change?

## Guided Practice

Count by 1s. Write the numbers. Use a hundred chart to help you.

1. 14, __15__, __16__, __17__, __18__

2. 21, _____, _____, _____, _____

3. 33, _____, _____, _____, _____

4. _____, _____, 49, _____, _____

**Topic 7** | Lesson 1

Name _____

Count by 1s. Write the numbers. Use a hundred chart to help you.

5. _____, 65, _____, _____, _____

6. _____, 52, _____, _____, _____

7. _____, _____, 83, _____, _____

8. 40, _____, _____, _____, _____

9. _____, _____, _____, _____, 79

10. _____, _____, _____, _____, 98

11. _____, _____, _____, _____, 91

12. _____, _____, _____, 12, _____

**Extend Your Thinking** Look at each part of the hundred chart.
Write the missing numbers.

13.

| 34 |    | 36 |    |
|----|----|----|----|
|    | 45 |    | 47 |

14.

|    | 48 |    |    |
|----|----|----|----|
| 57 |    |    | 60 |

# Problem Solving  Use the hundred chart to solve each problem.

| 1 | 2 | 3 | 4 | 5 | 6 | 7 | 8 | 9 | 10 |
|---|---|---|---|---|---|---|---|---|---|
| 11 | 12 | 13 | 14 | 15 | 16 | 17 | 18 | 19 | 20 |
| 21 | 22 | 23 | 24 | 25 | 26 | 27 | 28 | 29 | 30 |
| 31 | 32 | 33 | 34 | 35 | 36 | 37 | 38 | 39 | 40 |
| 41 | 42 | 43 | 44 | 45 | 46 | 47 | 48 | 49 | 50 |
| 51 | 52 | 53 | 54 | 55 | 56 | 57 | 58 | 59 | 60 |
| 61 | 62 | 63 | 64 | 65 | 66 | 67 | 68 | 69 | 70 |
| 71 | 72 | 73 | 74 | 75 | 76 | 77 | 78 | 79 | 80 |
| 81 | 82 | 83 | 84 | 85 | 86 | 87 | 88 | 89 | 90 |
| 91 | 92 | 93 | 94 | 95 | 96 | 97 | 98 | 99 | 100 |

**15.** Billy counts forward to 50. What are the next 5 numbers he counts? Write the numbers.

50, _____, _____, _____, _____, _____

**16.** Sasha counts forward to 65. What are the next 5 numbers she counts? Write the numbers.

65, _____, _____, _____, _____, _____

**17.** Gina counts pennies. She counts to 79. What number will Gina say next?

○  70

○  78

○  80

○  90

**18. Extend Your Thinking** Pick a number from the hundred chart. Count forward. Write the numbers.

_____, _____, _____, _____, _____,

_____, _____, _____, _____, _____

Name _____

 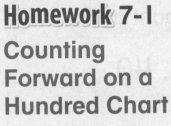

**Another Look** You can use a hundred chart to count forward.

| 1 | 2 | 3 | 4 | 5 | 6 | 7 | 8 | 9 | 10 |
|---|---|---|---|---|---|---|---|---|---|
| 11 | 12 | 13 | 14 | 15 | 16 | 17 | 18 | 19 | 20 |
| 21 | 22 | 23 | 24 | 25 | 26 | 27 | 28 | 29 | 30 |
| 31 | 32 | 33 | 34 | 35 | 36 | 37 | 38 | 39 | 40 |
| 41 | 42 | 43 | 44 | 45 | 46 | 47 | 48 | 49 | 50 |
| 51 | 52 | 53 | 54 | 55 | 56 | 57 | 58 | 59 | 60 |
| 61 | 62 | 63 | 64 | 65 | 66 | 67 | 68 | 69 | 70 |
| 71 | 72 | 73 | 74 | 75 | 76 | 77 | 78 | 79 | 80 |
| 81 | 82 | 83 | 84 | 85 | 86 | 87 | 88 | 89 | 90 |
| 91 | 92 | 93 | 94 | 95 | 96 | 97 | 98 | 99 | 100 |

What number comes after 33? __34__

What number comes after 34? __35__

What number comes after 35? __36__

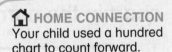

**HOME CONNECTION**
Your child used a hundred chart to count forward.

**HOME ACTIVITY** Write the following series of numbers: 15, 16, _____, 18, _____, 20. Have your child write the missing numbers. If necessary, create a portion of a hundred chart on a sheet of paper for your child to use while filling in the missing numbers. Repeat with other numbers.

33, __34__, __35__, __36__

Count by 1s. Write the numbers. Use a hundred chart to help you.

1. 71, _____, _____, _____, _____

2. _____, _____, _____, 61, _____

3. _____, _____, _____, _____, 51

4. _____, _____, 65, _____, _____

Count by 1s. Write the numbers. Use a hundred chart to help you.

5. 40, _____, _____, _____, _____

6. _____, _____, _____, 32, _____

7. Which shows part of the hundred chart in the correct order?
- ○ | 31 | 33 | 35 | 37 | 39 |
- ○ | 94 | 93 | 92 | 91 | 90 |
- ○ | 45 | 55 | 65 | 75 | 85 |
- ○ | 66 | 67 | 68 | 69 | 70 |

8. Which shows part of the hundred chart in the correct order?
- ○ | 22 | 25 | 28 | 31 | 34 |
- ○ | 82 | 83 | 84 | 85 | 86 |
- ○ | 16 | 26 | 36 | 46 | 56 |
- ○ | 30 | 35 | 40 | 45 | 50 |

**Extend Your Thinking** Write the missing numbers. Look for patterns.

9.
|    |    |    | 85 |    |    | 88 |    | 90 |
|----|----|----|----|----|----|----|----|----|
| 92 |    | 94 |    | 96 |    |    | 99 |    |

10.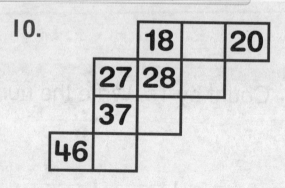

© Pearson Education, Inc. 1

Name _____

☆ ☆
**Solve & Share**

Pick a number from the hundred chart. Write the number in the box. What number is next when you count back? Write that number. Then write the next 3 numbers when you count back.

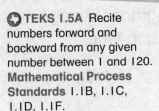

**TEKS I.5A** Recite numbers forward and backward from any given number between 1 and 120. **Mathematical Process Standards** I.IB, I.IC, I.ID, I.IF.

| 1 | 2 | 3 | 4 | 5 | 6 | 7 | 8 | 9 | 10 |
|---|---|---|---|---|---|---|---|---|---|
| 11 | 12 | 13 | 14 | 15 | 16 | 17 | 18 | 19 | 20 |
| 21 | 22 | 23 | 24 | 25 | 26 | 27 | 28 | 29 | 30 |
| 31 | 32 | 33 | 34 | 35 | 36 | 37 | 38 | 39 | 40 |
| 41 | 42 | 43 | 44 | 45 | 46 | 47 | 48 | 49 | 50 |
| 51 | 52 | 53 | 54 | 55 | 56 | 57 | 58 | 59 | 60 |
| 61 | 62 | 63 | 64 | 65 | 66 | 67 | 68 | 69 | 70 |
| 71 | 72 | 73 | 74 | 75 | 76 | 77 | 78 | 79 | 80 |
| 81 | 82 | 83 | 84 | 85 | 86 | 87 | 88 | 89 | 90 |
| 91 | 92 | 93 | 94 | 95 | 96 | 97 | 98 | 99 | 100 |

Digital Resources at PearsonTexas.com

Solve  Learn  Glossary  Check  Tools  Games

_____ , _____ , _____ , _____

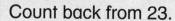

Use a hundred chart to count back. Count back from 19.

| 1 | 2 | 3 | 4 | 5 | 6 | 7 | 8 | 9 | 10 |
|---|---|---|---|---|---|---|---|---|---|
| 11 | 12 | 13 | 14 | 15 | 16 | 17 | 18 | 19 | 20 |
| 21 | 22 | 23 | 24 | 25 | 26 | 27 | 28 | 29 | 30 |

The ones digit in each number changes each time.

19, 18, 17, 16

Count back from 23.

| 1 | 2 | 3 | 4 | 5 | 6 | 7 | 8 | 9 | 10 |
|---|---|---|---|---|---|---|---|---|---|
| 11 | 12 | 13 | 14 | 15 | 16 | 17 | 18 | 19 | 20 |
| 21 | 22 | 23 | 24 | 25 | 26 | 27 | 28 | 29 | 30 |

The ones digit in each number changes here, too.

23, 22, 21, 20

Count back from 30.

| 1 | 2 | 3 | 4 | 5 | 6 | 7 | 8 | 9 | 10 |
|---|---|---|---|---|---|---|---|---|---|
| 11 | 12 | 13 | 14 | 15 | 16 | 17 | 18 | 19 | 20 |
| 21 | 22 | 23 | 24 | 25 | 26 | 27 | 28 | 29 | 30 |

Both digits change when you count back from a number that ends in 0.

30, 29, 28, 27

## Do You Understand?

**Show Me!** How do the numbers change when you count back by 1s from 40?

☆ **Guided Practice** ☆   Count back by 1s. Write the numbers. Use a hundred chart to help you.

1. 19, __18__, __17__, __16__, __15__, __14__

2. 27, ____, ____, ____, ____, ____

3. 39, ____, ____, ____, ____, ____

4. ____, ____, 11, ____, ____, ____

**Topic 7** | Lesson 2

Name _____

# Independent
## ☆ Practice

Count back by 1s. Write the numbers. Use a hundred chart to help you.

5. 66, ____, ____, ____, ____, ____

6. 55, ____, ____, ____, ____

7. ____, ____, ____, ____, ____, 82

8. ____, 39, ____, ____, ____

9. 75, ____, 73, ____, ____, ____

10. 98, ____, ____, ____, ____

11. 90, ____, ____, 87, ____, 85

12. ____, 9, ____, ____, ____

**Extend Your Thinking** Look at each part of a hundred chart.
Write the missing numbers.

13.

| | | 69 | |
|---|---|---|---|
| | 78 | | 80 |

14.

| 33 | | | 36 |
|---|---|---|---|
| | | 45 | |

**15.** Bob spills water on his hundred chart.
Some numbers rub off.
Use the hundred chart to help
Bob fill in the missing numbers.

| | 47 | | | 50 |
|---|---|---|---|---|
| | | | 59 | 60 |

**16.** Helen and Karl count back from 56.
Helen says the next number is 55.
Karl says the next number is 57.

Circle the name of the student who
is correct.

**Helen**        **Karl**

**17.** Thomas counts back from 47.
He stops counting at 42.
Write the numbers he counted.

47, _____, _____, _____, _____, 42

**18.** Judy counts back from 84.
Write the next 5 numbers she counts.

84, _____, _____, _____, _____, _____

**19.** Meg looks at a hundred chart.
⭐ She counts back from 37.
Which number does Meg say next?

38        36        35        37
○         ○         ○         ○

**20. Extend Your Thinking** Pick a number.
Count back. Write the numbers.

_____, _____, _____, _____, _____,

_____, _____, _____, _____, _____

© Pearson Education, Inc. 1

Name _____

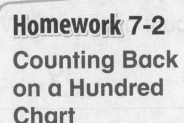

**Another Look** You can use a hundred chart to count back by 1s.

Start at 29. Count back to 23. Write the missing numbers.

| 11 | 12 | 13 | 14 | 15 | 16 | 17 | 18 | 19 | 20 |
|----|----|----|----|----|----|----|----|----|----|
| 21 | 22 | 23 | 24 | 25 | 26 | 27 | 28 | (29) | 30 |
| 31 | 32 | 33 | 34 | 35 | 36 | 37 | 38 | 39 | 40 |

29, 28, _27_, _26_, 25, _24_, 23

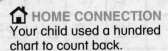

**HOME CONNECTION**
Your child used a hundred chart to count back.

**HOME ACTIVITY** Write the following series of numbers: 38, 37, ___, 35, ___, 33. Have your child write the missing numbers. If necessary, create a portion of a hundred chart on a sheet of paper for your child to use while filling in the missing numbers. Repeat with other number series.

Count back by 1s. Write the numbers.

| 61 | 62 | 63 | 64 | 65 | 66 | 67 | 68 | 69 | 70 |
|----|----|----|----|----|----|----|----|----|----|
| 71 | 72 | 73 | 74 | 75 | 76 | 77 | 78 | 79 | 80 |
| 81 | 82 | 83 | 84 | 85 | 86 | 87 | 88 | 89 | 90 |

1. 81, _____, _____, _____, _____

2. 72, _____, _____, _____, _____

Count back by 1s. Write the numbers. Use the hundred chart to help you.

3. _____, 39, _____, _____, _____

4. 76, _____, _____, _____, _____

| 1 | 2 | 3 | 4 | 5 | 6 | 7 | 8 | 9 | 10 |
|---|---|---|---|---|---|---|---|---|----|
| 11 | 12 | 13 | 14 | 15 | 16 | 17 | 18 | 19 | 20 |
| 21 | 22 | 23 | 24 | 25 | 26 | 27 | 28 | 29 | 30 |
| 31 | 32 | 33 | 34 | 35 | 36 | 37 | 38 | 39 | 40 |
| 41 | 42 | 43 | 44 | 45 | 46 | 47 | 48 | 49 | 50 |
| 51 | 52 | 53 | 54 | 55 | 56 | 57 | 58 | 59 | 60 |
| 61 | 62 | 63 | 64 | 65 | 66 | 67 | 68 | 69 | 70 |
| 71 | 72 | 73 | 74 | 75 | 76 | 77 | 78 | 79 | 80 |
| 81 | 82 | 83 | 84 | 85 | 86 | 87 | 88 | 89 | 90 |
| 91 | 92 | 93 | 94 | 95 | 96 | 97 | 98 | 99 | 100 |

5. Lin looks at a hundred chart.
⭐ She counts back from 53.
Which number does Lin say next?

54 ○    52 ○    51 ○    53 ○

6. Max looks at a hundred chart.
⭐ He counts back from 31.
Which number does Max say next?

32 ○    21 ○    41 ○    30 ○

7. **Extend Your Thinking** Lori counts back from 67. She counts 66, 64, 62, 63, 61. Is Lori correct? Explain.

8. **Extend Your Thinking** Joel counts back from 79. He stops at 65. Cross out the numbers that Joel does **not** count.

77  72  70  82  67  62  80

**Solve & Share**

Count by 10s. Color the numbers you count yellow. What pattern do you see?

Count by 5s. Draw a blue circle around the numbers.
Count by 2s. Draw a red square around the numbers.
Describe the patterns for each.

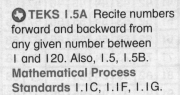

★ TEKS 1.5A Recite numbers forward and backward from any given number between 1 and 120. Also, 1.5, 1.5B. Mathematical Process Standards 1.1C, 1.1F, 1.1G.

| 1 | 2 | 3 | 4 | 5 | 6 | 7 | 8 | 9 | 10 |
|---|---|---|---|---|---|---|---|---|-----|
| 11 | 12 | 13 | 14 | 15 | 16 | 17 | 18 | 19 | 20 |
| 21 | 22 | 23 | 24 | 25 | 26 | 27 | 28 | 29 | 30 |
| 31 | 32 | 33 | 34 | 35 | 36 | 37 | 38 | 39 | 40 |
| 41 | 42 | 43 | 44 | 45 | 46 | 47 | 48 | 49 | 50 |
| 51 | 52 | 53 | 54 | 55 | 56 | 57 | 58 | 59 | 60 |
| 61 | 62 | 63 | 64 | 65 | 66 | 67 | 68 | 69 | 70 |
| 71 | 72 | 73 | 74 | 75 | 76 | 77 | 78 | 79 | 80 |
| 81 | 82 | 83 | 84 | 85 | 86 | 87 | 88 | 89 | 90 |
| 91 | 92 | 93 | 94 | 95 | 96 | 97 | 98 | 99 | 100 |

Digital Resources at PearsonTexas.com

    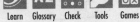

Solve    Learn    Glossary    Check    Tools    Games

Topic 7 | Lesson 3
Digital Resources at PearsonTexas.com
three hundred eighty-one    381

You can **skip count** on a hundred chart to find a pattern.

| 1 | 2 | 3 | 4 | 5 | 6 | 7 | 8 | 9 | 10 |
|---|---|---|---|---|---|---|---|---|---|
| 11 | 12 | 13 | 14 | 15 | 16 | 17 | 18 | 19 | 20 |
| 21 | 22 | 23 | 24 | 25 | 26 | 27 | 28 | 29 | 30 |
| 31 | 32 | 33 | 34 | 35 | 36 | 37 | 38 | 39 | 40 |
| 41 | 42 | 43 | 44 | 45 | 46 | 47 | 48 | 49 | 50 |
| 51 | 52 | 53 | 54 | 55 | 56 | 57 | 58 | 59 | 60 |
| 61 | 62 | 63 | 64 | 65 | 66 | 67 | 68 | 69 | 70 |
| 71 | 72 | 73 | 74 | 75 | 76 | 77 | 78 | 79 | 80 |
| 81 | 82 | 83 | 84 | 85 | 86 | 87 | 88 | 89 | 90 |
| 91 | 92 | 93 | 94 | 95 | 96 | 97 | 98 | 99 | 100 |

Skip count by 10s.

10, 20, 30, 40

Skip count by 5s.

5, 10, 15, 20

Skip count by 2s.

2, 4, 6, 8, 10, 12

## Do You Understand?

**Show Me!** Compare counting by 5s and by 10s. How are the patterns alike? How are the patterns different?

## Guided Practice

Skip count by 5s. Circle the numbers you say.

1.

| 1 | 2 | 3 | 4 | (5) | 6 | 7 | 8 | 9 | (10) |
|---|---|---|---|---|---|---|---|---|---|
| 11 | 12 | 13 | 14 | 15 | 16 | 17 | 18 | 19 | 20 |
| 21 | 22 | 23 | 24 | 25 | 26 | 27 | 28 | 29 | 30 |
| 31 | 32 | 33 | 34 | 35 | 36 | 37 | 38 | 39 | 40 |
| 41 | 42 | 43 | 44 | 45 | 46 | 47 | 48 | 49 | 50 |

© Pearson Education, Inc. I

Name _____

☆ Independent
☆ Practice
Write the numbers to continue each pattern.
Use a hundred chart to help you.

2. Skip count by 10s.

10, 20, 30, _____, _____, _____, _____

3. Skip count by 5s.

5, 10, 15, _____, _____, _____, _____

4. Skip count by 2s.

2, 4, 6, _____, _____, _____, _____, _____

5. **Extend Your Thinking**  Use a blue and green crayon.
Draw the missing part of the pattern.

What pattern do you notice?

_____

_____

three hundred eighty-three  **383**

# Problem Solving — Solve each problem below.

**6.** Anita walks her dog every 2 days to earn money. How many times does Anita walk her dog in 20 days?

Use the chart to skip count.
Write the number.

| 1 | 2 | 3 | 4 | 5 | 6 | 7 | 8 | 9 | 10 |
|---|---|---|---|---|---|---|---|---|----|
| 11 | 12 | 13 | 14 | 15 | 16 | 17 | 18 | 19 | 20 |

_____ times

**7.** Matt starts swimming lessons on Day 5. He goes every 5 days. How many lessons will Matt go to in 30 days?

Use the chart to skip count.
Write the number.

| 1 | 2 | 3 | 4 | 5 | 6 | 7 | 8 | 9 | 10 |
|---|---|---|---|---|---|---|---|---|----|
| 11 | 12 | 13 | 14 | 15 | 16 | 17 | 18 | 19 | 20 |
| 21 | 22 | 23 | 24 | 25 | 26 | 27 | 28 | 29 | 30 |

_____ lessons

**8.** Tim plays soccer on Day 15. He plays soccer every 5 days. Which is the next day Tim will play?

| 1 | 2 | 3 | 4 | 5 | 6 | 7 | 8 | 9 | 10 |
|---|---|---|---|---|---|---|---|---|----|
| 11 | 12 | 13 | 14 | 15 | 16 | 17 | 18 | 19 | 20 |

○ Day 10

○ Day 15

○ Day 20

○ Day 25

**9. Extend Your Thinking** Anna skip counts to 30. She only uses 3 numbers. Did Anna skip count by 2s, 5s, or 10s? Use pictures, numbers, or words to explain.

© Pearson Education, Inc. I

Name _____

**Another Look** You can skip count on a hundred chart. When you skip count by 10s, all the numbers end with a 0. When you skip count by 5s, all the numbers end with either a 5 or a 0.

| 1 | 2 | 3 | 4 | 5 | 6 | 7 | 8 | 9 | 10 |
|---|---|---|---|---|---|---|---|---|---|
| 11 | 12 | 13 | 14 | 15 | 16 | 17 | 18 | 19 | 20 |
| 21 | 22 | 23 | 24 | 25 | 26 | 27 | 28 | 29 | 30 |
| 31 | 32 | 33 | 34 | 35 | 36 | 37 | 38 | 39 | 40 |
| 41 | 42 | 43 | 44 | 45 | 46 | 47 | 48 | 49 | 50 |
| 51 | 52 | 53 | 54 | 55 | 56 | 57 | 58 | 59 | 60 |
| 61 | 62 | 63 | 64 | 65 | 66 | 67 | 68 | 69 | 70 |
| 71 | 72 | 73 | 74 | 75 | 76 | 77 | 78 | 79 | 80 |
| 81 | 82 | 83 | 84 | 85 | 86 | 87 | 88 | 89 | 90 |
| 91 | 92 | 93 | 94 | 95 | 96 | 97 | 98 | 99 | 100 |

What numbers will you say when you skip count by 10s?

10, 20, 30, _40_, _50_, _60_, _70_

What numbers will you say when you skip count by 5s?

5, 10, 15, _20_, _25_, _30_, _35_

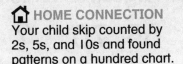

🏠 **HOME CONNECTION**
Your child skip counted by 2s, 5s, and 10s and found patterns on a hundred chart.

**HOME ACTIVITY** Practice orally skip counting by 2s, 5s, and 10s with your child. If necessary, have him or her use a hundred chart. Ask: "What patterns do you see when you skip count by 2s?"

Write the numbers to continue each pattern. Use a hundred chart to help you.

**1.** Skip count by 5s.

30, 35, ____, ____, ____, ____

**2.** Skip count by 2s.

2, 4, ____, ____, ____, ____

Write the numbers to continue each pattern. Use a hundred chart to help you.

**3.** Skip count by 10s.

10, 20, ____, ____, ____, ____

**4.** Skip count by 2s.

24, 26, ____, ____, ____, ____

**5. Algebra** Which is the missing number?

65, 70, __?__, 80, 85

| 72 | 73 | 74 | 75 |
|----|----|----|----|
| ○ | ○ | ○ | ○ |

**6.** Jamie skip counts by a number.
He counts: 54, 56, 58, 60.
Which number did Jamie skip count by?

| 2 | 3 | 5 | 10 |
|---|---|---|----|
| ○ | ○ | ○ | ○ |

**7. Extend Your Thinking** Write **Yes** or **No**. Vicky has baseball practice every 5 days. She starts on May 5. Will she have practice on May 19? _____

How do you know?

_____

_____

| May | | | | | | |
|---|---|---|---|---|---|---|
| Sunday | Monday | Tuesday | Wednesday | Thursday | Friday | Saturday |
| | 1 | 2 | 3 | 4 | 5 | 6 |
| 7 | 8 | 9 | 10 | 11 | 12 | 13 |
| 14 | 15 | 16 | 17 | 18 | 19 | 20 |
| 21 | 22 | 23 | 24 | 25 | 26 | 27 |
| 28 | 29 | 30 | 31 | | | |

Write 3 more dates that Vicky will have practice.

_____

_____

**Solve & Share**

Jane is making 5 toy robots.
She wants to put 2 mittens on each robot.
How can you use skip counting to find
the number of mittens Jane needs in all?

⊕ TEKS 1.5B Skip count
by twos, fives, and tens
to determine the total number
of objects up to 120 in a set.
Also, 1.5. Mathematical
Process Standards 1.1B,
1.1E, 1.1G.

Digital Resources at PearsonTexas.com

Solve    Learn    Glossary    Check    Tools    Games

Jane needs _____ mittens.

Lucy wants to make 5 robots. Each robot has 10 buttons, 5 wheels, and 2 mittens.

50 buttons for 5 robots.

She can skip count by 10s.

10 20 30 40 50

She can skip count by 5s.

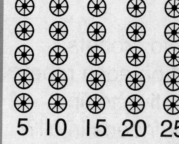

5 10 15 20 25

25 wheels for 5 robots.

She can skip count by 2s.

10 mittens for 5 robots.

2 4 6 8 10

## Do You Understand?

**Show Me!** How do you know that everything has been counted when you skip count?

☆ **Guided Practice** ☆ Use the picture to skip count. Write the numbers.

1. Buttons: __10__, __20__, _____, _____, _____, _____

2. Wheels: _____, _____, _____, _____, _____, _____

© Pearson Education, Inc. 1

Name _____

Use the picture to skip count. Write the missing numbers.

3. Lights: _____, _____, _____, 40

4. Mittens: 2, _____, _____, 8

Look at the skip-counting pattern. Write the missing numbers.

5. 30, _____, 40, 45, 50, _____, _____, _____, 70

6. **Extend Your Thinking** Mrs. Wheeler's class plays a game. Each student has a partner to form a team of 2. There are 15 teams in all. Draw a picture to show how many students are in Mrs. Wheeler's class.

How did you find how many students are in Mrs. Wheeler's class?

_____

_____

_____

_____ students

**7.** Jane makes 6 bracelets.
She put 10 beads on each bracelet.
How many beads did Jane use in all?

Skip count to solve.

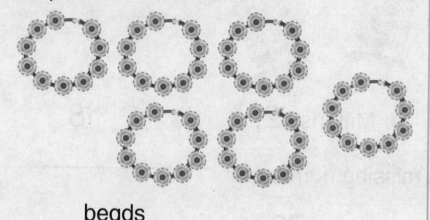

_____ beads

**8.** Rick has 7 bags.
There are 10 blocks inside each bag.
How many blocks does Rick have
in all?

_____ blocks

How did you find your answer?

_____

_____

_____

**9.** Count by 2s. How many mittens
☆ are there in all?

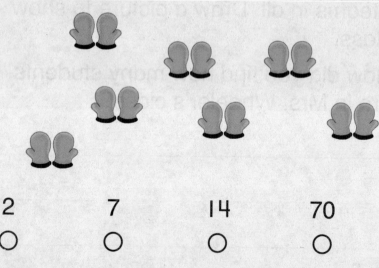

    2        7        14        70
    ○        ○        ○        ○

**10. Extend Your Thinking** Sara has
3 boxes. There are 5 toys inside each
box. Skip count to find how many toys
Sara has in all. Draw a picture
to show your work.

_____ toys

Name _____

**Another Look** You can skip count to find how many in all.

Skip count by 2s, or keep adding 2 to the last number.

2, __4__, __6__, __8__, __10__

    add 2   add 2   add 2   add 2

There are __10__ cherries in all.

🏠 **HOME CONNECTION**
Your child used skip counting to find the total number of items arranged in sets of 2s, 5s, and 10s.

**HOME ACTIVITY** Have your child practice skip counting orally by 2s, 5s, and 10s. Then say, "There are 10 bags. Each bag has 5 apples inside it. How many apples in all?" Have your child draw pictures to check his or her answer. Repeat with several other sets.

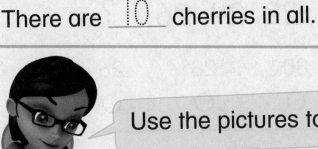

Use the pictures to skip count.

1. How many rabbit ears are there in all? Skip count by 2s.

2, ____, ____, ____, ____, ____, ____, ____, ____, ____,

2. How many cans are there in all? Skip count by 5s.

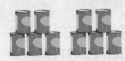        

5, ____, ____, ____, ____, ____, ____, ____, ____,

Use the pictures to skip count.

3. How many baseballs are there in all? Skip count by 10s.

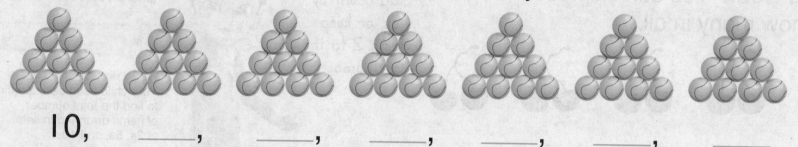

10, _____, _____, _____, _____, _____, _____

Look for a pattern. Find the missing number.

4. 75, 70, 65, 60, 55, ___?___

     35      40      45      50

     ○      ○      ○      ○

5. 18, 20, 22, 24, 26, ___?___

     32      30      28      26

     ○      ○      ○      ○

6. **Extend Your Thinking** Ben has 8 bags. He puts 5 marbles in each bag. How many marbles does Ben have in all? Draw a picture to solve.

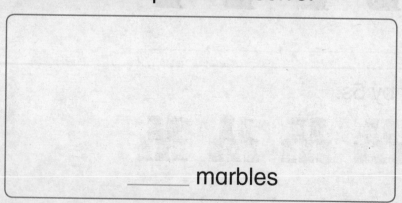

_____ marbles

7. **Extend Your Thinking** How many pencils are there in all?

Skip count by _____. There are _____ pencils.

© Pearson Education, Inc. 1

Name _____

☆ **Solve & Share** ☆

There are 6 students in line for lunch. Each student is wearing 2 shoes. How can you find the number of shoes they are wearing in all? Complete the table to help you solve the problem.

⭐ **TEKS 1.1F** Analyze mathematical relationships to connect and communicate mathematical ideas. Also, 1.5B. Mathematical Process Standards 1.1A, 1.1B, 1.1C.

**Digital Resources at PearsonTexas.com**

Solve    Learn    Glossary    Check    Tools    Games

| Number of Students | | | | | | |
|---|---|---|---|---|---|---|
| Number of Shoes | | | | | | |

## Analyze

Each child has 2 markers. There are 4 children. How many markers are there in all?

## Plan

Make a table to find a pattern.

| Number of Children | 1 | | | |
|---|---|---|---|---|
| Number of Markers | 2 | | | |

## Solve and Justify

The pattern shows 2 markers for each child.

| Number of Children | 1 | 2 | 3 | 4 |
|---|---|---|---|---|
| Number of Markers | 2 | 4 | 6 | 8 |

There are 8 markers in all.

## Evaluate

You can skip count by the pattern number to check your answer.

I can count by 2s to check: 2, 4, 6, 8.

## Do You Understand?

**Show Me!** How can you use skip counting to find the number of socks that 8 children wear?

## ☆ Guided Practice

Find the pattern. Write the numbers to complete the table. Solve.

1. Ellen counts the number of ladybugs on 5 leaves. There are 2 ladybugs on each leaf. How many ladybugs does Ellen count in all?

| Number of Leaves | 1 | | | | |
|---|---|---|---|---|---|
| Number of Ladybugs | 2 | | | | |

_____ ladybugs

© Pearson Education, Inc. 1

## ☆ Independent ☆ Practice

Find the pattern. Write the numbers to complete the table. Solve.

**2.** A bookcase has 8 shelves. There are 10 books on each shelf. How many books are there in all?

| Number of Shelves | | | | | | | | | |
|---|---|---|---|---|---|---|---|---|---|
| Number of Books | | | | | | | | | |

_____ books

**3.** 10 vases are on a table. There are 2 flowers in each vase. How many flowers are there in all?

| Number of Vases | | | | | | | | | |
|---|---|---|---|---|---|---|---|---|---|
| Number of Flowers | | | | | | | | | |

_____ flowers

**4. Extend Your Thinking** Ray's class collects 24 cans of food. The cans can go inside brown or white boxes. Brown boxes can hold 8 cans. White boxes can hold 3 cans. If Ray's class wants to use the most boxes, which boxes should they use? Why?

_____

_____

_____

# Problem Solving  Solve each problem below.

**5.** A farm has 4 hens. Each hen lays the same number of eggs. There are 20 eggs in all. How many eggs does each hen lay?

| Number of Hens | | | | |
|---|---|---|---|---|
| Number of Eggs | | | | |

_____ eggs

**6.** Kevin has 4 cats. He feeds each cat some treats. Use the table to answer each question.

| Number of Cats | 1 | 2 | 3 | 4 |
|---|---|---|---|---|
| Number of Treats | 2 | 4 | 6 | 8 |

How many treats does Kevin feed each cat? _____ treats

In all, how many treats were fed to the cats? _____ treats

**7.** There are 6 sacks of potatoes left in a store. Each sack holds 10 potatoes. How many potatoes are there in all?

4     16     30     60
○      ○      ○      ○

**8. Extend Your Thinking** Write a story about the table.

| Number of Bees | 1 | 2 | 3 | 4 |
|---|---|---|---|---|
| Number of Wings | 4 | 8 | 12 | 16 |

_____

_____

© Pearson Education, Inc. 1

Name _____

## Another Look

I made a table and found a number pattern. I skip counted by 10s to solve the problem.

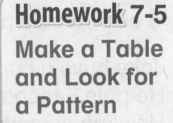

There are 6 buses.
10 people ride on each bus.
In all, how many people ride the bus? _60_

| Number of Buses | 1 | 2 | 3 | 4 | 5 | 6 |
|---|---|---|---|---|---|---|
| Number of Riders | 10 | 20 | 30 | 40 | 50 | 60 |

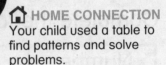

🏠 **HOME CONNECTION**
Your child used a table to find patterns and solve problems.

**HOME ACTIVITY** Tell your child this number story: "There are 6 cars. There are 3 people in each car. How many people are there in all?" Help your child make a table. Then have him or her find a pattern and solve the problem. Make up additional stories for your child to solve.

Find the pattern. Write the numbers to complete the table. Solve.

1. There are 5 bicycles. Each bicycle has 2 wheels. How many wheels are there in all?

_____ wheels

| Number of Bicycles | | | | | |
|---|---|---|---|---|---|
| Number of Wheels | | | | | |

Solve each problem below.

**2.** Jake buys a bookcase with 4 shelves. He puts 5 model cars on each shelf. How many model cars does Jake have in all?

Complete the table to solve.

| Number of Shelves | 1 | | | |
|---|---|---|---|---|
| Number of Cars | 5 | | | |

_____ model cars

**3.** There are 7 wagons on the farm. Each wagon can hold 10 jugs of milk.

How many jugs of milk can all 7 wagons hold?

○ 3

○ 17

○ 50

○ 70

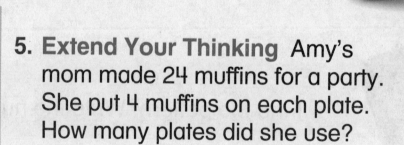

You can make a table to find the answer.

Make a table to solve each problem.

**4. Extend Your Thinking** 30 students in Mr. Chen's class play a game. There are 5 students on each team. How many teams of students are there?

_____ teams

**5. Extend Your Thinking** Amy's mom made 24 muffins for a party. She put 4 muffins on each plate. How many plates did she use?

_____ plates

© Pearson Education, Inc. 1

Name _____

Think about how **drawing a picture** can help you solve problems.

**1.** Draw a picture to show the problem.

Gina has 3 vases. Each vase needs 5 flowers. Gina uses 2 different colors of flowers to fill the vases.

**2.** Skip count or add to find the total number of flowers Gina uses.

_____ , _____ , _____

_____ + _____ + _____ = _____

Gina uses _____ flowers.

**3.** Complete the model to show the total number of flowers and different colors Gina uses.

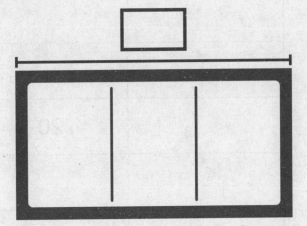

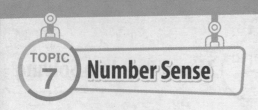

## Make a List

1. Tessa has eggs in 6 baskets. Each basket has the same number of eggs. She skip counts to find that the total number of eggs is 30.

Use a pattern to find the missing numbers in Tessa's list.

| Number of Baskets | Number of Eggs |
|---|---|
| 1 | 5 |
| | |
| 3 | |
| | 20 |
| | |
| 6 | |

## How Do You Know?

2. Tessa writes the number sentence below. Is she right? Explain.

$$5 + 5 + 5 = 10 + 5$$

_____

_____

_____

_____

## Complete It!

3. Fill in the missing numbers.

_____ is 10 less than 55.

62 is 1 more than _____.

93 is 10 more than _____.

© Pearson Education, Inc. 1

Name _____

Set A

You can use a hundred chart
to count backward.

| 1 | 2 | 3 | 4 | 5 | 6 | 7 | 8 | 9 | 10 |
|---|---|---|---|---|---|---|---|---|---|
| 11 | 12 | 13 | 14 | 15 | 16 | 17 | 18 | 19 | 20 |
| 21 | 22 | 23 | 24 | 25 | 26 | 27 | 28 | 29 | 30 |

Count back by 1s.

24, _23_, _22_, _21_

Use a hundred chart.
Count back by 1s.
Write the numbers.

1. 30, _____, _____, _____

2. 21, _____, _____, _____

3. 88, _____, _____, _____

4. 63, _____, _____, _____

Set B

You can skip count on a hundred
chart to find a pattern.

| 1 | 2 | 3 | 4 | 5 | 6 | 7 | 8 | 9 | 10 |
|---|---|---|---|---|---|---|---|---|---|
| 11 | 12 | 13 | 14 | 15 | 16 | 17 | 18 | 19 | 20 |
| 21 | 22 | 23 | 24 | 25 | 26 | 27 | 28 | 29 | 30 |
| 31 | 32 | 33 | 34 | 35 | 36 | 37 | 38 | 39 | 40 |

Skip count by 5s.

5, 10, _15_, _20_, _25_

Use a hundred chart.
Continue the pattern.

5. Skip count by 10s.

10, _____, _____, _____, _____

6. Skip count by 2s.

2, _____, _____, _____, _____

How many shoes are there?
You can skip count by 2s.

2    4    6    8    10

There are __10__ shoes.

Solve the problem below.

7. Skip count by 2s.
   How many mittens are there?

There are _____ mittens.

Set D

You can use a table to find a pattern.

| Number of Dogs | 1 | 2 | 3 | 4 |
|---|---|---|---|---|
| Number of Bones | 2 | 4 | 6 | 8 |

The number of dogs goes up by __1__.

The number of bones goes up by __2__.

4 dogs have __8__ bones.

Complete the table to answer the questions.

| Number of Tanks | 1 | 2 | 3 | |
|---|---|---|---|---|
| Number of Fish | 5 | 10 | 15 | |

8. The number of tanks increases by _____.

9. The number of fish increases by _____.

10. How many fish do 4 tanks have? _____

Name _____

1. Mrs. Brown sells 3 baskets. There are 2 apples in each basket.

Which number tells how many apples Mrs. Brown sold?
Use the table to help you.

| Number of Baskets | 1 | 2 | 3 | 4 |
|---|---|---|---|---|
| Number of Apples | 2 | 4 | ? | 8 |

○ 4

○ 6

○ 8

○ 10

Use the part of the hundred chart below to solve each problem.

| 71 | 72 | 73 | 74 | 75 | 76 | 77 | 78 | 79 | 80 |
|---|---|---|---|---|---|---|---|---|---|
| 81 | 82 | 83 | 84 | 85 | 86 | 87 | 88 | 89 | 90 |
| 91 | 92 | 93 | 94 | 95 | 96 | 97 | 98 | 99 | 100 |

2. Cathy counts pennies by 1s.
She counts to 88.
Which number will Cathy say next?

80      89      90      98
○       ○       ○       ○

3. Sam skip counts to make the pattern below. Which number is missing from the pattern?

84, 88, __?__, 96

89      90      92      94
○       ○       ○       ○

**4.** Henry counts back by 1s.
Which is the missing number?

56, 55, 54, __?__, 52

- ○ 51
- ○ 53
- ○ 55
- ○ 56

**5.** Kristen writes the pattern below.
What number comes next?

10, 15, 20, 25, __?__

- ○ 45
- ○ 40
- ○ 35
- ○ 30

**6.** Alex makes the pattern below.
Draw what comes next.

What pattern do you notice?

_____

_____

# TOPIC 8

## Tens and Ones

**Essential Question:** How can you count and add using tens and ones?

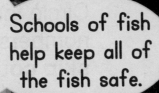

Some fish swim in groups called schools.

Schools of fish help keep all of the fish safe.

Wow! Let's do this project and learn more.

## Math and Science Project: Schools of Fish

**Find Out** Talk to friends and relatives about why fish might swim in groups. Ask them to help you make a list of fish that do **not** swim in groups.

**Journal: Make a Book** Show what you found out. In your book, also:

- Draw different schools of fish with at least 10 fish in each.
- Write number sentences to show how many fish there are in all.

Topic 8

four hundred five  **405**

# Review What You Know

## Vocabulary

**1.** Circle the **tens digit**.

17

**2.** Circle the **ones digit**.

35

**3.** Circle the set of numbers that shows **skip counting** by 2s.

14, 16, 18, 20, 22

15, 20, 25, 30, 35

30, 40, 50, 60, 70

---

## Count Forward and Backward by 1

**4.** Write the next 3 numbers.

45, 46, 47, _____, _____, _____

**5.** Count back. Write the next 3 numbers.

84, 83, 82, _____, _____, _____

## Skip Counting

**6.** Write a pattern that shows skip counting by 5s.

_____, _____, _____, _____, _____

## tens

35 has 3 **tens.**

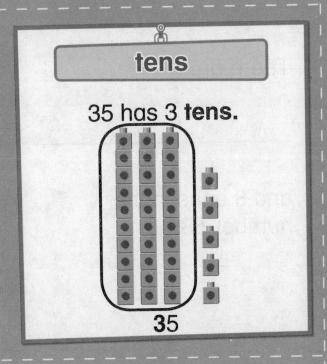

35

## ones

42 has 2 **ones.**

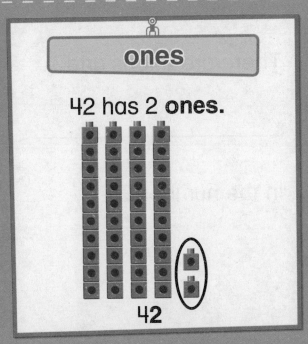

42

## standard form

using digits to write a number

28

## expanded form

breaking apart a number to show the value of each digit

20 + 8 = 28

## break apart a ten

1 ten = 10 ones

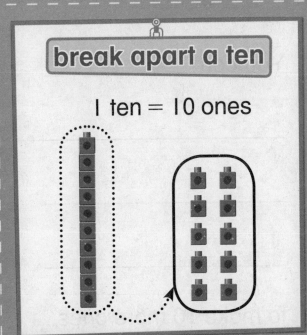

# My Word Cards

Use what you know to complete the sentences.
Extend learning by writing your own sentence using each word.

_____

_____

is a way to write a number using only digits.

---

There are 2 tens and 7

_____

in the number 27.

---

There are 6

_____

and 8 ones in the number 68.

---

You can _____

_____

_____

_____

to make 10 more ones.

---

_____

_____

shows the value of each digit.

Name _____

**Solve & Share**

How many groups of 10 can you make with 34 cubes?

Show your work in the space below.
Then fill in the blanks.

⭐ TEKS 1.2B Use ... models to compose and decompose numbers up to 120 in more than one way as so many hundreds, so many tens, and so many ones. Also, 1.2C. Mathematical Process Standards 1.1B, 1.1C, 1.1E, 1.1F.

Digital Resources at PearsonTexas.com

Solve    Learn    Glossary    Check    Tools    Games

_____ groups of 10

_____ left over

Count 23 cubes.

How many groups of 10 are there? How many are left over?

You can make groups of 10.

There are 2 groups of 10.

Count how many are left over.

There are 3 left over.

23 is __2__ groups of 10 and __3__ left over.

So, 23 is 2 groups of 10 and 3 left over.

## Do You Understand?

**Show Me!** Why does 37 have 3 groups of 10 and not 4 groups of 10?

## ☆ Guided Practice ☆    Circle groups of 10. Write the numbers.

1.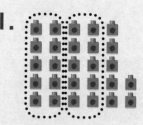

__27__ is __2__ groups of 10 and __7__ left over.

2.

____ is ____ groups of 10 and ____ left over.

© Pearson Education, Inc. 1

Name _____

Circle the groups of 10. Write the number.

3.

4 groups of 10 and 3 left over is _____.

4.

3 groups of 10 and 5 left over is _____.

5.

1 group of 10 and 6 left over is _____.

6.

4 groups of 10 and 8 left over is _____.

Draw a picture to solve. Then write the numbers.

7. **Extend Your Thinking** There is more than 1 group of 10 cubes and several cubes left over. There are 25 cubes in all. How many groups of 10 and leftover ones are there?

25 is _____ groups of 10 and _____ left over.

**Topic 8** | Lesson 1

four hundred eleven  **411**

**8.** The monkeys have 32 bananas. 10 bananas are in each bunch.

How many bunches are there? _____

How many bananas are left over? _____

**9.** The dogs have 21 bones. 10 bones are in each bowl.

How many bowls are there? _____

How many bones are left over? _____

**10.** ⭐ There are 5 bunches of grapes at the store. Each bunch has 10 grapes. How many grapes are there in all?

55       50       15       5

○        ○        ○        ○

**11. Extend Your Thinking** Read the clues. Write the number.

Amil has a number. His number has more than 5 groups of 10. His number has less than 6 groups of 10. What number could Amil have?

_____

© Pearson Education, Inc. 1

Name _____

**Another Look** You can count by 10s and then the leftover 1s.

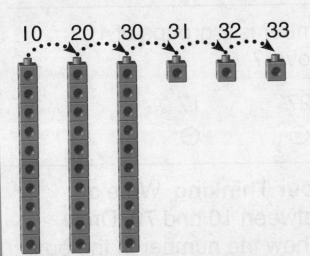

10   20   30   31   32   33

3 groups of 10   3 left over

33 in all

10  11  12  13  14

__1__ group of 10   __4__ left over

__14__ in all

🏠 **HOME CONNECTION**
Your child counted large groups of objects by making groups of 10 and then counting the leftovers.

**HOME ACTIVITY** Place 25 pennies in a pile. Have your child make groups of 10 pennies. Ask, "How many groups of 10 pennies? How many pennies are left over?" Repeat with up to 40 pennies.

Count by 10s and 1s. Write the numbers.

1. _____

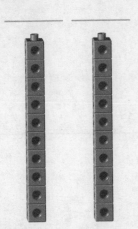

_____ groups of 10

_____ left over

_____ in all

2. _____

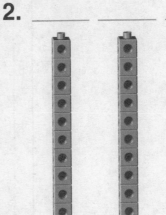  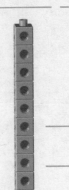

_____ groups of 10

_____ left over

_____ in all

Write the missing number.

3. _____ is 1 group of 10 and 2 left over.

4. 31 is _____ groups of 10 and 1 left over.

5. Which number is 1 group of 10 and 4 left over?

| 5 | 14 | 21 | 41 |
|---|----|----|----|
| ○ | ○ | ○ | ○ |

6. Which number is 2 groups of 10 and 7 left over?

| 37 | 27 | 17 | 15 |
|----|----|----|----|
| ○ | ○ | ○ | ○ |

7. **Extend Your Thinking** 10 beads fit on a bracelet. Ben has some red beads, some green beads, and some yellow beads. He has 34 beads in all.

Draw a picture to show the bracelets he can make with his beads. Then draw the beads that will be left over.

8. **Extend Your Thinking** Write a number between 10 and 70. Draw cubes to show the number in the box. Then write the missing numbers.

My number is _____.

_____ groups of 10

_____ left over

© Pearson Education, Inc. 1

Name _____

**Solve & Share**

Guess how many cubes are in your bag. Then empty the bag in the space below. Without counting each cube, guess how many cubes there are. Write each guess.

Now count the cubes and write the total number of cubes.

TEKS 1.2B Use ... models to compose and decompose numbers up to 120 in more than one way as so many hundreds, so many tens, and so many ones. Also, 1.2C. Mathematical Process Standards 1.1A, 1.1C, 1.1E.

Digital Resources at PearsonTexas.com

Solve   Learn   Glossary   Check   Tools   Games

Guess 1: _____ cubes

Guess 2: _____ cubes

Actual amount:

_____ cubes

35 stands for 3 tens and 5 ones.

The 3 in 35 is the tens digit.
The 5 in 35 is the ones digit.

35 has 2 digits.

| Tens | Ones |
|------|------|
| 3 tens | 5 ones |

| Tens | Ones |
|------|------|
| 3 | 5 |

35

You can use a model to show the tens and ones.

The tens digit goes on the left. The ones digit goes on the right.

## Do You Understand?

**Show Me!** How are these numbers alike? How are they different?

| 46 | 64 |
|----|----|

☆ **Guided Practice** ☆ Count the tens and ones. Then write the numbers.

1.
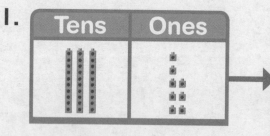

| Tens | Ones |
|------|------|
| 3 | 8 |

38

2.
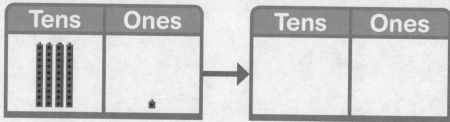

| Tens | Ones |
|------|------|
|  |  |

_____

© Pearson Education, Inc. 1

Name _____

Count the tens and ones. Then write the numbers.

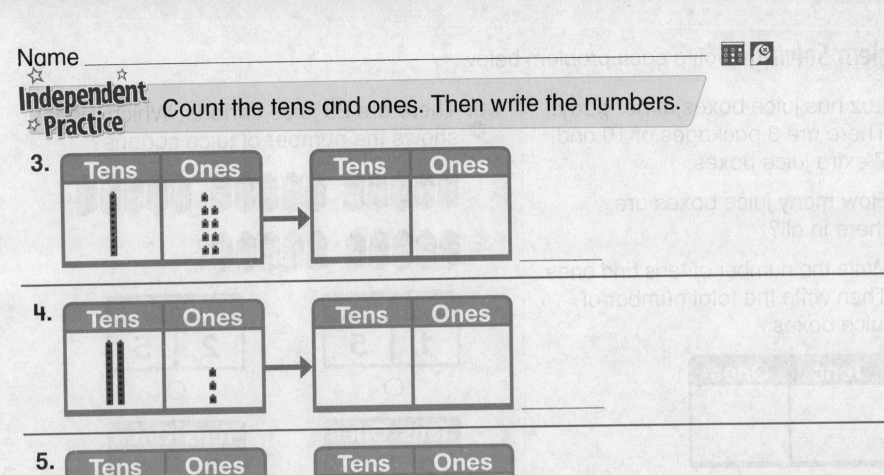

3.

4.

5.

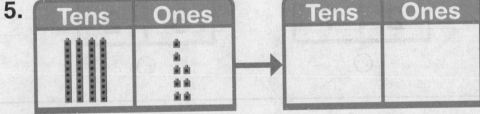
Draw a picture to solve.
Write the number.

6. **Extend Your Thinking** Bill has a number.
It has the same number of tens and ones.
What could Bill's number be?

## Problem Solving  Solve each problem below.

**7.** Luz has juice boxes at her party. There are 3 packages of 10 and 7 extra juice boxes.

How many juice boxes are there in all?

Write the number of tens and ones. Then write the total number of juice boxes.

| Tens | Ones |
|------|------|
|      |      |

_____ juice boxes

**8.** There are 25 juice cartons. Which model shows the number of juice cartons?

| Tens | Ones |
|------|------|
| 1    | 5    |

○

| Tens | Ones |
|------|------|
| 2    | 5    |

○

| Tens | Ones |
|------|------|
| 2    | 7    |

○

| Tens | Ones |
|------|------|
| 5    | 2    |

○

**9. Extend Your Thinking**  Draw a picture to show a number greater than 25 and less than 75. Then write the number.

My number is _____.

© Pearson Education, Inc. 1

Name _____

**Another Look** You can use a workmat to show tens and ones.

| Tens | Ones |
|------|------|
|      |      |

3 tens   4 ones

3 tens is 30.

4 ones is 4.

$30 + 4 = 34$

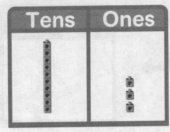

__1__ ten __3__ ones

1 ten is __10__.

3 ones is __3__.

__10__ + __3__ = __13__

🏠 **HOME CONNECTION**
Your child wrote two-digit numbers and used the terms *ones* and *tens* to describe how many.

**HOME ACTIVITY** Draw 2 squares side by side. Write a 3 in the left square and label it "Tens." Write a 4 in the right square and label it "Ones." Have your child draw a picture to show the number. Ask him or her to use the terms *ones* and *tens* to describe how many.

Count the tens and ones.
Then write the numbers.

**I.**

| Tens | Ones |
|------|------|
|      |      |

____ tens and ____ ones

____ tens is ____.

____ ones is ____.

____ + ____ = ____

**2.**

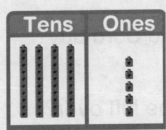

____ tens and ____ ones

____ tens is ____.

____ ones is ____.

____ + ____ = ____

Count the tens and ones. Then write the numbers.

**3.**

| Tens | Ones |
|------|------|

→

| Tens | Ones |
|------|------|
|      |      |

_____

**4.** Which is **not** the same as 72?

○ 7 tens and 2 ones

○ 70 + 2

○ 2 groups of 10 and 7 left over

○ 7 groups of 10 and 2 left over

**5.** Which is the missing number?
6 tens and ___?___ ones is the same as 60.

| 0 | 6 | 10 | 60 |
|---|---|----|----|
| ○ | ○ | ○  | ○  |

**6. Extend Your Thinking** Draw a picture to solve the questions.
Sara needs 48 apples. There are 10 apples in each box.
How many boxes should Sara buy?

_____ boxes

How many apples will be left over?

_____ apples

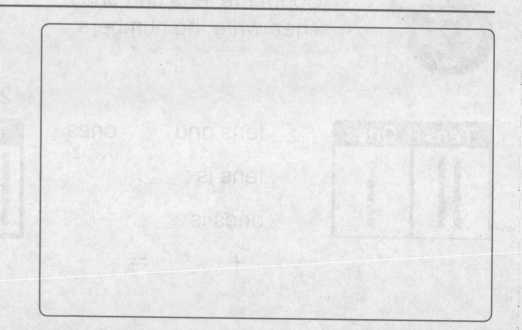

© Pearson Education, Inc. 1

Name _____

**Solve & Share**

How can you use a hundred chart to find the sum of 8 + 40? Show your work and tell how you found the sum.

| 1 | 2 | 3 | 4 | 5 | 6 | 7 | 8 | 9 | 10 |
|---|---|---|---|---|---|---|---|---|---|
| 11 | 12 | 13 | 14 | 15 | 16 | 17 | 18 | 19 | 20 |
| 21 | 22 | 23 | 24 | 25 | 26 | 27 | 28 | 29 | 30 |
| 31 | 32 | 33 | 34 | 35 | 36 | 37 | 38 | 39 | 40 |
| 41 | 42 | 43 | 44 | 45 | 46 | 47 | 48 | 49 | 50 |
| 51 | 52 | 53 | 54 | 55 | 56 | 57 | 58 | 59 | 60 |
| 61 | 62 | 63 | 64 | 65 | 66 | 67 | 68 | 69 | 70 |
| 71 | 72 | 73 | 74 | 75 | 76 | 77 | 78 | 79 | 80 |
| 81 | 82 | 83 | 84 | 85 | 86 | 87 | 88 | 89 | 90 |
| 91 | 92 | 93 | 94 | 95 | 96 | 97 | 98 | 99 | 100 |

⭐ TEKS 1.3A Use concrete and pictorial models to determine the sum of a multiple of 10 and a one-digit number in problems up to 99. **Mathematical Process Standards 1.1B, 1.1C, 1.1F, 1.1G.**

Digital Resources at PearsonTexas.com

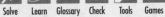
Solve   Learn   Glossary   Check   Tools   Games

You can use a hundred chart to add tens and ones.

| 1 | 2 | 3 | ④ | 5 | 6 | 7 | 8 | 9 | 10 |
|---|---|---|---|---|---|---|---|---|----|
| 11 | 12 | 13 | 14 | 15 | 16 | 17 | 18 | 19 | 20 |
| 21 | 22 | 23 | 24 | 25 | 26 | 27 | 28 | 29 | 30 |

$4 + 20 = ?$

Start on 4.

For every ten you add, move down 1 row.

20 is 2 tens. Move down 2 rows.

$4 + 20 = 24$

| 1 | 2 | 3 | ④ | 5 | 6 | 7 | 8 | 9 | 10 |
|---|---|---|---|---|---|---|---|---|----|
| 11 | 12 | 13 | 14 | 15 | 16 | 17 | 18 | 19 | 20 |
| 21 | 22 | 23 | 24 | 25 | 26 | 27 | 28 | 29 | 30 |

Check your work.
Start at 4.
Skip count by 10s.

4 ,  14 ,  24

So, 24 is 2 groups of 10 and 4 left over.

## Do You Understand?

**Show Me!** When you add 50 to 6, why is 6 the ones digit in the sum? Explain.

## ☆ Guided Practice ☆

Use the part of the hundred chart to add tens and ones.

1. $2 + 10 =$ __12__

2. $5 + 30 =$ ____

3. $7 + 20 =$ ____

4. $9 + 40 =$ ____

5. $6 + 30 =$ ____

| 1 | 2 | 3 | 4 | 5 | 6 | 7 | 8 | 9 | 10 |
|---|---|---|---|---|---|---|---|---|----|
| 11 | 12 | 13 | 14 | 15 | 16 | 17 | 18 | 19 | 20 |
| 21 | 22 | 23 | 24 | 25 | 26 | 27 | 28 | 29 | 30 |
| 31 | 32 | 33 | 34 | 35 | 36 | 37 | 38 | 39 | 40 |
| 41 | 42 | 43 | 44 | 45 | 46 | 47 | 48 | 49 | 50 |

Name _____

Use the part of the hundred chart to add tens and ones.

| 1 | 2 | 3 | 4 | 5 | 6 | 7 | 8 | 9 | 10 |
|---|---|---|---|---|---|---|---|---|---|
| 11 | 12 | 13 | 14 | 15 | 16 | 17 | 18 | 19 | 20 |
| 21 | 22 | 23 | 24 | 25 | 26 | 27 | 28 | 29 | 30 |
| 31 | 32 | 33 | 34 | 35 | 36 | 37 | 38 | 39 | 40 |
| 41 | 42 | 43 | 44 | 45 | 46 | 47 | 48 | 49 | 50 |

6. $7 + 40 =$ _____

7. $8 + 30 =$ _____

8. $9 + 10 =$ _____

9. $5 + 10 =$ _____

10. $3 + 20 =$ _____

11. $1 + 40 =$ _____

Use the part of the hundred chart above to solve.

12. **Extend Your Thinking** Sue had some stickers in a book. She bought 30 more stickers. Now she has 36 stickers in her book. How many stickers did Sue have in the book at the start?

_____ stickers

13. **Extend Your Thinking** There are 40 people at a baseball game in the morning. Some more people come to the game in the afternoon. Now there are 43 people at the game. How many people came to the game in the afternoon?

_____ people

# Problem Solving   Use the hundred chart to solve each problem below.

| 1 | 2 | 3 | 4 | 5 | 6 | 7 | 8 | 9 | 10 |
|---|---|---|---|---|---|---|---|---|---|
| 11 | 12 | 13 | 14 | 15 | 16 | 17 | 18 | 19 | 20 |
| 21 | 22 | 23 | 24 | 25 | 26 | 27 | 28 | 29 | 30 |
| 31 | 32 | 33 | 34 | 35 | 36 | 37 | 38 | 39 | 40 |
| 41 | 42 | 43 | 44 | 45 | 46 | 47 | 48 | 49 | 50 |
| 51 | 52 | 53 | 54 | 55 | 56 | 57 | 58 | 59 | 60 |
| 61 | 62 | 63 | 64 | 65 | 66 | 67 | 68 | 69 | 70 |
| 71 | 72 | 73 | 74 | 75 | 76 | 77 | 78 | 79 | 80 |
| 81 | 82 | 83 | 84 | 85 | 86 | 87 | 88 | 89 | 90 |
| 91 | 92 | 93 | 94 | 95 | 96 | 97 | 98 | 99 | 100 |

**14.** Some hens laid 8 eggs. Then they laid 60 more eggs. How many eggs did the hens lay in all?

_____ eggs

**15.** 4 students made it to the town fair early. More students made it there on time. There are 74 students at the fair. How many students made it to the fair on time?

_____ students

**16.** 8 people are on a bus. 50 people are on a different bus. Which number sentence shows how many people are on both buses?

- ○ $80 + 5 = 85$
- ○ $8 + 5 = 13$
- ○ $8 + 50 = 58$
- ○ $80 + 8 = 88$

**17. Extend Your Thinking** Write a number story for $3 + 40$.

**424**  four hundred twenty-four

© Pearson Education, Inc. 1

**Topic 8** | Lesson 3

Name _____

## Another Look

When you add tens and ones on a hundred chart, you can skip count by 10s.

The ones digit in each number is the same as the one-digit number you started from.

The tens digit of each number is 1 more than the tens digit of the number before it.

| 1 | 2 | 3 | 4 | 5 | (6) | 7 | 8 | 9 | 10 |
|---|---|---|---|---|---|---|---|---|---|
| 11 | 12 | 13 | 14 | 15 | (16) | 17 | 18 | 19 | 20 |
| 21 | 22 | 23 | 24 | 25 | (26) | 27 | 28 | 29 | 30 |
| 31 | 32 | 33 | 34 | 35 | (36) | 37 | 38 | 39 | 40 |
| 41 | 42 | 43 | 44 | 45 | (46) | 47 | 48 | 49 | 50 |
| 51 | 52 | 53 | 54 | 55 | (56) | 57 | 58 | 59 | 60 |
| 61 | 62 | 63 | 64 | 65 | (66) | 67 | 68 | 69 | 70 |
| 71 | 72 | 73 | 74 | 75 | (76) | 77 | 78 | 79 | 80 |
| 81 | 82 | 83 | 84 | 85 | (86) | 87 | 88 | 89 | 90 |
| 91 | 92 | 93 | 94 | 95 | (96) | 97 | 98 | 99 | 100 |

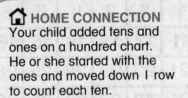

**HOME CONNECTION** Your child added tens and ones on a hundred chart. He or she started with the ones and moved down 1 row to count each ten.

**HOME ACTIVITY** Use a hundred chart. Give your child a one-digit number, such as 7. Have him or her add a multiple of 10, such as 30. Repeat with other one-digit numbers and other multiples of 10.

Start at 6 and skip count by 10s:

6, 16, _26_, _36_, _46_, _56_, _66_, _76_, _86_, _96_

Use a hundred chart to add tens to 3.

1.
$$\begin{array}{r} 3 \\ +10 \\ \hline \end{array}$$

2.
$$\begin{array}{r} 3 \\ +20 \\ \hline \end{array}$$

3.
$$\begin{array}{r} 3 \\ +30 \\ \hline \end{array}$$

4.
$$\begin{array}{r} 3 \\ +40 \\ \hline \end{array}$$

5.
$$\begin{array}{r} 3 \\ +50 \\ \hline \end{array}$$

6.
$$\begin{array}{r} 3 \\ +60 \\ \hline \end{array}$$

Skip count by 10s to find each missing number.

7. 5, 15, _____, 35, _____

8. 9, _____, 29, 39, _____

Use the hundred chart to solve each problem.

| 1 | 2 | 3 | 4 | 5 | 6 | 7 | 8 | 9 | 10 |
|---|---|---|---|---|---|---|---|---|---|
| 11 | 12 | 13 | 14 | 15 | 16 | 17 | 18 | 19 | 20 |
| 21 | 22 | 23 | 24 | 25 | 26 | 27 | 28 | 29 | 30 |
| 31 | 32 | 33 | 34 | 35 | 36 | 37 | 38 | 39 | 40 |
| 41 | 42 | 43 | 44 | 45 | 46 | 47 | 48 | 49 | 50 |
| 51 | 52 | 53 | 54 | 55 | 56 | 57 | 58 | 59 | 60 |
| 61 | 62 | 63 | 64 | 65 | 66 | 67 | 68 | 69 | 70 |
| 71 | 72 | 73 | 74 | 75 | 76 | 77 | 78 | 79 | 80 |
| 81 | 82 | 83 | 84 | 85 | 86 | 87 | 88 | 89 | 90 |
| 91 | 92 | 93 | 94 | 95 | 96 | 97 | 98 | 99 | 100 |

9. Which number sentence is **not** true?

○ $1 + 10 = 11$          ○ $8 + 70 = 78$

○ $3 + 70 = 73$          ○ $8 + 40 = 84$

10. **Algebra** Which is the missing number?

$6 + \underline{\ ?\ } = 76$

○ 70          ○ 10

○ 60          ○ 7

11. **Extend Your Thinking** Mike has 8 marbles. He bought some more. Now he has 28 marbles. How many marbles did Mike buy?

Draw a picture to solve.

Mike bought _____ marbles.

© Pearson Education, Inc. 1

Name _____

Solve & Share

How can you find the sum of 50 + 5?

Use cubes to help you find the sum. Then use numbers and pictures to show your work.

⭐ **TEKS 1.3A** Use concrete and pictorial models to determine the sum of a multiple of 10 and a one-digit number in problems up to 99. **Mathematical Process Standards 1.1C, 1.1D, 1.1E, 1.1F.**

**Digital Resources at PearsonTexas.com**

Solve   Learn   Glossary   Check   Tools   Games

$$50 + 5 = \underline{\phantom{00}}$$

You can count on from a ten to add ones.

$30 + 5 = ?$

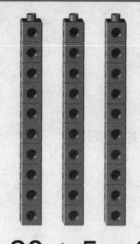

$30 + 5 = ?$

Start with 30.
Count by 1s to add 5.

30, ___31___,

___32___, ___33___,

___34___, ___35___

$30 + 5 = 35$

The tens digit stays the same. The ones digit changes.

---

## Do You Understand?

**Show Me!** Which digit changes when you add 3 to 70? How does it change?

☆ **Guided Practice** ☆   Complete each number sentence.

1.

___20___ + ___4___ = ___24___

2.

_____ + _____ = _____

3.

|

_____ + _____ = _____

4.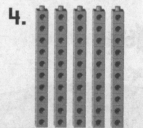

7

_____ + _____ = _____

© Pearson Education, Inc. 1

**Topic 8** | Lesson 4

Name _____

Complete each number sentence.

5.  9

___ + ___ = ___

6.  6

___ + ___ = ___

7.  8

___ + ___ = ___

8.  3

___ + ___ = ___

9.  5

___ + ___ = ___

10. 2

___ + ___ = ___

Look for a pattern to help you
find the missing numbers.

**11. Extend Your Thinking** Write the missing numbers. Then write the last
addition problem in the pattern.

```
  4 0          4 0          ☐ ☐          4 0          4 0          ☐ ☐
+   ☐        +   5        +   6        +   7        +   ☐        +   ☐
─────        ─────        ─────        ─────        ─────        ─────
  4 4        ☐ ☐            4 6        ☐ ☐            4 8        ☐ ☐
```

**12.** Jamal has 30 coins in his piggy bank. Jamal's dad gives him 4 coins. How many coins does Jamal have now?

_____ + _____ = _____

_____ coins

**13.** Julie sells some muffins on Monday. She sells 20 muffins on Friday. She sold 28 muffins in all. How many muffins did Julie sell on Monday?

_____ + _____ = _____

_____ muffins

**14.** Liza has 7 ribbons. She gets 4 more packs of ribbons. Each pack has 10 ribbons. How many ribbons does Liza have now?

Which addition sentence matches the story?

7

○ 10 + 7 = 17          ○ 30 + 7 = 37

○ 20 + 7 = 27          ○ 40 + 7 = 47

**15. Extend Your Thinking** Jake has 9 marbles. He gets some more packs of marbles. Each pack has 10 marbles. Now Jake has 29 marbles. How many packs of marbles did Jake get? Draw a picture to solve.

_____ packs of marbles

Name _____

**Another Look** You can count on by 1s to add.

30 + 3

3 ones

$+1$　$+1$　$+1$

30, _31_ , _32_ , _33_

$30 + 3 = 33$

Count on by 1s to add. Write the numbers.

1.

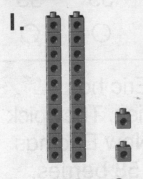

20 + 2

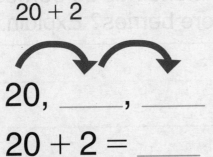

20, _____, _____

20 + 2 = _____

2.

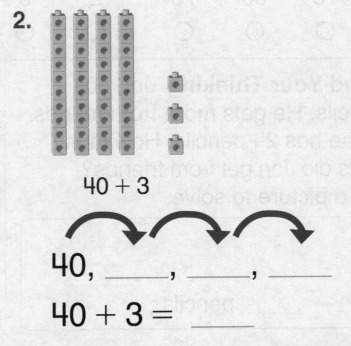

40 + 3

40, _____, _____, _____

40 + 3 = _____

Write an addition sentence to solve each problem.

3. Andy has 9 markers. He gets 20 more markers. How many markers does Andy have now?

_____ = _____ + _____

_____ markers

4. There are 30 pears in a basket. Then Mrs. Miller puts 5 more pears in the basket. How many pears are in the basket now?

_____ = _____ + _____

_____ pears

Find the missing number for each problem.

5. Algebra ✪

$70 + \underline{\ ?\ } = 76$

| 6 | 10 | 60 | 70 |
|---|----|----|----|
| ○ | ○ | ○ | ○ |

6. Algebra ✪

$\underline{\ ?\ } + 8 = 28$

| 2 | 8 | 10 | 20 |
|---|---|----|----|
| ○ | ○ | ○ | ○ |

7. Algebra ✪

$50 + 3 = \underline{\ ?\ }$

| 10 | 30 | 35 | 53 |
|----|----|----|----|
| ○  | ○  | ○  | ○  |

8. **Extend Your Thinking** Jon has 4 pencils. He gets more from friends. Now he has 24 pencils. How many pencils did Jon get from friends? Draw a picture to solve.

_____ pencils

9. **Extend Your Thinking** Eric has 6 berries. Marie has 8 berries. They pick berries in the afternoon. Now Eric has 46 berries and Marie has 58 berries. Who picked more berries? Explain.

_____

_____

**432** four hundred thirty-two

© Pearson Education, Inc. 1

**Topic 8** | Lesson 4

Name ____________________

## Lesson 8-5
## Expanded Form

**Solve & Share**

Write how many tens and ones are in the two-digit number. You may use cubes to help you.

**25**

____ tens and ____ ones

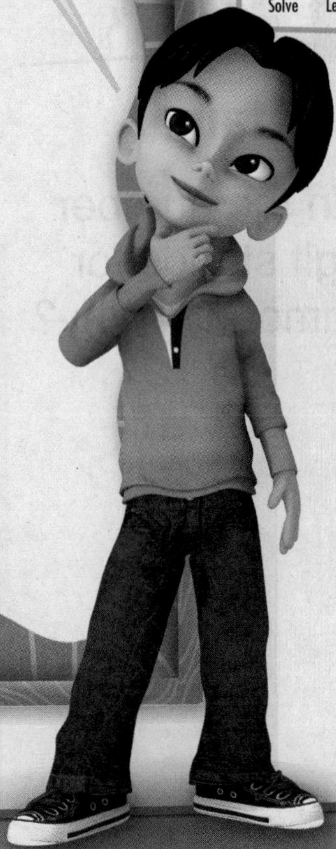

**TEKS 1.2C** Use objects, pictures, and expanded and standard forms to represent numbers up to 120. Also, 1.2B. **Mathematical Process Standards** 1.1B, 1.1C, 1.1D, 1.1G.

Digital Resources at PearsonTexas.com

Solve | Learn | Glossary | Check | Tools | Games

Two-digit numbers can be shown in different ways.

There are 26 cubes.

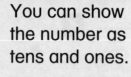

You can show the number as tens and ones.

| Tens | Ones |
|------|------|
| | |

2 tens    6 ones

You can show the value of the tens and ones.

| Tens | Ones |
|------|------|
| | |

20    6

2 tens is 20.
6 ones is 6.

The number can be written as the tens added to the ones.

When we write it this way, we call it standard form.

26

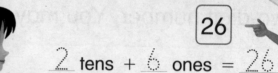

$\underline{2}$ tens + $\underline{6}$ ones = $\underline{26}$
$\underline{20}$ + $\underline{6}$ = $\underline{26}$

When we write it this way, we call it expanded form.

## Do You Understand?

**Show Me!** In the number 49, which digit stands for the greater amount? Why?

☆ **Guided Practice** ☆   Draw the tens and ones. Then fill in the blanks.

1. 37

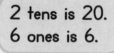

| Tens | Ones |
|------|------|
| | |

$\underline{3}$ tens + $\underline{7}$ ones = $\underline{37}$

$\underline{30}$ + $\underline{7}$ = $\underline{37}$

2. 54

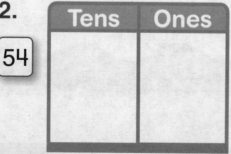

| Tens | Ones |
|------|------|
| | |

___ tens + ___ ones = ___

___ + ___ = ___

**Topic 8** | Lesson 5

Name _____

Draw the tens and ones. Then fill in the blanks.

**3.**

| Tens | Ones |
|------|------|
|      |      |

29

___ tens + ___ ones = ___

___ + ___ = ___

**4.**

| Tens | Ones |
|------|------|
|      |      |

16

___ ten + ___ ones = ___

___ + ___ = ___

**5.**

| Tens | Ones |
|------|------|
|      |      |

41

___ tens + ___ one = ___

___ + ___ = ___

Draw a picture to solve.
Write the numbers.

**6. Extend Your Thinking** Think of
a two-digit number that is less than 30.
Draw the number as tens and ones.
Write the expanded form of your number.
Then write the standard form.

| Tens | Ones |
|------|------|
|      |      |

_____ + _____

**expanded form**

_____

**standard form**

**7.** Guess the number. It has 8 tens. The ones digit is 1 more than the tens digit.

| Tens | Ones |
|------|------|
|      |      |

____

**8.** Guess the number. It has 7 ones. The tens digit is 1 less than the ones digit.

| Tens | Ones |
|------|------|
|      |      |

____

**9.** ⭐ There are 28 dogs. Which answer shows the number of dogs?

- ○ 20 + 3
- ○ 30 + 3
- ○ 20 + 8
- ○ 30 + 8

**10. Extend Your Thinking** Think of a two-digit number less than 50. Draw the number as tens and ones. Then write the number in 2 different ways.

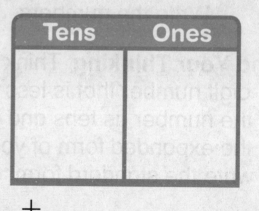

| Tens | Ones |
|------|------|
|      |      |

____ + ____
**expanded form**

____
**standard form**

Name _____

## Another Look

Two-digit numbers are made up of tens and ones.

27 is a two-digit number.

2 is in the tens column.

7 is in the ones column.

| Tens | Ones |
|------|------|
| 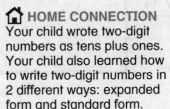 | |

$\overset{2}{\underset{\text{tens}}{\curvearrowright}}$ $\quad$ $\overset{7}{\underset{\text{ones}}{\curvearrowright}}$

__2__ tens + __7__ ones = __27__

$$20 + 7 = 27$$

**expanded form** $\qquad$ **standard form**

 Count the tens and ones. Then fill in the blanks.

**I.**

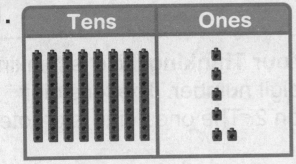

| Tens | Ones |
|------|------|

_____ tens + _____ ones = _____

_____ + _____

_____ tens $\qquad$ _____ ones

Draw the tens and ones. Then fill in the blanks.

**2.**

| Tens | Ones |
|------|------|

54

_____ tens + _____ ones = _____

_____ + _____ = _____

**3.**

| Tens | Ones |
|------|------|

68

_____ tens + _____ ones = _____

_____ + _____ = _____

**4.** Jen has 57 crayons. Which is **not** another way to write 57?

○ 5 tens + 7 ones
○ 50 + 7
○ 7 + 50
○ 7 tens + 5 ones

**5.** Which is the missing number?

3 tens + _____?_____ ones = 35

○ 5
○ 4
○ 3
○ 0

**6. Extend Your Thinking** George is thinking of a two-digit number. The tens digit is greater than 6. The ones digit is 4. What could George's number be?

_____

**7. Extend Your Thinking** Lisa is thinking of a two-digit number. The tens digit is less than 2. The ones digit is greater than 8.

_____

Name ______________________________

## Lesson 8-6
## Ways to Make Numbers

**Solve & Share**

You can make 46 with 46 ones.
Show another way to make 46 with tens and ones.
Use cubes to show your work. Then fill in the blanks.

TEKS 1.2B Use concrete and pictorial models to compose and decompose numbers up to 120 in more than one way as so many hundreds, so many tens, and so many ones. Also, 1.2C.
**Mathematical Process Standards** 1.1D, 1.1E, 1.1G.

Digital Resources at PearsonTexas.com
Solve Learn Glossary Check Tools Games

____ tens and ____ ones

| Tens | Ones | | Tens | Ones | | Tens | Ones | | Tens | Ones |
|---|---|---|---|---|---|---|---|---|---|---|
| 3 tens | 7 ones | | 2 tens | 17 ones | | 1 ten | 27 ones | | 0 tens | 37 ones |

$37 = 30 + 7$    $37 = 20 + 17$    $37 = 10 + 27$    $37 = 0 + 37$

You can make 37 in different ways.

Break apart a ten to make 10 more ones.

Break apart another ten into ones.

This is another way to make 37.

## Do You Understand?

**Show Me!** How are 2 tens and 6 ones the same as 1 ten and 16 ones?

★ **Guided Practice** ★ Count the tens and the ones. Show 2 different ways to make the number.

1.

$23 = \underline{20} + \underline{3}$
$23 = \underline{10} + \underline{13}$
$23 = \underline{0} + \underline{23}$

2.

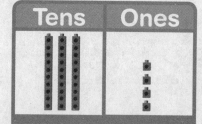

| Tens | Ones |
|---|---|

$34 = \underline{\phantom{00}} + \underline{\phantom{00}}$
$34 = \underline{\phantom{00}} + \underline{\phantom{00}}$
$34 = \underline{\phantom{00}} + \underline{\phantom{00}}$

**Independent ☆ Practice**

Count the tens and the ones. Show 2 different ways to make the number.

3.

| Tens | Ones |
|---|---|

68 = _____ + _____

68 = _____ + _____

68 = _____ + _____

4.

| Tens | Ones |
|---|---|

51 = _____ + _____

51 = _____ + _____

51 = _____ + _____

5.

| Tens | Ones |
|---|---|

78 = _____ + _____

78 = _____ + _____

78 = _____ + _____

6. **Extend Your Thinking** Write 32 as tens and ones in 4 different ways. Use cubes to help you solve.

_____ + _____ = _____

_____ + _____ = _____

_____ + _____ = _____

_____ + _____ = _____

7. **Extend Your Thinking** Carla writes a number greater than 20 and less than 30. The tens digit is greater than the ones digit. What number did Carla write? Draw a picture to show the number.

Carla's number is _____.

Look at each model. Write the number.
Then write the addition sentence.

**8.** What number does the model
show? _____

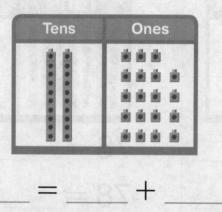

_____ = _____ + _____

**9.** What number does the model
show? _____

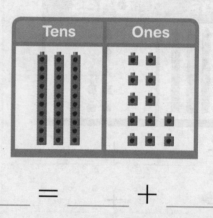

_____ = _____ + _____

---

**10.** Which of these is **not** a way to
⭐ show 35?

○  10 + 25

○  20 + 15

○  30 + 5

○  30 + 15

**11. Extend Your Thinking** Write
numbers in the models to show 61
in 3 different ways.

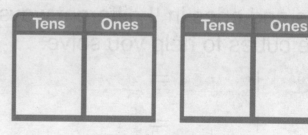

| Tens | Ones |
|------|------|
|      |      |

© Pearson Education, Inc. 1

**Topic 8** | Lesson 6

Name _____

**Another Look** You can use cubes to show the same number a different way.

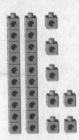

is the same as

27

2 tens 7 ones

27 = 20 + 7

27

____1____ ten ____17____ ones

27 = ____10____ + ____17____

🏠 **HOME CONNECTION**
Your child learned how to use tens and ones to make numbers in different ways.

**HOME ACTIVITY** Give your child 50 small objects, such as paper clips or buttons. Ask him or her to make groups of tens and ones to show 48. Then ask your child to show 48 with a different number of tens and ones. Repeat with other two-digit numbers up to 50.

Draw cubes to show a different way to make the number. Then fill in the blanks.

1.

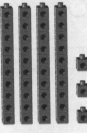

is the same as

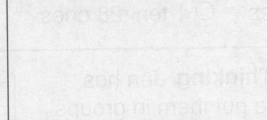

43

43

_____ tens _____ ones

43 = _____ + _____

_____ tens _____ ones

43 = _____ + _____

Complete the number sentence to show a different way to make each number.

**2.**

| Tens | Ones |
|------|------|

$37 = 30 + 7$

Break apart a ten into ones.

$37 = 20 + \underline{\phantom{000}}$

**3.**

| Tens | Ones |
|------|------|

$24 = 10 + 14$

Make a ten with 10 ones.

$24 = \underline{\phantom{000}} + 4$

**4.** Mario draws a picture to show 4 tens and 8 ones. Which is another way to show the same number?

○ 6 tens 6 ones    ○ 3 tens 18 ones

○ 3 tens 9 ones    ○ 1 ten  28 ones

**5.** Which is the missing number?

$$80 + 3 = 70 + \underline{\,?\,}$$

3          13          23          33

○           ○           ○           ○

**6. Extend Your Thinking** Jen has 42 buttons. She put them in groups of tens and ones. Jen shows 2 tens. Draw a picture to show how many ones.

© Pearson Education, Inc. 1

Name _____

**Solve & Share**

Barry showed the number 42 with cubes. What are some of the ways he could have shown 42?

Write the tens and ones to show the ways. You may use cubes to help you.

⭐ **TEKS 1.1E** Create and use representations to organize, record, and communicate mathematical ideas. Also, 1.2B. Mathematical Process Standards 1.1B, 1.1D.

Digital Resources at PearsonTexas.com

Solve   Learn   Glossary   Check   Tools   Games

| Tens | Ones |
|------|------|
|      |      |
|      |      |
|      |      |
|      |      |
|      |      |

## Analyze

How many ways can you show the number 38 with tens and ones?

# 38

## Plan

I can make a list of all the different ways.

| Tens | Ones |
|------|------|
|      |      |
|      |      |
|      |      |

## Solve and Justify

There are 4 ways to show 38 with tens and ones.

| Tens | Ones |
|------|------|
| 3    | 8    |
| 2    | 18   |
| 1    | 28   |
| 0    | 38   |

## Evaluate

Skip count by 10s to check.

| Tens | Ones |
|------|------|
| 3    | 8    |
| 2    | 18   |
| 1    | 28   |
| 0    | 38   |

I count 38 for each way.

---

## ☆ Guided Practice ☆

Make a list to solve. You can use cubes to help you.

## Do You Understand?

**Show Me!** How many ways can you show 18? What are they? How do you know that you found all the ways?

1. Carly lists all the ways to show 25 as tens and ones. What ways does she list?

| Tens | Ones |
|------|------|
| 2    | 5    |
|      |      |
|      |      |

2. Andy wants to show 31 as tens and ones. What are all the ways?

| Tens | Ones |
|------|------|
|      |      |
|      |      |
|      |      |

---

Name _____

## Independent Practice

Make a list to solve. You can use cubes to help you.

3. Alma lists all the ways to show 46 as tens and ones. What ways does she list?

| Tens | Ones |
|------|------|
|      |      |
|      |      |
|      |      |
|      |      |

4. Seth wants to show 33 as tens and ones. What are all the ways?

| Tens | Ones |
|------|------|
|      |      |
|      |      |
|      |      |

5. **Extend Your Thinking** Dana says there are 8 ways to show 63 using tens and ones. Is she right? How do you know?

Make a list to help you.

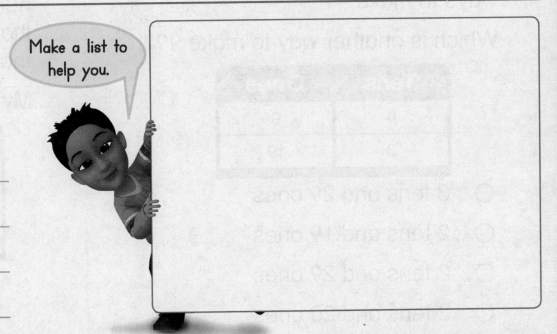

_____

_____

_____

**6.** Andrew writes 4 ways to make 27. Is he correct?

Yes          No

Cross out the way that does **not** show 27.

| Tens | Ones |
|------|------|
| 2 | 7 |
| 2 | 17 |
| 1 | 17 |
| 0 | 27 |

**7.** Josie needs to find all the ways to make 68. She found 4 ways. Help Josie find the other 3 ways. Write the numbers in the chart.

| Tens | Ones |
|------|------|
| 6 | 8 |
| 5 | 18 |
| 4 | 28 |
| 3 | 38 |
|  |  |
|  |  |
|  |  |

**8.** Connie's list shows some ways to make 49.

Which is another way to make 49?

| Tens | Ones |
|------|------|
| 4 | 9 |
| 3 | 19 |

○   3 tens and 29 ones

○   2 tens and 19 ones

○   2 tens and 29 ones

○   2 tens and 20 ones

**9. Extend Your Thinking** Choose a number greater than 40 and less than 100. List 3 different ways you can make the number with tens and ones.

My number is _____.

| Tens | Ones |
|------|------|
|  |  |
|  |  |
|  |  |

Name _____

**Another Look** You can make a list to solve problems.

What are all the ways you can make 49 as tens and ones?

| Tens | Ones |
|------|------|
| 4 | 9 |
| 3 | 19 |
| 2 | 29 |
| 1 | 39 |
| 0 | 49 |

Making a list can help you find all the ways.

🏠 **HOME CONNECTION**
Your child used groups of tens and ones to show and write a two-digit number.

**HOME ACTIVITY** Give your child a two-digit number. Ask, "How many ways can you show the number?" Have him or her make a list of the tens and ones he or she would use to show each way. Continue with several two-digit numbers.

Make a list to solve each problem. You can use cubes to help you.

1. Mark wants to show 34 as tens and ones. What are all the ways?

| Tens | Ones |
|------|------|
| | |
| | |
| | |
| | |

2. Maya wants to show 28 as tens and ones. What are all the ways?

| Tens | Ones |
|------|------|
| | |
| | |
| | |

Make a list to solve each problem. You can use cubes to help you.

**3.** Miguel writes some ways to make 56 as tens and ones. Help Miguel find other ways. Write the numbers in the chart.

| Tens | Ones |
|------|------|
| 4 | 16 |
| 1 | 46 |
| 0 | 56 |
| | |
| | |
| | |

**4.** Brad writes some ways to make 31.

Cross out the way that is **not** correct.

Write 1 more way to make 31.

| Tens | Ones |
|------|------|
| 3 | 1 |
| 2 | 11 |
| 2 | 21 |
| 1 | 21 |
| | |

**5.** Frank knows he can make 22 with 2 tens and 2 ones. Which is another way he can make 22?

○   3 tens and 2 ones
○   2 tens and 12 ones
○   1 ten and 12 ones
○   0 tens and 12 ones

**6.** Anna knows she can make 56 with 4 tens and 16 ones. Which is another way she can make 56?

○   3 tens and 16 ones
○   5 tens and 16 ones
○   2 tens and 6 ones
○   1 ten and 46 ones

**7. Extend Your Thinking** There are 47 marbles in a jar. How many ways can the marbles be grouped as tens and ones? _____ ways

| Tens | Ones |
|------|------|
| | |
| | |
| | |
| | |
| | |
| | |

Make a list to show all the ways.

© Pearson Education, Inc. 1

Name _____

**Use the model** to solve the problem.

1. Cross out the model that does **not** match the problem.

Zach and Todd share some cubes.
Zach has 43 cubes. He gets
20 more cubes from Todd.

How many cubes does
Zach have now?

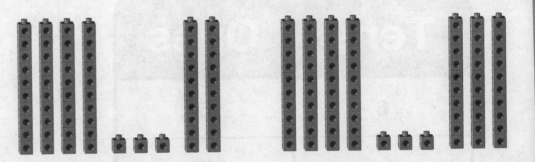

2. Start at 43. Count by 10s to find how many cubes Zach has in all. You can use the model in Exercise 1 to help you.

_____ , _____ , _____

Zach has _____ cubes.

3. Write how many cubes Zach has in the box. Todd has fewer cubes than Zach. Solve to find how many cubes Todd has.

The tens digit is 1 less than 4.
Double 3 to find the ones digit.
Write the number in Todd's box.

**Zach**

☐

**Todd**

☐

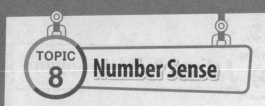

## Make a List

1. There are 7 ways to make 65 with tens and ones. Use the pattern to find the missing numbers.

| Tens | Ones |
|:---:|:---:|
| 6 | 5 |
|  | 15 |
| 4 |  |
| 3 | 35 |
|  | 45 |
| 1 |  |
| 0 | 65 |

## What's Wrong?

2. Cross out the number sentence that **can't** be right. Complete the number sentence that can be right.

34

3 tens + _____ ones = _____

4 tens + _____ ones = _____

## Complete It!

3. Fill in the missing numbers.

2 tens = _____

4 tens = _____

_____ tens = 70

_____ tens = 80

Set A

You can group objects by 10 to count.

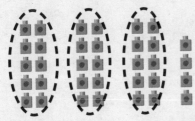

34 is __3__ groups of 10
and __4__ ones left over.

Circle groups of 10.
Write the numbers.

1.

25 is _____ groups of 10
and _____ ones left over.

2.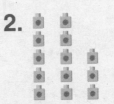

13 is _____ group of 10
and _____ ones left over.

Set B

You can show a two-digit number as tens and ones.

| Tens | Ones |
|------|------|

4 3

4 tens and 3 ones is 43.

Count the tens and ones.
Then write the number.

3.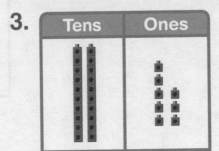

_____

4.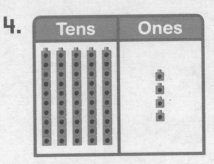

_____

## You can break apart tens to show a number in more than one way.

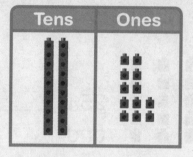

$32 = 30 + 2$

$32 = 20 + 12$

## Show 3 other ways to make each number. Use cubes to help you.

**5.**

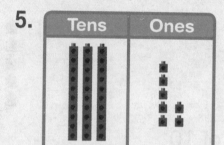

____ + ____ = 37

____ + ____ = 37

____ + ____ = 37

**6.**

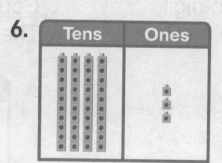

____ + ____ = 43

____ + ____ = 43

____ + ____ = 43

© Pearson Education, Inc. 1

Set D

You can use part of the hundred chart to add tens and ones.

$3 + 40 = ?$

| 1 | 2 | ③ | 4 | 5 | 6 | 7 | 8 | 9 | 10 |
|---|---|---|---|---|---|---|---|---|----|
| 11 | 12 | 13 | 14 | 15 | 16 | 17 | 18 | 19 | 20 |
| 21 | 22 | 23 | 24 | 25 | 26 | 27 | 28 | 29 | 30 |
| 31 | 32 | 33 | 34 | 35 | 36 | 37 | 38 | 39 | 40 |
| 41 | 42 | 43 | 44 | 45 | 46 | 47 | 48 | 49 | 50 |

$3 + 40 = \underline{43}$

Reteaching
Continued

Use the part of the hundred chart to add tens and ones.

| 1 | 2 | 3 | 4 | 5 | 6 | 7 | 8 | 9 | 10 |
|---|---|---|---|---|---|---|---|---|----|
| 11 | 12 | 13 | 14 | 15 | 16 | 17 | 18 | 19 | 20 |
| 21 | 22 | 23 | 24 | 25 | 26 | 27 | 28 | 29 | 30 |
| 31 | 32 | 33 | 34 | 35 | 36 | 37 | 38 | 39 | 40 |
| 41 | 42 | 43 | 44 | 45 | 46 | 47 | 48 | 49 | 50 |
| 51 | 52 | 53 | 54 | 55 | 56 | 57 | 58 | 59 | 60 |

7. $4 + 50 = $ _____

8. $8 + 30 = $ _____

Set E

You can use different ways to add tens and ones. You can use cubes to help you find the ways.

I know 3 tens = 30 and 9 ones = 9. I can write a 3 as the tens digit and a 9 as the ones digit.

$30 + 9 = \underline{39}$

Add the tens and the ones. Use cubes to help you.

9. $80 + 3 = $ _____

10. $70 + 4 = $ _____

11. $20 + 5 = $ _____

A number can be written in standard form and expanded form.

**36**

~~36~~
standard form

~~30~~ + ~~6~~ = 36
expanded form

Solve each problem below.

12. Choose 2 numbers. Write the numbers in standard form.

_____      _____

13. Write 82 in expanded form.

_____ + _____ = _____

You can use a list to show all the ways to make a number with tens and ones.

32

| Tens | Ones |
|------|------|
| 3 | 2 |
| 2 | 12 |
| 1 | 22 |
| 0 | 32 |

There are 4 ways to show 32 with tens and ones.

Complete the models to show different ways to make each number.

14. 29

| Tens | Ones |
|------|------|
| 2 | |
| 1 | |
| 0 | |

15. 54

| Tens | Ones |
|------|------|
| 5 | |
| 4 | |
| 3 | |
| 2 | |
| 1 | |
| 0 | |

1. __?__ is 1 group of 10 and 4 left over.

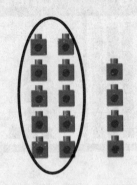

| 4 | 6 | 14 | 40 |
|---|---|----|----|
| ○ | ○ | ○ | ○ |

2. 42 is __?__ groups of 10 and 2 left over.

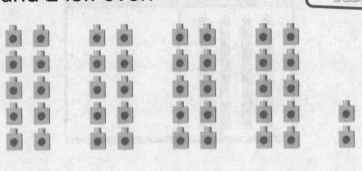

| 2 | 4 | 20 | 40 |
|---|---|----|----|
| ○ | ○ | ○ | ○ |

3. Which number sentence matches the picture?

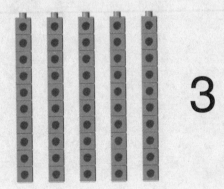

3

○ 5 + 3 = 8      ○ 50 + 3 = 53

○ 5 + 30 = 35    ○ 50 + 30 = 80

4. Count the tens and ones. Which number does the model show?

| Tens | Ones |
|------|------|

○ 5        ○ 57

○ 55       ○ 75

**5.** How many tens and ones are shown in the model?

| Tens | Ones |
|------|------|
| ||||| |

- ⭘ 4 tens and 5 ones
- ⭘ 4 tens and 2 ones
- ⭘ 3 tens and 2 ones
- ⭘ 2 tens and 2 ones

**6.** Which number does the model show?

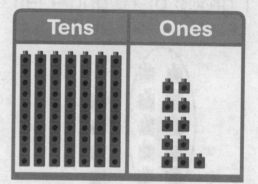

- ⭘ 79
- ⭘ 80
- ⭘ 81
- ⭘ 90

**7.** Which number sentence matches the picture?

- ⭘ $77 = 79 - 2$
- ⭘ $72 = 70 + 2$
- ⭘ $27 = 20 + 7$
- ⭘ $27 = 10 + 17$

Name _____

Use the part of the hundred chart to solve each problem.

| 1 | 2 | 3 | 4 | 5 | 6 | 7 | 8 | 9 | 10 |
|---|---|---|---|---|---|---|---|---|----|
| 11 | 12 | 13 | 14 | 15 | 16 | 17 | 18 | 19 | 20 |
| 21 | 22 | 23 | 24 | 25 | 26 | 27 | 28 | 29 | 30 |
| 31 | 32 | 33 | 34 | 35 | 36 | 37 | 38 | 39 | 40 |

**8.** $4 + 20 = ?$

- ○ 60
- ○ 42
- ○ 24
- ○ 14

**9.** $9 + 30 = ?$

- ○ 93
- ○ 39
- ○ 21
- ○ 11

**10.** Which number sentence shows 91 written in expanded form?

- ○ $90 + 1 = 91$
- ○ $90 - 1 = 89$
- ○ $10 + 9 = 19$
- ○ $19 - 9 = 10$

**11.** Which shows a number written in standard form?

- ○ $70 + 8 = 78$
- ○ 7 tens and 8 ones
- ○ 78
- ○ $70 + 0$

**12.** Which of these is **not** a way to show 36?

○ 20 + 16

○ 60 + 3

○ 10 + 26

○ 0 + 36

**13.** Ken writes 63 as tens and ones. Which number is missing in the chart?

○ 24

○ 23

○ 22

○ 21

| Tens | Ones |
|------|------|
| 6 | 3 |
| 5 | 13 |
| 4 | ? |
| 3 | 33 |
| 2 | 43 |
| 1 | 53 |
| 0 | 63 |

**14.** Start at 80. Count by 1s to add 6.

——— , ——— , ——— , ——— , ——— , ——— , ———

80 + 6 = ———

**15.** Nicole found 2 ways to make 41. Complete the list to show all of the ways.

| Tens | Ones |
|------|------|
| 4 | 1 |
| | |
| 2 | 21 |
| | |
| | |

# Glossary

**0 less than**

0 less than 8 is 8.

$$8 - 0 = 8$$

**1 less**

4 is 1 less than 5.

**1 less than**

1 less than 8 is 7.

$$8 - 1 = 7$$

**1 more**

5 is 1 more than 4.

**10 less**

20 is 10 less than 30.

**10 more**

10 more than a number has 1 more ten or 10 more ones.

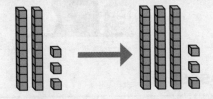

**2 less than**

2 less than 8 is 6.

$$8 - 2 = 6$$

**add**

When you add, you find out how many there are in all.

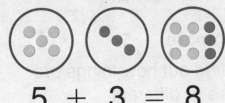

$$5 + 3 = 8$$

**addend**

the numbers you add together to find the whole

$$2 + 3 = 5$$

**addition fact**

$$9 + 8 = 17$$

**addition sentence**

$$3 + 4 = 7$$

**balance**

To balance the scale, both sides need to have the same number of cubes.

## bar graph

a graph that uses bars to show data

## break apart a ten

### I ten 10 ones

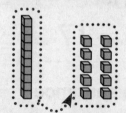

Break apart a ten to make 10 more ones.

## cent

1¢

A penny is worth 1 cent.

## charity

Charity is helping people in need.

## closest 10

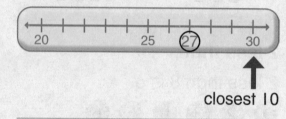

closest 10

## column

| 1 | 2 | 3 | 4 | 5 |
| 11 | 12 | 13 | 14 | 15 |
| 21 | 22 | 23 | 24 | 25 |
| 31 | 32 | 33 | 34 | 35 |

column

## compare

to find out how things are alike or different

## cone

## corner

## cube

## cylinder

## data

information you collect

## difference

the amount that is left after you subtract

$$4 - 1 = 3$$

The difference is 3.

## digits

Numbers have 1 or more digits.

43 has 2 digits.
The tens digit is 4.
The ones digit is 3.

## dime

10 cents or 10¢

front        back

## double

an addition fact with the same addends

$$4 + 4 = 8$$

4 and 4 is a double.

## doubles-plus-1 fact

The addends are 1 apart.

$$3 + 4 = 7$$
addends

## doubles-plus-2 fact

The addends are 2 apart.

$$3 + 5 = 8$$
addends

## edge

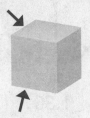

## equal parts

4 equal parts

## equal sign (=)

$$2 + 3 = 5$$

equal sign

## equals

5 + 2 equals 7.

## estimate

a close guess

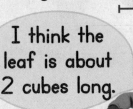

I think the leaf is about 2 cubes long.

## expanded form

breaking apart a number to show the value of each digit

$$20 + 8 = 28$$

## face

## fact family

a group of related addition and subtraction facts

$3 + 5 = 8$
$5 + 3 = 8$
$8 - 3 = 5$
$8 - 5 = 3$

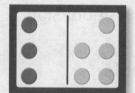

## flat surface

## fourths

The square is divided into fourths.

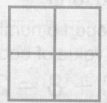

## greater than (>)

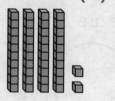 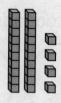

42 is greater than 24.

## greatest

the number or group with the largest value

23 is the greatest number.

## half hour

A half hour is 30 minutes.

1:30

## halves

The circle is divided into halves.

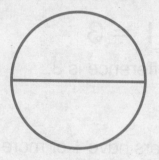

## hexagon

## hour

An hour is 60 minutes.

2:00

## hour hand

The short hand on a clock is the hour hand.
The hour hand tells the hour.

It is 3:00.                    hour hand

## hundred chart

A hundred chart shows all of the numbers from 1 to 100.

| 1 | 2 | 3 | 4 | 5 | 6 | 7 | 8 | 9 | 10 |
|---|---|---|---|---|---|---|---|---|---|
| 11 | 12 | 13 | 14 | 15 | 16 | 17 | 18 | 19 | 20 |
| 21 | 22 | 23 | 24 | 25 | 26 | 27 | 28 | 29 | 30 |
| 31 | 32 | 33 | 34 | 35 | 36 | 37 | 38 | 39 | 40 |
| 41 | 42 | 43 | 44 | 45 | 46 | 47 | 48 | 49 | 50 |
| 51 | 52 | 53 | 54 | 55 | 56 | 57 | 58 | 59 | 60 |
| 61 | 62 | 63 | 64 | 65 | 66 | 67 | 68 | 69 | 70 |
| 71 | 72 | 73 | 74 | 75 | 76 | 77 | 78 | 79 | 80 |
| 81 | 82 | 83 | 84 | 85 | 86 | 87 | 88 | 89 | 90 |
| 91 | 92 | 93 | 94 | 95 | 96 | 97 | 98 | 99 | 100 |

## in all

There are 4 birds in all.

## income

You can earn income by working.

## inside

The dogs are inside the dog house.

## join

to put together

3 and 3 is 6 in all.

## least

the number or group with the smallest value

7 is the least number.

## length

the distance from one end of an object to the other end

## less

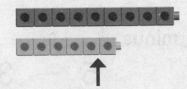

The yellow row has less.

## less than (<)

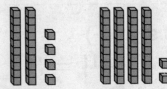

24 is less than 42.

## make 10

$7 + 4 = ?$

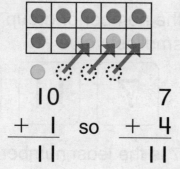

$$\begin{array}{ccc} 10 & & 7 \\ +\ 1 & so & +\ 4 \\ \hline 11 & & 11 \end{array}$$

## measure

You can measure the length of the shoe.

## minus

$$5 - 3$$

5 minus 3

This means 3 is taken away from 5.

## minus sign (−)

$$7 - 4 = 3$$

## minute

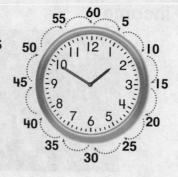

60 minutes is 1 hour.

## minute hand

The long hand on a clock is the minute hand.
The minute hand tells the minutes.

minute hand

It is 3:00.

## missing part

the part that is not known

5

?

2 is the missing part.

## more

The red row has more.

## near double

an addition fact that has an addend that is 1 or 2 more than the other addend

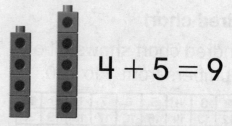

$$4 + 5 = 9$$

$4 + 4 = 8$. 8 and 1 more is 9.

## need

You need food to live.

## nickel

5 cents or 5¢

front      back

## number line

A number line is a line that shows numbers in order from left to right.

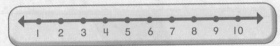

## number sentence

$6 + 4 = 10$     $6 - 2 = 4$

$10 = 6 + 4$     $4 = 6 - 2$

## o'clock

8:00

8 o'clock

## ones

The ones digit shows how many ones are in a number.

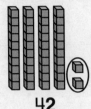 42 has 2 ones.

42

## ones digit

The ones digit in 43 is 3.

ones digit

## order

60    61    62    63

least             greatest

Numbers can be put in counting order from least to greatest or from greatest to least.

## outside

5 dogs are playing outside of the dog house.

## part

a piece of a whole

2 and 3 are parts of 5.

## pattern

You can arrange 5 objects in any pattern, and there will still be 5 objects.

## penny

1 cent or 1¢

front    back

## picture graph

a graph that uses pictures to show data

Favorite Pets

| Cat | | | |
| Dog | | | |

## plane shape

a flat shape

circle  rectangle  square  triangle

## plus

5 + 4

5 plus 4

This means 4 is added to 5.

## plus sign (+)

$$6 + 2 = 8$$

## quarter

25 cents or 25¢

front    back

## quarters

The square is divided into quarters, another word for fourths.

## rectangular prism

## related facts

addition facts and subtraction facts that have the same numbers

$$2 + 3 = 5$$
$$5 - 2 = 3$$

These facts are related.

## rhombus

a shape with 4 sides that are the same length

## row

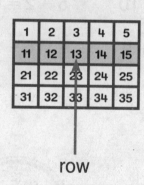

| 1 | 2 | 3 | 4 | 5 |
| 11 | 12 | 13 | 14 | 15 |
| 21 | 22 | 23 | 24 | 25 |
| 31 | 32 | 33 | 34 | 35 |

row

## save

You can save money to buy things you want or need.

## scale

A scale is used to measure how much things weigh.

## separate

When you subtract, you can separate one group from another.

## side

These shapes have straight sides.

## skip count

You can skip count by 5s to 25.

# 5, 10, 15, 20, 25

## solid figure

a figure that has length, width, and height

These are all solid figures.

## sort

to group objects according to how they are similar

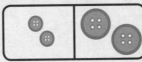

The buttons are sorted by size.

## spend

When you buy something, you spend money.

## sphere

## standard form

a number shown in digits

28

## subtract

When you subtract, you find out how many are left.

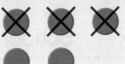

5 − 3 = 2

## subtraction sentence

$$12 - 4 = 8$$

## sum

$$2 + 3 = \underset{\uparrow}{5}$$

sum

## survey

to gather information

## T-chart

a chart that uses tally marks to show data

| Walk | School Bus |
|------|-----------|
| 卌 || | 卌 卌 |

## take away

| Start With | Take Away | Have Left |
|:----------:|:---------:|:---------:|
| 6 | 3 | 3 |

$$6 - 3 = 3$$

To take away is to remove or subtract.

## tally mark

marks that are used to record data

| Cats | 卌 |
|------|----|
| Dogs | || |

There are 5 cats and 2 dogs.

## tens digit

The tens digit shows how many groups of 10 are in a number.

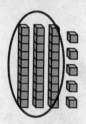

35 has 3 tens.

35

## trapezoid

## triangular prism

## value

how much something is worth

1¢     5¢     10¢     25¢

## vertex (vertices)

a point where 3 or more edges meet

vertex

## want

items you would like to have, but do not need to live

## whole

You add parts to find the whole.

5

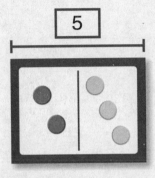

The whole is 5.